GOD'S ADVENTURER

The story of Stuart Windsor and the
persecuted church

STUART WINDSOR
AND GRAHAM JONES

MONARCH
BOOKS

Oxford, UK & Grand Rapids, Michigan, USA

First published in the UK in 2011 by Monarch Books
(a publishing imprint of Lion Hudson plc)
Wilkinson House, Jordan Hill Road, Oxford OX2 8DR, England
Tel: +44 (0)1865 302750 Fax: +44 (0)1865 302757
Email: monarch@lionhudson.com   www.lionhudson.com

ISBN 978 1 85424 999 9 (print)
ISBN 978 0 85721 099 9 (Kindle)
ISBN 978 0 85721 100 2 (ePub)
ISBN 978 0 85721 101 9 (PDF)

Distributed by:
UK: Marston Book Services, PO Box 269, Abingdon, Oxon, OX14 4YN
USA: Kregel Publications, PO Box 2607, Grand Rapids, Michigan 49501

Photographs of Sam Yeghnazar, Hossein Soodmand, Haik Hovsepian Mehr and Mehdi Dibaj courtesy of Elam Ministries. Photograph of children at Barnado's home courtesy of Dr Barnado's. Other photographs courtesy of Stuart Windsor/CSW.

The text paper used in this book has been made from wood independently certified as having come from sustainable forests.

British Library Cataloguing Data
A catalogue record for this book is available from the British Library.

Printed in Great Britain by Clays Ltd, St Ives plc.

Speak up for those
who cannot speak for
themselves,
for the rights of all
who are destitute.
Speak up and judge fairly;
defend the rights of the
poor and needy.

PROVERBS 31:8–9

Contents

Foreword

By Jonathan Aitken

Every so often God raises up someone who becomes a rock in the stream: entirely himself, a character of such timbre and individuality that life is never quite the same after you meet him.

I first got to know Stuart Windsor when we shared a platform together over ten years ago on a speaking tour of Scotland in support of the persecuted church. I immediately recognised his great gifts of communication as a public speaker, as a spiritual leader, as a prayer-giver, and above all as a warm and loveable human being. More recently Stuart and I have worked closely together as senior colleagues in Christian Solidarity Worldwide. As honorary president of CSW I have been filled with admiration for Stuart's unique contribution to the organisation as a life-force of energy, brotherly love and Christian leadership at its finest.

Stuart is a man of tremendous vision, humble but determined, cheerful and capable. It is simply a pleasure to spend time in his company. His genius is that he likes people, and values their uniqueness. He is very hard to say "no" to! His enthusiasm, and his evident willingness to please and be pleased, have got him into some amazing hot spots, but have also called forth generosity and affection in the most unlikely quarters.

His unflagging support for the persecuted church has saved countless lives and blessed so many believers around the world. I am so grateful to him for his willingness to get involved in every detail, to follow up every lead, so that those whose voices cannot be heard in their own lands may nevertheless come to the attention of the international community. Stuart serves a

God who cares for the unnoticed people, those whom the media ignore. God has honoured his efforts.

I am so pleased that he has written his own story! This series of remarkable adventures will open your eyes and strengthen your faith. I wholeheartedly commend it to your attention.

Jonathan Aitken
March 2011

1

Into the Blizzard

The doors slid shut on the Ilyushin IL-76 and the giant aircraft nosed across the tarmac of Amsterdam's Schiphol Airport.

In the pilot's seat sat a square-jawed man in his late fifties with deep-set eyes and silver hair swept thickly back from his forehead. In a different setting he might have been a TV anchorman or an ageing Hollywood actor. With some deference, the co-pilot introduced him as General Boris Volynov, former Russian test pilot and cosmonaut with two Soyuz missions to his credit. "He is very famous," added the co-pilot as instructions crackled in from the control tower. "A Hero of the Soviet Union."[1]

From the cockpit jump seat I glanced at the profile of this Soviet Hero and wondered what he made of our mission today. Stacked in the fuselage behind us were fifty tonnes of food and medical aid for Nagorno Karabakh, that tiny Armenian enclave that looks on the map like a coiled foetus in the belly of Azerbaijan. Our destination was the Armenian capital, Yerevan, where our cargo would be loaded onto trucks and driven through the high mountain passes that separate Nagorno Karabakh from Armenia proper.

I'd never flown in a Russian aircraft before, though I knew the IL-76 from my days in the Royal Air Force during the Cold War. As part of my training, I'd had to learn the different types of Russian aircraft, and the IL-76 had always commanded our respect. Bigger than an RAF Hercules and designed to withstand the Siberian winter, this beast of a plane could pack the equivalent of five double-decker buses in its cargo bay and carry it more than 5,000 kilometres. I recalled that the four massive engines consumed ten tonnes of fuel per hour. Glancing at the gauges, I was relieved to see they registered full.

Today was the last day of 1992, a year on from the collapse of the Soviet Union. Thanks to the desperate state of the Russian economy, it was now possible to hire an IL-76 and its pilot – even a former cosmonaut – at a bargain-basement price. Which must have been why Sam Yeghnazar had chosen to charter this ageing Soviet aircraft.

Sam now came forward and joined me in the cockpit. A handsome man in his late forties, Sam was born in Iran to Armenian parents. After national service in the Iranian army, he had left his homeland to work for the United Bible Societies in the Philippines and later Lebanon. Fluent in English, Farsi and Armenian, he now headed the Iranian Christian Fellowship in London. A man passionate for freedom and justice, especially among his own people, he had personally raised the money and organized the flight to take aid to his fellow Armenian Christians in Nagorno Karabakh.

It was thanks to Sam that I, too, was on the flight. Working as a Pentecostal minister in Widnes in Cheshire, I'd got to know Sam in the process of running a small film unit that specialized in recording Christian conferences. Knowing it would help his fund-raising efforts to have his trip on video, he'd asked if I could bring a camera and a sound man and film his mission.

"Of course," I'd said. "Where's Nagorno Karabakh?"

He'd given me a rough idea – inside Azerbaijan, next to Armenia, in a region encircled by Georgia, Turkey and Iran. What he failed to mention at the time was the bitter ethnic conflict raging in and around the enclave. With my sound engineer, Frank Walsh, Sam and I were now on our way to a war zone.

"Something's wrong," muttered Sam, staring out at the tarmac.

"How do you mean?" I replied.

"Well, how long is it since we started moving?"

I checked the time. "About forty minutes."

"Exactly. And we haven't got to the runway yet. I think he's lost."

I smiled at the thought of our two-time cosmonaut and Soviet Hero failing to find the runway at Amsterdam. But then, Schiphol is a very large airport and the general could well have had trouble following directions in English from the control tower. I just hoped he knew the way to Armenia.

Twenty minutes later, the rising note of the engines signalled that we'd found the runway and were preparing for take-off. As we picked up speed and lumbered into the wintry Dutch sky, I smiled at Sam and made myself comfortable for the five-hour flight to Yerevan.

We were still swinging out over the North Sea when the general turned to face us and explained in his heavily accented English that we had a problem. Because we'd been so late taking off from Schiphol (he didn't say why), there now wasn't time to fly to Yerevan.

"But why not?" asked Sam.

"It is New Year's Eve," he explained, as though the reason were obvious. "I am base commander of Domodedevo."

I knew the name from the Cold War. Now Moscow's international airport, Domodedevo was then one of Russia's military transport bases. But I still didn't understand why we couldn't go to Yerevan.

"Tonight we have party," continued the general. "As base commander, I cannot miss party with my men. So now we fly to Moskva. Tomorrow, Yerevan."

As the IL-76 droned towards Moscow, the general grew more talkative. When he found out I'd been in the RAF, he began describing the test flights he'd made to the Arctic and back with the aim of extending the distances it was possible to fly without refuelling. It was clear he was an exceptional pilot.

What he didn't tell me – not least because the state had forbidden him to tell anyone – was the story of his fiery return to earth at the end of his Soyuz 5 mission in January 1969. The 34-year-old cosmonaut was alone in his craft after docking in space with Soyuz 4 and transferring two of his crew to the other vehicle. As he re-entered the earth's atmosphere, a redundant module failed to detach as it should and Volynov found himself pointing the wrong way, with his heat shield now useless against the 5,000-degree heat of re-entry. As the temperature climbed and flames licked the inside of his capsule, he continued to make notes in his log. Seconds before being incinerated (or so he thought), he tore out the last few pages and stuffed them deep inside his jacket in the hope that they might be found when his barbecued body hit the ground.

He survived because the capsule turned the right way round at the last moment. He landed in snow in the Ural Mountains, 2,000 kilometres off course, with no injuries apart from losing some of his teeth on impact. But now he faced the opposite problem. The temperature on the ground was minus thirty-eight Centigrade, and he knew he'd die of cold if he didn't move quickly. Climbing out of his still-sizzling capsule, he staggered to a peasant's hut for shelter until the rescuers from mission control could reach him.

Like all mishaps in the Soviet space programme, Volynov's near-disaster was kept secret from the world. It was only in 1997, five years after I met him, that the details were made public and Volynov could start to tell his story. Had I known then what I know now, my admiration would have been even greater.

The celebrations to welcome 1993 began even before we touched down. As we neared Domodedevo some three hours after taking off from Schiphol, the co-pilot produced a bottle of vodka and poured a large tumbler. He handed it to Sam who passed it on to me.

There was a time when I'd have downed a glass of vodka in a few gulps. But for thirty years I'd been teetotal. *"Niet, niet,"* I stuttered, but my protestations went unheard. With the Russian crew all now joining in, the party mood was taking hold.

"You've got to," hissed Sam.

I smiled nervously over the rim and took a decorous sip. It was too late now to worry about not getting to Yerevan. If we were going to spend the night in Moscow, we might as well enjoy it.

When Sam, Frank and I finally emerged into the freezing Russian night at Domodedevo air base, it became clear that we, too, were expected to take part in the festivities.

So began one of the jolliest New Year celebrations I've ever experienced. With Christmas abolished by the Soviets, Russians at the time had little opportunity for merriment other than the holidays inspired by the Communist Revolution. Not surprisingly, October Revolution Day and the Day of International Solidarity for the Working Class were not noted for their gaiety and fun. As the one public holiday free of political ideology, New Year was traditionally the happiest of all the year's celebrations.

The welcome at Domodedevo from our one-time Cold War enemies was like being enfolded in a warm, Russian bear hug. Getting by on miniscule sips of vodka, we raised our glasses to innumerable toasts and hummed along to the Russian national anthem and the Russian military's entire repertoire of drinking songs. We sang "Kalinka", made famous by the Russian Army Male Voice Choir, and "The Bear Song", whose tune I remembered from an old film about the Russian military threat. And we responded in kind with the British national anthem and a selection of choruses and hymns.

Watching our Russian hosts swaying along to "What a friend we have in Jesus", I relished the humanity that unites us all, whatever our nationality and politics.

The sight that greeted us the following morning after three hours' sleep was not encouraging. Woken at 6 a.m. for take-off at 7.30, we stepped outside into a Russian New Year's Day and a temperature of minus twenty degrees. The IL-76 was where it had been parked the night before, but the fuselage was now thickly encrusted with ice. I was surprised to see a ladder propped against the tailplane and a small figure (it turned out to be the young co-pilot) chipping ice off the tailfin rudders with an ice-pick.

The general obviously had other duties (or perhaps he was sleeping off the effects of the night before), because our pilot today was a charming officer called Mikhail Mikhailovitch – Michael son of Michael, as he explained to us in his excellent English.

Eventually the co-pilot removed enough ice to allow us to take off and we set course due south across the Caucasus to Yerevan – a flight we expected to take about two and a half hours.

Three hours later, somewhat to our surprise, the IL-76 was still circling Yerevan Airport. Peering through the windows, I could see nothing but dense, freezing fog. We might have been at 30,000 feet or 30 – there was no way of telling. Mikhail Mikhailovitch and his co-pilot were anxiously scanning the controls. Lights I knew to be warning lights were flashing on the cockpit display. Apart from the unnerving bleep of alarm buzzers, the only sounds in the cockpit were the odd burst of Russian from the Yerevan control tower and Mikhail Mikhailovitch's terse replies.

As a former·RAF man, I could see what was happening.

"He can't find the runway," I thought. "His navigation aids are useless in these conditions. If he goes any slower he's going to stall and we'll crash."

I prayed – and could see that Sam was praying too. This was not how I wanted our mission to end. Simultaneously, I found myself wondering whether some NATO listening post was picking up our movements. Why would an IL-76 fly all the way from Moscow to Yerevan and simply circle? I'd seen the scenario many times before in my RAF days when we'd tracked unusual flight patterns and tried to work out what those devious Soviets were up to. I wondered if any of my former colleagues were watching and listening to our flight. They'd be surprised to know I was on it.

Still we circled, the tension in the cockpit rising by the second. Eventually, Mikhail Mikhailovitch spoke:

"*Niet.* Impossible to land. Back to Moscow."

The engine note changed and I felt the aircraft straightening and lifting as Mikhail Mikhailovitch aborted his landing and set off home to Domodedevo.

Our eventual arrival in Yerevan came later that evening after we'd flown back to Moscow, waited until late afternoon and taken off again – once more in the company of Mikhail Mikhailovitch.

Sam had now briefed me more fully on the situation in Nagorno Karabakh. Although the enmities in the region are centuries old, the conflict of the 1990s could be traced to Stalin's decision to place the enclave of Nagorno Karabakh – historically part of Armenia – under the control of neighbouring Azerbaijan. While the Soviet Union remained intact, Armenia and Azerbaijan had largely buried their differences. But once the Soviets withdrew in the late 1980s, the Karabakhis – overwhelmingly Armenian – began calling for unification with the mother country. In 1988, reports of violence against local Azeris were followed by a massacre of

Armenians in the Azeri city of Sumgait.

The conflict escalated, with the Azeris invading the enclave and laying siege to its capital, Stepanakert. One result was a mass movement of refugees. Azeris living in Armenia and Nagorno Karabakh fled across the borders into Azerbaijan, while Armenians in Azerbaijan retreated west into Armenia. The spring of 1991 saw Azeri forces, supported by the Soviet Fourth Army, deporting Armenians from villages in the enclave. The atrocities were appalling. Starvation, burnings, dismemberments and beheadings were all used to terrorize the Karabakhi population and force them off the land.

As we touched down in Yerevan that first evening of 1993, the 150,000 Armenian Karabakhis were still at war with 7 million Azeris whose country entirely surrounded their little enclave. Constantly under attack from Azerbaijan's professional army and air force, most could muster little more than hunting rifles.

Yerevan wore the battered, derelict look of a city at war. Armenia's economy had ground to a halt, with Azerbaijan cutting power and transport connections from the east and the Turks (ethnic cousins to the Azeris) doing likewise from the west. The pipelines bringing gas from Russia passed through Georgia to the north and were constantly being blown up by Georgian and Azeri terrorists. Electricity was limited to two hours a day. The shops were empty. Food was scarce. With temperatures hovering at minus twenty, life in Armenia in January 1993 was bleak in the extreme.

Sam, Frank and I were now joined by Michael Sookias of the Iranian Christian Fellowship, who had arrived in Yerevan a few days earlier. The four of us shivered through the night at Yerevan's Hotel Armenia, a grey, Soviet-era edifice that seemed colder inside than out. When we came to unload the IL-76 in the morning, we found that the airport had no handling equipment – or none that worked – and that all fifty tonnes of aid would need to be lifted off the aircraft by hand. Fortunately, the resourceful Sam had contacts with some of the churches in Yerevan and managed to find fifty volunteers who set to with enthusiasm.

As we lugged the boxes off the aircraft, I was alarmed at the state of the five dilapidated Soviet trucks that were due to transport the aid through the Lachin mountain corridor into Nagorno Karabakh. The threadbare tyres were particularly worrying. I also wondered where the diesel was going to come from. With Armenia starved of fuel by Azeri and Turkish blockades, the only supplies were those coming in by lorry from Iran. To fill up, Sam explained, you looked for one of these vehicles parked by the roadside and bought your fuel direct from the driver.

"But not in our case," he added with a smile. "I wouldn't use that stuff. It's terrible. We're going to use quality diesel."

A short while later I was surprised to see one of the truck drivers filling a container from one of the fuel outlets on the IL-76. It turned out that the excellent Mikhail Mikhailovitch had allowed the convoy to use some of his aircraft fuel.

Loading the trucks took all day, so it wasn't until the morning of 3 January, after another freezing night at the Hotel Armenia, that our ramshackle convoy creaked and rattled out of Yerevan towards the eastern mountains. Sam and Mike led the way in a car lent by a local pastor. Frank and I followed with two Armenian drivers in a Uri, a six-wheeled vehicle similar to a personnel carrier. This belonged to Spitak, a mountain rescue service that operated from bases in Yerevan and Nagorno Karabakh and was Sam's contact on the ground. Piled in the back were our camera and sound gear along with first-aid equipment, puncture repair kits, boxes of Bibles and teaching materials for Karabakhi churches and some of the aid that wouldn't fit anywhere else. The five rattling trucks brought up the rear.

The terrain grew steeper and the roads windier. In the course of the day we toiled over three mountain ranges and under the lee of Mount Ararat, where Noah's Ark came to rest after the flood. The short winter day was already spent by the time we reached Goris, the little town much strafed by the Azeri air force that marks the border between Armenia and Azerbaijan and the start of the heavily-fought Lachin corridor into Nagorno Karabakh.

A little way past Goris, Sam pulled in and stopped. As we drew up behind him, he stepped out of the car and walked back to the Uri. He said something to the drivers in Armenian. He looked worried.

"Stuart," he said, turning to me. "We've got a problem."

"What's that?"

"We've lost our trucks."

It took some time to make radio contact with the missing vehicles and find out what had happened. It seemed those tyres were as dodgy as I'd thought, because all five trucks had come to a stop with punctures at different points along the route. And the puncture repair kits were here with us in the Uri.

Although it was now getting dark, it was vital to send the Uri back as quickly as possible to get the trucks moving again. The question was whether Frank and I should go with it or stay here by the roadside with Sam and Mike until it returned.

We prayed for guidance as to what to do.

"I have this strong feeling you should stay," said Sam. I agreed, and Frank and I stepped out onto the icy verge. The Spitak drivers turned the Uri around and disappeared down the road in the direction of Yerevan.

As the night hours ticked by, the temperature plunged again to minus twenty. We debated whether to huddle in Sam's car, but the scene on that mountain pass was so ravishingly beautiful, with snowy, moonlit peaks on every side and the winter sky brilliant with stars, that we preferred to wait outside. For twelve hours we prayed and sang and talked and paced up and down to keep warm as we waited for the Uri to return.

The first vehicle to make it up the road was not the Uri but an Armenian police car which came by at about 5 a.m. An officer rolled down his window and spoke to Sam.

"There's a vehicle gone over a drop about forty minutes back. Anything to do with you?"

"I don't know," said Sam. "What kind of vehicle?"

The policeman shrugged. "Hard to say. It's pretty smashed up. Perhaps you should come and have a look."

The four of us squeezed into Sam's car and followed the police back down the road. After twenty or so winding kilometres, our escort pulled over and indicated a spot where something had clearly gone over the edge. Dawn was now breaking and the grey light revealed tyre tracks and scarred vegetation where a vehicle had plunged off the road. Stomachs tight with apprehension, we got out and walked to the rim of the precipice.

The Uri was forty metres below at the foot of an almost sheer drop. It lay on its roof, its windows smashed, its doors ripped away and its front end a tangle of twisted metal. The middle section, where Frank and I would have been sitting if we'd been aboard, was punched in like a crushed tin can. Had we been inside, we would certainly have died.

I took in the rest of the scene. The luggage lay scattered along the ravine, the boxes split and the contents strewn across the rocks. I could see my camera case in the snow, some distance from the vehicle.

There was no sign of the two drivers. But it seemed impossible that anyone could have survived.

After a moment's shocked silence we scrambled down the side of the ravine, dreading the sight that surely awaited us when we got to the cab. Sam – brave as always – forged ahead to confirm the worst. While he did so, I picked up my camera and found it was undamaged. To make sure, I started to film the wreckage. It was so cold, my finger froze to the button.

"Stuart, come over here!" yelled Sam.

I stopped filming and hurried over. The cab where I expected to see the bodies of the brave men from Spitak Rescue was empty. I glanced up the side of the ravine, thinking they must have been thrown clear as the Uri fell.

"They survived," said Sam. I followed his pointing finger and saw a ragged trail of blood leading up the slope away from the wreckage.

Following the blood, we traced the drivers to a small hospice a little further down the road. Miraculously, they'd suffered nothing more than cuts, bruises and broken ribs and had managed to drag themselves out of the ravine and find help.

"We hit some black ice and went over," they explained as they lay in bed, bandaged and still dazed. "It's amazing we weren't killed." They assured us that all they needed was a few days to convalesce and that Spitak Rescue would then send a vehicle to collect them. I marvelled at the toughness of these mountain-bred Armenians, and also at the supernatural protection we'd surely just experienced. As one convinced of the existence of angels – of which there's more to tell later – I was certain our angels had been active that night.

Fortunately for our mission, the Uri had crashed on its way back from fixing the broken-down trucks. Before long we heard the grinding of engines and our rickety convoy slowly appeared around the side of the mountain. When it caught up, Sam and Mike again led the way in the car while Frank and I climbed into the cab of one of the trucks. I sat next to the driver and Frank took the seat on the right-hand side.

If our angels were busy during the night, I'm sure they were working overtime as we crossed the eight-kilometre strip of Azerbaijan – the Lachin corridor – that separates Armenia from Nagorno Karabakh. I quickly became convinced that our young Armenian driver was insane. Either that or drunk. As we dropped towards the enclave, his knuckles whitened on the wheel and his eyes took on a maniacal glitter. Hunched forward in his seat, he took to accelerating down icy hills with hairpin bends at the bottom and drops of hundreds of metres on one side or the other. I found myself praying constantly while Frank, ashen faced, gripped the side of the cab and groaned softly, "Oh, dear God. Oh God. Oh my God!"

Eventually I decided I had to do something. I made the driver stop – he didn't want to do so and kept revving as we paused – and Frank and I changed places. I thought if either of us was going to be thrown out over a precipice, it ought to be me. Sam, who had pulled over when he saw us stopping, then swapped places with Frank, who staggered to the car in relief. On we went. As we once more hurtled down the inclines, Sam remarked through gritted teeth that he now understood why Frank had been so terrified and ordered the driver to slow down. A little further on, Frank and Sam swapped back. The nightmare journey began again and I don't believe Frank or I drew a complete breath until we rolled into Stepanakert.

When Sam later spoke to the driver, he found he was neither crazy nor drunk. He'd heard, apparently, that Azeri snipers were still in position along the corridor and wanted to get through as quickly as possible.

"But I thought you said the Armenian army had cleared the snipers out and the road was safe," I said to Sam.

He shrugged. "Maybe I was wrong."

Our contact in Stepanakert had the wonderful if unlikely name of Aslan – Aslan Krikorian, a devout Armenian Orthodox Christian who ran the Karabakhi end of Spitak Rescue. Rugged, dark-haired and immensely brave, he was also a skilled mountaineer. Before the conflict, when national differences didn't matter, he'd skied for Azerbaijan in the Winter Olympics. Now he led a team of paramedics that sneaked out into the war zones and brought back injured Karabakhis for treatment. Along with the leader of Armenia's Pentecostals, a prominent scientist by the name of Sergei Georgov, Aslan was to be our host.

As it was too late in the day to unload, Aslan suggested dinner. Even in the direst conditions, the Armenians have a genius for eating and drinking. In a town where the shops were empty, the Christians of Stepanakert had made enormous sacrifices to lay on a meal. From out of nowhere they'd managed to produce a feast of lamb, rice, yogurt, tomatoes and the one thing never in short supply – Karabakhi brandy. The toasts flowed, thirty or forty in all, each followed by long, sentimental speeches provoking tears and hilarity in equal measure. We toasted England, we toasted the Queen and Windsor Castle and we toasted the Armenian Orthodox Christmas, just two days away on 6 January.

Most of all we toasted peace, none of us knowing when the day would ever arrive.

The following morning revealed the true horrors of life in Stepanakert. For more than four years the town had been regularly strafed by Russian ground-attack aircraft and pounded by Azeri artillery and Grad BM-21 missiles. Although banned by international convention, Grads had been used to bloody effect by the Russians in Afghanistan. The name means "hail". Fired in clusters from the back of a truck, Grads fall indiscriminately and explode in a firestorm of shrapnel that can rip a building to shreds.

The Azeris had taken control of the nearby heights at Shusha which commanded deadly views of the town. From here they rained down their Grads – 400 a day at times – on the defenceless population. We learned that missiles and munitions were being stored in Shusha's Armenian Orthodox church and that the Azeri gunners had marked out the houses they intended to occupy and were directing their fire at other parts of the town. A Grad hit Aslan's house the day after we left, damaging the roof but fortunately injuring no one.

This was a town of shattered and pock-marked buildings, gradually subsiding into rubble. People slept in basements and emerged briefly between bombardments to scrounge the necessities of life. There was almost no electricity or running water and very little food. According to Aslan, old people in Stepanakert were dying of starvation in their homes. Hospitals had run out of medicines and were having to perform operations without anaesthetics.

What made the situation even more unbearable was the knowledge that the Azeri capital, Baku, was then a magnet for aid agencies, Western businesses and visiting international dignitaries. Why? Because Azerbaijan had oil. It seemed the Karabakhis faced not only the hostility of their well-armed Azeri neighbours but also the indifference of the world community. ("We have oil interests in Azerbaijan," said one British minister when pressed to explain his government's disregard for the plight of Nagorno Karabakh.) Against so much suffering, our own tiny convoy seemed just a drop in the bucket.

Even so, the small amount we had to offer was desperately and gratefully received. Once we'd unloaded, again with help from the local churches, Sam, Mike, Frank and I criss-crossed the town with Aslan handing out the aid. One of our journeys took us along a road on which two young Karabakhis had hit a mine the previous day. Both had lost limbs.

Our last visit on 5 January, the Armenian Orthodox Christmas Eve, took us to a compound where starving people clamoured at the gate and almost rioted as we drove in. Aslan was forced to fire his gun in the air and bellow at the crowd: "Remember your dignity! We are Christians and Armenians. This is not the way we behave." The people were so hungry, it was heartbreaking.

The distribution done, there was no time to waste. We had to be back in Yerevan the following day to catch our Armenian

Aeroflot flight to Paris.

Our transport this time was a jeep-style Lada Niva. The driver made a number of stops around Stepanakert to find whatever fuel he could, then set off through the forest towards the mountains. The sunlit beauty of the Lachin corridor made it hard to believe that a vicious war was being waged along its length. Despite the talk of snipers, I felt I could relax and enjoy the journey home.

The first hint of trouble occurred once we were back in Armenia, a little way beyond Goris and not far from the spot where we lost the Uri. As daylight faded, the clouds grew low and heavy and the first flurries of snow began to hit the windscreen. We made it on to Zange Zhor, translated as "The Place of Bells". In daylight it's one of the most scenic points of the route, 2,100 metres high with breathtaking views down the mountainside. But the view was the last thing on our minds. By now the wind was shrieking and the snow had turned to blizzard, sweeping across the terrain and obliterating the route.

After struggling on for another twenty minutes, the Lada ploughed to a stop and its engine cut out, defeated by the extreme cold and a broken head gasket. The driver tried to restart, but the engine growled and died. Peering through the blizzard at the rising snow level, we could see we were trapped.

"He who watches over you will not slumber," murmured Sam, immediately turning to the Bible to steady his mind and fortify our spirits.

"The Lord will keep you from all harm," I continued, recalling the words of Psalm 121. "He will watch over your life. The Lord will watch over your coming and going…"

"And your being stuck," added Frank grimly.

That night, the temperature at Zange Zhor fell to minus twenty-three, with the wind chill dragging it down to minus fifty. Unable to start the engine to keep warm, we shivered in our overcoats and tried to endure the vicious cold that cut through our bodies and numbed our feet and hands. Just as we'd done two nights before on this same stretch of road, we prayed and sang and put our trust in God.

"I guess we've missed our flight to Paris," said Frank helpfully.

Gazing at the cascading snow, we agreed that this was likely. Given that the next scheduled flight from Yerevan wasn't for another week, we were looking at a serious change of plan – if indeed we got through the night alive and didn't freeze to death in our little metal tomb.

"I've been thinking," said Frank a little later. "This is the fourth time I've nearly died on this crazy trip."

"Remind me," I replied.

"Well, the first was circling over Yerevan and nearly crashing. Then there was you and I deciding not to go back in the Uri. Then the journey to Stepanakert with the lunatic driver. And now stuck in a blizzard. All in five days."

We fell silent, wondering if this would be the time we finally didn't make it. Yes we trusted God to protect us, but always if it was his will. We knew that one day it might be his will that we didn't survive.

Frank turned to more basic matters. "I'm desperate for a pee," he said, fumbling at the door catch with his gloved hand.

The driver spoke rapidly in Armenian and Sam translated. "He says you'd better be careful. There are wolves out there."

Frank thought he might try and wait.

I glanced at my watch. "It's gone midnight," I said. "Happy Christmas, everyone."

I later discovered that my wife, Ethel, had spent the afternoon of 5 January in an odd state of unease. She knew in her heart that something had gone wrong, but had no way of finding out what the trouble was. As the feeling persisted, she went and spoke to her friend, Sonia MacDonald, who ran a newspaper shop near our home in Widnes in Cheshire.

"I just know Stuart's in trouble," she said. "Would you come and pray with me?" Sonia agreed to shut the shop early and she and Ethel spent the evening together praying for our safekeeping. They must have been hard at it as midnight ticked past in Armenia, four hours ahead of the UK, and the Orthodox Christmas Day began. When she later learned what had happened – that at that moment I'd been trapped with my companions in a mountain blizzard – her response was typical of her rock-like faith: "I knew I had to pray," she said. "God doesn't make mistakes."

When morning dawned, we found we were not alone at Zange Zhor. Several vehicles coming the other way had also hit the blizzard and come to a stop overnight. Among them was an old red bus, trapped in a deep drift about a hundred metres ahead of us.

There was something else as well – a telephone relay station, its mast breaking the horizon a couple of kilometres along the side of the mountain. It was little more than a concrete shack, but the coil of smoke from its chimney told us there'd be warmth and maybe some way of getting help if only we could reach it.

We decided to go for it.

The hour that followed was, I think, the only time in my life that I've seriously wanted to die. Hauling one foot in front of the other through knee-deep snow, my body crying out from cold and exhaustion, I thought how tempting it would be to lie down, fall asleep and never wake up. I didn't know it at the time, but my ears were turning black with frostbite. I thought back to Sam's call inviting me on this lunatic adventure, and wished I'd never picked up the phone. I craved an escape – any escape – from the frozen desolation in which we were trapped.

"Dear God, this is madness! Why have you brought me to such a place?"

It's not exactly true that your life flashes in front of your eyes at moments like that, but I did find my thoughts turning to the past – to my childhood, my friends, my wife and the chain of events that had brought me to this bleak Armenian mountainside to die. As far as I can remember, my uppermost feeling was one of faint surprise. "So today I'll be in heaven. Who would have thought it would end like this?"

I squinted up at the relay station, apparently no nearer than when we'd started, then back at the stricken bus below us. I wondered who was on it and whether they'd survived that terrible night.

Miraculously they had, as I later discovered. In ways I could never have guessed, one of the occupants of that snowbound bus would help set the future direction of my life.

2

Barnardo's Boy

Wandering runs in the family. My paternal grandmother, Beatrice Windsor, was the daughter of an Italian immigrant, a pedlar by the name of Louis Devoto who plied his trade in Cornwall and Somerset. My other grandmother was born Emily Derx, daughter of Conrad Derx who arrived in London from Germany in the nineteenth century and, with his brother Balthazar, became a master sugar baker in the East End.

The Derxes made their home in Kingston, Surrey. While other members of the family climbed the social ladder (one of Conrad's grandsons was a Director of Glaxo and another became a Member of Parliament for Wimbledon), Emily – for reasons I've never discovered – ended up as a domestic servant in the London borough of Surbiton. There she met a butler called Eric Taylor, bore him a daughter and then abandoned them both to marry a chauffeur.

That daughter was my mother, Irene – the illegitimate child whose existence was kept secret from the Derx family until many years later. (The Derxes, it seems, disapproved of Emily and had nothing to do with her in her later life.) Brought up by her father, the butler, the young Irene married Norman Windsor in 1941 and settled in Sherbourne in Dorset. There she had five children – myself, the oldest, born in 1943, then Maureen, Brian, Reg and Janet.

In an echo of the Derx story, my father never did as well professionally as his two brothers. Uncles Ken and Arthur were both grammar school boys who reached senior positions in the civil service – Ken in the Foreign & Commonwealth Office and Arthur at the Admiralty Surface Weapons Establishment in Portsmouth. My father, by contrast, had been a sickly child who suffered educationally from having to spend a lot of time off school and whose illness left him with a limp for the rest of his life. While his brothers' careers flourished, he made a modest living as a sales assistant in the drapery department at Denners department store in Yeovil, Somerset.

Along with post-war food rationing and family holidays with Grandma Windsor in Yeovil, my early memories are of playing football in the street with my brother, Brian, and the other neighbourhood kids. We all supported the local team, Yeovil Town, who in 1948 pulled off the fantastic feat of beating First Division Sunderland at home in the FA Cup. I was there at the age of five on Yeovil's notoriously sloping pitch, cheering the local boys to their gloriously unexpected two–one victory. (The next round was less glorious for Yeovil – an eight–nil defeat against Sir Matt Busby's Manchester United. But at least, by then, we'd earned our reputation as the giant-killers of the Southern League.)

I don't recall when the tensions between my mother and father began to surface. I've since learned that financial problems probably contributed and that various neighbours helped us out when money was tight. And I do remember the increasingly frequent visits of George Roots, a short, portly man with a bow tie who lived in Salisbury and came calling in his car. The civic records describe him as a waste reclamation dealer. We knew him as the rag-and-bone man.

The realization that my parents' marriage had collapsed

came suddenly and brutally when I was ten. Rushing home from school one day, eager to get out and play football, I found my nine-year-old sister, Maureen, in the kitchen. She was trying to make dinner – a job that would normally have been Mother's.

"Where's Mother?" I asked.

Maureen put down her pan, looked at me intently and broke the news. "She came to see me in the playground. She said she was off and she was taking baby Janet with her. She said she'd left a note to explain and to make sure I showed it to Father."

The note still lay on the table, waiting for Father's return.

"Mother's left us," continued Maureen. "She's not coming back."

Over half a century later, I can still hear Maureen's unbearably sad voice and feel the shock of those words. I was stunned. I couldn't understand why our mother would want to leave us. Indeed, it was only later that I realized she'd run away with George Roots. Without wishing to sensationalize (parents splitting up is common enough today, though far less common then), I can testify to the trauma of having your mother ripped from your life at the age of ten. Nothing is the same ever again. You spend your nights in tears and your days crippled by anxiety. You feel different to other children. The sense of loss and betrayal is overwhelming.

Mother's departure left a host of practical problems. It was clear that Father couldn't continue working and look after four young children – still less five when Janet was returned to the family shortly afterwards. I remember Uncle Ken and his wife coming and cooking for us, and various neighbours providing a roast dinner on Sundays. But these were temporary measures. Someone had to decide what to do with five motherless Windsor children in the long term.

The decision was a joint one between Father, Uncle Ken and Uncle Arthur. Rather than splitting us up between different relatives, they chose to keep us together and put us into care.

We began by spending six months at temporary homes in Plymouth and Weymouth, which we hated. At one of those homes, we came back from school one day and peeked into the dining room to see it beautifully set out with balloons and fancy food. The owners' little daughter was having a party and we wondered for a brief moment if we were to be invited. Not so. When the owners discovered that we'd pried where we shouldn't have done, they cancelled the party and put us to bed early. So not only were we not invited, it was made very clear that we were responsible for ruining a little girl's birthday.

Eventually the five of us ended up at High Broom, the Dr Barnardo's home at Crowborough on the edge of the Ashdown Forest in Sussex. Built as a country house in 1825 and now an old people's residence, High Broom was my home between the ages of ten and sixteen.

Shortly after we moved in, Mother paid a surprise visit – the first time she'd seen us since she walked out. I'm told she wanted to take us away, but my father adamantly refused. That visit was the last time I ever saw or heard from her. I don't know if she attempted to make contact again and was perhaps prevented by the home or my father's side of the family. I do remember that Grandma Windsor, whom we all adored, was devastated at the break-up of the marriage and made it clear that she didn't want us seeing that wicked woman ever again. The only one brave enough to break the ban was Maureen, who once visited Mother in Salisbury. For my part, I think I was so worried about offending Grandma that I didn't try to do the same. It's a decision I've regretted ever since.

To be closer to the family, Father transferred from Yeovil to the linens department at Peter Jones in London's Sloane Square and came and saw us every week. Uncle Arthur would also come from Croydon and take us for rides in his car, and we used to go and stay both with him and with Uncle Ken at his home near Gatwick.

Despite the trauma of the family break-up, my memories of Barnardo's are happy ones on the whole. The fifty or so children at High Broom lived in three "families", each with a house mother whom I generally remember as being not a bad substitute for the real thing. Every morning in term time we formed a crocodile and walked the three miles to school, all dressed alike. Both at school and around the town, our clothes and the way we were organized marked us out as Barnardo's children and reinforced the feeling that we weren't the same as other children. Being different was something we learned to live with.

I was never much good at lessons, but I did enjoy football and played all over Sussex for the home and the school. I also played cricket and did a lot of boxing and cross-country running. My brothers and I sang in the choir at All Saints Church in Crowborough, where we used to get five shillings for performing at weddings and two-and-sixpence for funerals. Sundays meant three visits to church – morning service, Bible class and finally Evensong for those in the choir. I loved it all and developed a great affection for Anglican services. Even though we messed about in Mr Robertson's Scripture lessons, I was happy to be confirmed at the age of twelve. The Vicar of Crowborough, Gordon Clark, was a wonderful man who became a great hero of mine when he took me to White City in West London to watch the British Open Athletics Championship.

Earnings from the choir were supplemented by sixpence a week pocket money which typically went on coconut ice, cough candy, penny gobstoppers and everlasting strips of toffee at one of Crowborough's sweetshops. As people of my age like to say, you could buy a lot for sixpence in those days. Every Friday teatime we were treated to ice cream, sliced into small blocks and eaten with fresh fruit. It became a ritual to look out for the ice cream van racing up our very long drive and rattling to a halt at the kitchen door, just in time for the meal.

Maybe it's the softening effect of time, but many of my memories of High Broom come bathed in the sunlight of long Sussex summers. I remember endless afternoons playing on the spacious lawns of the house or exploring the nearby woods. We hiked across the Ashdown Forest, went camping at Newhaven on the south coast and, for two weeks every August, swapped homes with Barnardo's in Hastings, where we spent our days swimming, going on excursions and tramping over the South Downs.

The home was well supported by the public and we all had Barnardo's "uncles" and "aunts" who donated bulging sackfuls of toys every Christmas. I'm sure we did better for presents than many of our contemporaries in proper families in 1950s Britain. My brother Brian was fortunate to have a Barnardo's uncle who was head of Coca-Cola in the UK and who treated us to musicals in the West End. On one occasion he entertained us for a whole day at Coca-Cola's headquarters.

One of the highlights of my six years at Barnardo's was the day Princess Margaret came to visit us. It was my proud job to show her round. I remember her being very small and very posh, but interested in everything that was going on.

For all the happy memories, life in an institution had its less pleasant aspects. The chores, for example – washing up for fifty people or endlessly buffing the linoleum floors with orange Ronuk polish. Or being made to eat kedgeree, a concoction I've detested ever since. It's amazing how the childhood rhymes stick:

There is a mouldy dump
Down High Broom Lane,
Where we get bashed about
Sixty times a day.
Eggs and bacon we don't see;

We get sawdust in our tea.
That's why we're gradually
Fading away.

If we messed about or didn't eat all our food at mealtimes, one of the housemasters – usually the fearsome Mr Garner – would make us stand in a corner of the hall with our backs to the other children. This experience was also commemorated in verse:

Old Mr Garner thinks he's jolly good;
Stands us in the corner like a block of wood;
Gives us penny lectures, thinks we take it in.
All we do is turn around and give a little grin!

I'm sure those words are a terrible slur on a devoted staff and an institution that was, by and large, extremely caring. All the same, something prompted me at the age of twelve or thirteen to run away. I'd been told off, as I recall, and was convinced that no one would miss me. With one of the other boys, I decided to leg it one Saturday morning. Heading for London, we walked about ten miles and were north of Tunbridge Wells when a police car picked us up. The officers didn't believe we'd walked that far and were convinced that someone had sprung us from the home and given us a lift. Eventually they accepted that we were two kids on a jaunt and took us back.

That incident resurfaced many years later as I underwent vetting to be cleared to work in Signals Intelligence in the RAF.

"I see you've got a police record," said the investigating officer.

"What?" This was news to me.

"It says here, you ran away from Barnardo's."

I protested that the incident shouldn't be there, as I was under the age of criminal responsibility at the time. I'm happy to say that Her Majesty's Government was willing to overlook that particular blot on my record.

I've heard it said that the thoughts of soldiers injured in battle nearly always turn to their mothers. If a wounded soldier starts screaming for mum, the chances are he's done for. I don't know if that's true. But I can say that as I slogged across that snowy mountainside in Armenia, inwardly screaming to lie down and lose consciousness, I found myself thinking of the enigma that was my mother.

Irene Windsor divorced my father in 1954 and became Mrs George Roots. Two years and two daughters later, George died and left her homeless and penniless in Salisbury. She trudged the streets for two days with the girls in a pram before someone befriended her and took her in. She later fell in love with a Scot called James Buchanan who refused to marry her but left her with two further children – twin girls who were adopted and given new names by Dr Farr (of the Aberdeen haematology service) and his wife. A further relationship with a man called Victor Sillence produced two more sons. She then met Royston Alexander, to whom she was happily married for thirty years and who helped her bring up the two Roots girls and the two Sillence boys.

I was ignorant of all of this until 2003 when Meriel, one of the adopted daughters of the Scottish doctor, phoned my sister Maureen out of the blue.

"At last! We've found you!" she said.

It turned out that Meriel, knowing she was adopted, had spent many years tracking down her mother and half-siblings and had gradually uncovered the story. The result was the bombshell that we Windsors had six half-brothers and half-sisters that we never knew existed.

The eleven of us met for the first time just before my sixtieth birthday – a surreal, awkward but ultimately joyful occasion. By then our mother had been dead nearly ten years, but those who remembered her said at once that of all her children, I'm the one who most resembles her in looks and mannerisms. I'm pleased to think that that's the case.

I wish constantly that I'd met her again before she died and still find her story perplexing. It's odd how history repeated itself: Irene's mother abandoning her as a baby, and she walking out on her own young family; her own existence kept secret from the disapproving Derxes, and she then concealing her different families from one another; and the fact that both she and her mother knew what it was to be ostracised.

The mother I remember from my distant childhood was a large, jolly woman who undoubtedly loved her children. My half-brother Brian describes her as warm, loving and generous. Meriel recalls her standing on her doorstep, smiling broadly and flinging her arms wide when she met her for the first time as an adult. According to Meriel, she didn't talk much about her first family, beyond saying we were good children. "I always wanted someone to love," she once confided to Meriel. "But I made too many mistakes." While she seems to have gone from one doomed relationship to another in the first half of her life, I'm glad to think she eventually found the security she was seeking.

But I still wonder what kind of trauma she carried with her. I have a photograph of her as Mrs Royston Alexander, sitting with her later children on Weymouth beach in exactly the same spot where she sat with us, the Windsor family, and where we used play on Sunday School outings from Sherbourne. Was she thinking of us as the picture was being taken? And why, amazingly, did she call two of her sons Brian and give the second Brian the same middle name – Victor – that her first husband, our father, had had? Was she in some way recreating the family she'd lost? Or was this an admission that the original family was dead and gone? I shall never know.

As for my father, the break-up of the marriage broke his

heart and scarred him mentally for the rest of his life. He lived in Parson's Green in West London and I carried on seeing him as often as I could. His home was within walking distance of both the Fulham and Chelsea football grounds and we used to go to matches when one team or the other was playing at home. He remarried in 1958, but died of a stroke just four years later.

3

On Her Majesty's Service

When I reached sixteen, the question arose as to what I should do next. At school I'd sat five O Levels or equivalents and failed them all except physics. The superintendant of High Broom, a former Royal Navy Commander called George Luxton, believed that the services were a good next step for the boys in his care. Given that most had nowhere else to go after Barnardo's, he was probably right.

I was mad on aircraft, anyway, so the Royal Air Force looked like a good option. With my one, solitary exam pass, I didn't have the qualifications to fly, so applied to join on the lowest rung of all – that of Boy Entrant.

October 1959 saw me leaving Barnardo's and moving to RAF Cosford near the village of Albrighton, about fifteen miles from Wolverhampton. While other entrants trained as airframe mechanics, radar technicians or instrumentation specialists, someone decided that my field should be radio telegraphy. We started by learning the Morse Code. We then progressed to teleprinters, radio communications, and the Murray system in which each letter of the alphabet consists of five holes punched into a ticker tape which is then fed into a machine for the message to be transmitted. Over the next eighteen months, the training covered the main communications technologies used by the RAF in the late 1950s. I later retook my O Levels and even attempted A Levels, this time with far greater success.

As for flying, it happened just once, when I and the other boy entrants were taken on a short flight in a twin-engined Avro Anson cargo aircraft. We flew round the Wreakin, a big hill in Shropshire, waving excitedly at the people on the ground. And that was it. Although we were technically airmen, our training was strictly ground-based.

I quickly learned that the main purpose of the first three months at Cosford was to have the stuffing knocked out of us. We lived in billets – long wooden sheds with eighteen to twenty beds up each side, a stove for heating and a strip of linoleum flooring up the middle. The beds were precisely fifteen inches from the wall to allow room to walk behind them. That's because the floor itself was not for walking on: its sole purpose was to be polished. After Barnardo's, at least polishing a floor was something I knew how to do.

Every day had its kit inspection. The idea was to lay out your uniform and bedding with each item folded to precisely the right dimensions and arranged on the bed as per regulations. My contingent of entrants, the so-called "38th entry", had a reputation for being stroppy and in particular need of discipline, so the officers inevitably came down hard.

"Open the window, Boy Entrant Windsor!" The drill sergeant would holler the words, his face two inches from mine. I'd know what was coming.

"Right. Now throw your kit out the window!"

"But…"

"But? But what? I don't *care* if it's raining, Boy Entrant Windsor. That's an order!"

Out would go the bedding and the belt and boots that I'd just spent hours polishing. Or it might be that the billet itself wasn't scrupulously clean.

"What's this? Dust by your bed, Boy Entrant? Confined to

barracks for three days!"

Worst of all were the dreaded FFIs. At random times of day, the door of the billet would fly open and one of the sergeants would march in with the usual ninety-decibel rant: "Right, you lot! Foot and foreskin inspection! Strip off and stand to attention!"

Regulations allowed us to keep our underpants on, but we had to drop them as the sergeant paced along the line checking for signs of gonorrhoea or syphilis, which were endemic in the services. Unpleasant as it was, it drilled home the lesson of personal hygiene. If an entrant failed to wash and started getting smelly, he'd be forcibly bundled into a cold shower by the rest of the billet. Elsewhere, hygiene was less of a priority. After meals we washed our mess tins in a communal tank of greasy, lukewarm water which gave us all constant cold sores.

We lived in uniform (compulsory at all times except during our two-week annual leave) and were drilled endlessly up and down the parade ground. We were bawled at, belittled, given pointless orders and generally pushed to the limits of our endurance. Some of the entrants had breakdowns and one committed suicide while I was there. Not surprisingly, some took up the offer of paid weekends at the government's research establishment at Porton Down on Salisbury Plain. They believed they were taking part in tests to research the common cold, but there's evidence that some were exposed to nerve gas and other chemical and biological agents without their knowledge. A lot have suffered ill health ever since and various investigations have been launched.

My own preferred escape was not the cushy weekends at Porton Down but as much drinking as I could manage on a Saturday night. Our pay as boy entrants was just ten shillings a week, out of which we had to buy our own boot blacking and Duraglit buckle polish, so there wasn't much left over for boozing. In any case, drinking was illegal, on or off the base, except during leave. Undeterred, we'd sneak out to the pubs in Albrighton or, if we felt more daring, we'd get the train to Wolverhampton for a better choice of bars and clubs.

My companion for many of these outings was a ruddy-faced Devonian called Jan Trist (in the services, everyone from Devon was Jan, just as every Scotsman was Jock). I never discovered his real name, but we spent many uproarious Saturday nights in the local pubs. To be fair, the drinking was mainly on my part: Jan was great company but usually switched to orange juice after a couple of pints. The danger point was coming back to base. We had a staff sergeant called Hinds who was renowned for standing at the gate and sniffing your breath as you returned to barracks.

Sunday was a good day if I managed to dodge church parade. Beneath the barrack block was a hidey-hole, just big enough for the heathens, myself included, to huddle inside until church parade was over.

Life in the RAF became more interesting at the end of my initial training when I transferred to RAF Coltishall near Norwich, Norfolk, in 1961.

This was the height of the Cold War, just a year before the Cuban missile crisis, and Coltishall was home to a Gloucester Javelin fighter squadron and two Lightning squadrons that had to be in constant readiness for action against the Russians. During exercises that sometimes went on for three or four days, the pilots would fly their sorties, score "kills" by photographing their targets and return to base for refuelling. In the few minutes before they took off again, one of our jobs was to cycle out across the tarmac and collect the photographs so that kills could be verified. Many a time I was blown off my bike by the force of a Lightning exhaust.

As part of the communications team, it was also my job every afternoon to telex the Ministry of Defence with precise details of the operational readiness of all the aircraft on the airfield –

sometimes as many as a hundred. We also submitted hourly weather reports and handled the flow of messages in and out of the base. Today, the thought of Britain's air defences relying on messages sent by teleprinter over telegraph wires seems primitive in the extreme. But it worked. And from those military protocols developed in the early 1960s came the internet and wireless communications we know today.

It was exciting work for an eighteen-year-old – all the more so for the RAF legends we met. One was Group Captain Bird Wilson, Coltishall's Commanding Officer and a hero of World War II, which was still recent history. Another was Wing Commander Black, reputedly the best Lightning pilot in the RAF and famous for flying any aircraft to the limit of its capabilities. It was said that he once landed a Lightning with its tail hanging off after snapping it in mid air with the force of his G-turns.

As at Cosford, there were also the pleasures of drinking and dancing on evenings out. One of my favourite venues was Studio 5, a trad jazz club in Norwich where we danced and stomped to bands like The Temperance Seven, Kenny Ball and his Jazzmen and The Clyde Valley Stompers. Many times I missed the last bus to Coltishall and had to walk the ten miles back. It's a long way when you're tipsy.

After Coltishall, my next posting was a two-month secondment in 1962 to RAF Bishop's Court in Northern Ireland. This was the site of the huge Killard Point radar station, the most westerly in Britain, that tracked civilian aircraft as they left UK airspace and headed across the Atlantic. While I was there it was also tracking the test runs of the TSR-2, an experimental supersonic military jet that was being developed to counter the Warsaw Pact's MiG-21s and ground attack aircraft. A brilliant plane, conceived and built way ahead of its time, it sadly fell victim to bureaucratic wrangling and rising costs, and the project was eventually scrapped.

It was there that I met Russ Williams, a Welshman who was working on the base as part of his national service. I quickly noticed something different about Russ – a quality of stillness and peace that I hadn't seen in anyone else. It intrigued me.

One day when Russ came down to the telecommunications office and handed me a signal to send, I decided to get to the bottom of it. "Russ," I said. "Why are you not the same as the rest of us?"

He thought for a moment and answered quietly: "Maybe it's because I'm a Christian."

I was puzzled. "Well, I'm a Christian, aren't I? I've been christened. I've been confirmed. I live in England, for heaven's sake! Everyone's a Christian in England."

Russ pulled a heavily thumbed New Testament from his pocket and flipped through the pages. "There," he said, pointing to a verse in the letter to the Romans. "What does that say?"

I followed his finger on the page and read out the words: "All have sinned and fall short of the glory of God."

"Do you know what that means?"

I shook my head dumbly. Russ flicked on a couple of pages and pointed to another verse. Again I read it: "The wages of sin is death."

"Go on," he said.

"But the gift of God is eternal life in Christ Jesus our Lord." I still didn't see what he was getting at. "So are you saying I'm not a Christian?"

"All I can do is show you what the Bible says," replied Russ. "The point is, what are you doing with your life? Does it have a purpose?"

I had to admit that there wasn't much purpose in my life. Drinking? Stomping? Learning to be a good signals operator? There had to be more than that. Russ had unsettled me, and over the next few weeks I quizzed him further about this Christianity thing. Why was he so sure he was a Christian and I wasn't? Where did his inner peace come from? How could I get some of it for myself?

As I asked my questions, Russ patiently helped me to understand. We talked about God's love for me, personally; about the towering figure of Jesus Christ – God in human form – who suffered an excruciating death in which I was somehow implicated but which opened up the way to being forgiven; about the empty tomb – what did that mean? – and the need for a personal response. At times I was tempted to dismiss the whole thing as fantasy, but I couldn't argue with the quiet, inward conviction of the man talking to me.

Despite all my years at Sunday School and Bible class, the notion that Jesus Christ, dead for 2,000 years as I understood it, could in fact be alive and talking to me, Stuart Windsor, in 1962, was a shock and a revelation. On 6 May, my head still full of questions, I realized it was time to act.

"Russ," I said as we stood together in my office. "I'd like to become a Christian."

Russ smiled. I think he knew this was coming. He closed the door and he and I got down on our knees, elbows propped on a couple of chairs. He led me in a simple prayer in which I asked Jesus to come into my heart as Saviour and Lord and promised I would follow and obey him for the rest of my life. As I said the words, and meant them, I felt a surge of inner peace – a warm, gentle pulse that told me something real and important had happened in my soul and I'd never be the same again.

While talking to Russ, I'd become friends with one of the air traffic controllers – a Scotsman with the confusingly similar name of Ross. He and I spent much of our free time cycling together round County Down and I'd talked to him about my discussions with Russ.

Once I'd made my commitment, I told Ross what had happened. To my great surprise, he said he'd like to become a Christian as well. I thought this wasn't supposed to happen – not yet, not with me being so new in my own faith. Somewhat nervously, I took Ross through the prayer that I myself had prayed and was flabbergasted and delighted to see his life changed in the same way. I think Ross had a Scottish Presbyterian background which had no doubt sown the seeds of his eventual commitment.

Shortly afterwards, Russ the Welshman told me about a Christian outreach campaign taking place in the nearby town of Downpatrick. A Baptist evangelist called Currie Brennan was speaking at a series of meetings and Russ suggested we go and hear him.

I remember it being a fine summer's evening and the campaign tent was full to overflowing. Russ and I, along with Russ's wife Glenys, squeezed our way in and took a seat at the back. After some choruses and hymns and a few minutes' talk from the front, I was astounded to hear Currie Brennan mentioning my name.

"There's a young man here from across the water called Stuart Windsor. He's based at RAF Bishop's Court and he's just become a Christian. He's going to come up and tell us what this means to him."

There must have been about 300 people in that tent and here was I, totally unprepared, being asked to stand up and say something. I'd never spoken in public in my life. I stared at Russ, convinced he must have tipped Currie off. He probably had, but his face was a picture of amused innocence. Terrified, I waved my hands at the stage as if to say, "No! Please! Move on!", but people were now craning round to see who this Stuart Windsor was. There was no way out. With Currie beckoning me forward, I rose from my seat with a feeling of dread in my stomach and walked slowly to the stage.

Currie led me to the microphone and I looked down on a sea of expectant faces.

"Yes, it's true," I stammered when I could find my voice. "I did make a decision to become a Christian. I do believe God has done something in my heart and life, because now I feel completely different." I cast about for something else to say and remembered a verse that Russ had quoted again and again. "As it says in 2 Corinthians 5:17, 'If any person is in Christ, he is a new creation. Old things are passed away and behold, all things have become new.' I can tell you today that that's true. I know I'm different. I have a peace and joy that I never had before. I know my life has changed."

Whoever decides these things in the RAF now decreed that all of Cosford's 38th entry should be brought back from their postings around the country and put through what was called "special training" at RAF Digby in Lincolnshire. Though it seemed like a random, bureaucratic decision, I can see, looking back, that God was guiding me into the next stage of my life. I just didn't know it at the time.

The location was a clue as to what we'd be doing. At Coltishall we'd occasionally seen people from Digby's 591 Signals Unit setting up radio equipment in trucks at the end of the airfield to listen to communications to and from the aircraft. They never gave much away about what they were doing, but we knew it was something to do with monitoring the security of Coltishall's communications. Special training, it seemed, was all about listening – either to our own aircraft or, covertly, to the enemy – in collaboration with the national security agencies. As such, I later learned, it came under the control of Government Communications Headquarters or GCHQ. It turned out I was to join Digby's 399 Signals Unit whose role was to monitor Warsaw Pact air forces.

This was my introduction to Signals Intelligence – SIGINT

for short – which became my work for the next sixteen years. And much as I would love to say more, I can't alter the fact that I'm still bound by the Official Secrets Act and must slide over much of what I did. Suffice it to say, the work took me to Germany, Cyprus and the Persian Gulf and contributed, I hope, to maintaining the balance of power during the Cold War.

More immediately, the move to Digby in 1962 brought me back into contact with the old Cosford crowd, including Jan Trist, who arrived at about the same time as me. When Jan had learned of the transfer, he'd written to his parents to say he was unfortunately being sent to Digby – Digby also being the name of a mental institution two miles from their home. They'd written back to ask what was wrong with him. He told me the story with great amusement when we met and suggested we go for a drink. I said I'd come, but I'd stick to orange juice.

Jan was astounded. "What's up? Are you ill?"

"No, it's not that," I said. "I'm now a Christian, so I've stopped drinking."

Jan found this hard to take. Just like me a few months previously, he believed he had impeccable credentials for calling himself a Christian. Not only christened and confirmed, he'd been a choirboy, an altar server and a member of the Royal School of Church Music. In his view, you didn't get much more Christian than that, and to hear me talking about "becoming" a Christian was incomprehensible – even slightly offensive.

For me, stopping drinking was not a conscious decision or a point of principle. I simply found I no longer wanted to drink. And it seemed to me that if God had taken away the desire, he must have a reason and I might as well go along with it.

In talking to Jan since, I've learned that my not drinking was just one of the changes he noticed in me. He tells me I came to Digby with a new confidence and joy. I even looked different. I certainly behaved differently to the old Stuart. Jan and I were in the same billet and every night I'd kneel by my bed in front of the lads and say my prayers. That again was not a difficult decision, more a matter of obeying the impulse. I expected to be ribbed for it and was thankful when most people fell quiet and simply watched me doing it. Fortunately I was good at sport and this commanded a certain respect. If I hadn't been, I'm sure I'd have faced a torrent of ridicule.

In my new-found zeal, I was probably a pain to some of my fellow trainees. Apparently I used to tell them off if they swore on the football pitch. Jan insists that whenever he tried to light up, I'd flick the cigarette from his mouth and tell him he didn't need it. I'm grateful for the tolerance of the old 38th as I found my feet as a new Christian.

In Northern Ireland I'd attended the Baptist church in Newcastle, County Down, and a mission church in the east end of Belfast. When I left for the mainland, the Baptist elders recommended I join the Brethren church at Prospect Hall in Lincoln and sent me off with a letter of introduction.

On my very first Sunday, Bible under my arm, I boarded the country bus at Digby for the ride into Lincoln. A couple of stops later someone else got on, also with a Bible under his arm, and asked for a ticket to Prospect Hall. Once he'd sat down, I sidled over and introduced myself. His name was Bob Gordon. At one time he was the owner of King's Coaches in Norwich. Later, as Dr Bob Gordon, he became a prominent evangelist and conference speaker and an adviser to the Evangelical Alliance. He also worked for many years with Colin Urquhart at the Fountain Trust.

Bob took me under his wing. I was hungry to learn more of the Bible and Christian doctrine and how to evangelize and so much more in this new life that I'd discovered. In the following months, Bob became my mentor and a close friend. He was there at Prospect Hall on the day I was baptized and the elders gave me a verse from the book of Proverbs that has guided me ever since: "Trust in the Lord with all your heart, and do not rely on your own insight. In all your ways acknowledge him and he will make straight your paths" (3:5–6, RSV).

A few Sundays after my first visit, I persuaded Jan to come with me to Prospect Hall. A high Anglican by background, Jan found our humble Brethren chapel quite a culture shock. No candles. No robes. No Latin. But something touched him – a freedom in worship that he hadn't seen before. Not long afterwards, he made his own commitment. He says he did so in bed at Digby, still somewhat suspicious because this wasn't the kind of Christianity he'd grown up with, but realizing he had to act.

"Lord," he said, "if all this stuff is true, then I'd like to discover what Stuart has got."

He did.

Life in SIGINT is never stationary for long, and in January 1963 I was posted to Five Signals Wing at RAF Butzweilerhof on the edge of Cologne in Germany. Formerly a Luftwaffe air defence station for Cologne and now owned by Sony, it was then a vast Cold War listening station. Behind its gates was an area the size of a small town with mile after mile of antennae, some twice the height of an electricity pylon. The purpose of the base was to pick up high-frequency signals from distant enemy transmissions.

I'd never before spent any length of time outside the British Isles and I revelled in the strangeness of being in a foreign country. Even the Brethren church I started attending was unlike anything I'd known at home. It ran on very traditional lines with men and women sitting separately during the services and a rack at the back for the men to leave their pipes in as they entered. With so much that was new and odd, I was eager to discover more.

Exploring the centre of Cologne one Saturday afternoon,

I was intrigued to hear singing in the distance. I followed the sound and it led me into the city's main railway station. I started to pick out the words: *"Lies deine Bibel, bete jeden Tag"* (Read your Bible, pray every day).

"Christians," I thought. And there they were, six singers with a guitar and a few others handing out tracts at the edges of the crowd. Two middle-aged German ladies came up to me and put a tract in my hand.

"Entschuldigung," (Excuse me) I said. "I'm English. But I am a Christian."

They switched immediately to English. "Well, if you're a Christian, you should be up there with the others." And they pushed me towards the musicians. I wasn't going anywhere special, so was quite happy to join in and sing along as best I could.

After a couple more songs, the leader of the group – an elderly Baptist pastor – turned to me and said in English: "Welcome, my friend! If you'd now like to give your testimony, I will translate."

Nothing like being thrown in at the deep end, I thought. It was Downpatrick all over again. This time, though, I was more confident of my story and managed to speak to the crowd for a few minutes, drawing on various Bible verses to make my point.

"Thank you," said the pastor when I'd finished. "For a young man I can see you're well versed in the word of God. But I have a suggestion. When we've finished, I'd like you to come to my house and have supper. Then my wife and I will pray with you."

"Why not?" I thought. As the group dispersed, I left the station with the pastor and his wife, and we took a tram to their home not far from the centre. There they treated me to an excellent German supper of meat and sauerkraut.

"Now we pray," said the pastor as the meal came to an end.

"That's fine," I thought. "I like the idea of that."

"Also, we would like to lay hands on you as we pray."

I froze. Praying was one thing. Laying hands on people was not something we Brethren approved of. It smacked too much of dodgy Pentecostal practices like speaking in tongues, which the elders at Prospect Hall had taught us was from the flesh, if not the devil. "Stay away from those Pentecostals," they'd warned. "We don't believe in that sort of thing, not today in 1962!"[2]

Now here I was, about to pray with a rabid layer-on of hands.

"Please, no speaking in tongues," I stammered as we knelt on the floor. "I'm not into..."

As soon as the pastor and his wife placed their hands on my back, I felt a surge of power and warmth coursing through my body. With it came a heady, bubbling sensation, a mixture of laughter and excitement, along with an overwhelming sense of God's presence and the most intense feeling of love crackling between us like an electric shock. I'd felt God's presence before, right from the day I'd said that first prayer of commitment with Russ Williams. But this was another dimension. As I knelt and God's Spirit flooded through me, I did what I never thought I would. I spoke in tongues, praising Jesus in this new heavenly language I'd miraculously been given. And I carried on doing it, I'm told, for the next two hours.

When I was capable of concentrating, the pastor opened his Bible and led me through a number of passages to show that all this was perfectly biblical and, indeed, to be expected as part of God's empowering. "With this equipping you'll be able to walk more closely with God," he said. "You'll be able to pray and worship according to God's will. You'll understand the Scriptures better. Christ will become more real to you and your witness to unbelievers will become even more powerful."

His words touched a chord in my soul. This was what I'd craved without knowing it all my life. I'd come home. I'd discovered unconditional love.

Those feelings were reinforced when I went to church the next Sunday with Herte and her sister Trudy, the two ladies who'd handed me the tract in the railway station. They worshipped at the Pentecostal church in Porz, across the river from the centre of Cologne. Standing among the worshippers, captivated by God's reality and carried away by the joyfulness of the service, I knew I'd found my spiritual home.

Three months after my arrival in Cologne, I was delighted to find my old friend, Jan Trist, also assigned to Butzweilerhof. We spent a lot of time together until Jan suffered a serious car accident while back in England on leave. He spent several months in hospital with head and pelvis injuries and eventually made it back to Cologne in 1965. But the injuries had taken their toll. Assessments showed he could no longer perform his previous duties (he couldn't wear headphones, for one thing), and the RAF gave him the choice of being downgraded or leaving. He chose to leave and passed out of my life for the next twenty-seven years.

In the meantime, I'd formed a friendship with an RAF policeman called Fred Moore. I'd seen him on duty at the gate, but didn't realize he was a Christian until we met at the camp church. Once we'd got to know each other, Fred and I set up a camp fellowship that began to attract others on the base for a weekly prayer and Bible study meeting.

In the spring of 1963, Fred informed me that his wife's sister, Ethel, was coming from England for a holiday and would be staying at Butzweilerhof over the summer. "Lovely Christian girl," he said. "Could have had loads of boyfriends, but she's very choosy. You'll like her. Not sure she'll like you, though!"

I thought no more about Fred's visitor until a few weeks later when I'd just played a match for the camp football team. I came off the field and decided to cool off in the pool. I changed and plunged in. As I surfaced, there was Sue, Fred's wife, sitting at the poolside with an extremely pretty, dark-haired girl in a blue swimming costume.

The attraction was instant – on my side, anyway. Ethel and I met again at the camp Christian fellowship and I persuaded her to come on a date with me to Cologne Zoo. I'd like to say that love blossomed among the elephants and giraffes, but Ethel tells me it took a little longer than that. We kept in touch after she went home to Workington in Cumbria and, in the spring of 1965, we got engaged.

By now I was back at RAF Digby and the plan was to get married the following April. But the camp housing officer took me aside and explained that if we got married by Christmas, we'd be able to move straight into married quarters. If we delayed, there'd be more people coming back from abroad and we'd be shunted to the bottom of the list – which could mean having to live apart until the next vacancy came up.

The offer was too good to miss and Ethel and I were married in Workington in December 1965. Our first child, Stuart Junior, arrived in 1967 and we embarked on the challenging task of trying to forge a normal family life on a military base devoted to winning the Cold War.

International tensions were never far away. I well remember the time two black cars arrived at Digby from London and took away one of my colleagues, Chief Technician Doug Britten. He never came back. It turned out he'd been using his position in SIGINT to sell secrets to the Russians, a crime that earned him a twenty-one-year prison sentence.

It was in this heightened atmosphere that Stuart Junior went missing at the age of three. One morning he crawled through a gap in the privet hedge surrounding our garden and disappeared. When Ethel discovered he'd gone, she began frantically calling on the neighbours to see if they had him. Soon the camp police were on the case, spreading out from the immediate neighbourhood and knocking on more doors. Ethel and I became more and more anxious, torn between staying at home in case he turned up and getting out with the search party. Finally, at about 5 p.m., one of the camp sergeants arrived and told us that Stuart had been found. It seemed a car had dropped him off at the entrance to the base.

All Stuart could tell us was that a Mini van, "a car like Daddy's," had picked him up and taken him to the coast. We never did find out who the abductors were or why they took him and why they brought him back. Was it pranksters, or something more sinister related to the nature of my work? Though I thrived in the world of intelligence and national security, the work from then on was tinged with anxiety about the possible danger to my family.

4

God's Call

In 1978, after sixteen years in SIGINT and thirteen years of marriage, I was warned to stand by for a special signals project that would mean spending a long period overseas without the family. I'd already done a similar unaccompanied tour, leaving for the Persian Gulf at the end of December 1967 and coming back thirteen months later in January 1969. Baby Stuart had been two months old when I left and when I returned he didn't know me.

"Who's that funny man?" he kept asking. It was heart-breaking.

Now Stuart was eleven and his little sister, Elizabeth, was six. Though I didn't seriously think they'd forget me, the thought of another year or so away from Ethel and the family weighed heavily. In any case, I'd now served twenty years in the RAF. Should I now be considering something else?

At the time, Britain's Labour government was looking for cuts in the armed services and was offering generous pay-offs to people who agreed to retire early. As Ethel and I prayed about whether I should leave the RAF, I found a job advertised in The *Daily Telegraph*. The North West Water Authority was looking for a Staff Training and Development Officer at its headquarters in Warrington, Lancashire.

Although I didn't have a degree, I did know about training. In 1975 I'd completed the RAF's Training Officers course and learned a lot about using closed-circuit TV for training purposes. Since then I'd been training personnel at the RAF's School of Advanced Telecommunications at North Luffenham in Lincolnshire. I didn't see why the same skills shouldn't transfer from military communications to the water and sewerage business. Not an obvious connection, I agree, but training is training in any field.

So I applied and was called to Warrington for interview. I found I was one of 120 candidates, most of them graduates. I was surprised, therefore, to be shortlisted and even more so when North West Water eventually offered me the job. Starting work in September 1978, I lived in temporary lodgings for the first six months until we were able to buy a house in nearby Runcorn and Ethel and the children moved up to join me.

Runcorn lies on the southern shores of the River Mersey between Warrington and Liverpool. Along with Widnes on the opposite bank, it forms the Borough of Halton. Now Halton is full of wonderful people, but I hope they'll forgive me if I say that no one would choose to live there without good reason. This is chemical industry heartland – or *was* before much of it was closed down. It was here that ICI and Mond and about twenty other chemical firms conducted the smellier end of their business. Chlorine plants dominated the borough, blighting the landscape and poisoning the atmosphere. After the clean air and wide horizons of Lincolnshire, I wondered at times if bringing the family here had been such a good move.

My new life had its compensations, however. After two decades of covert telecommunications work in the RAF during which I couldn't even tell Ethel what I was doing, it was a welcome change not to have to be evasive when people asked me my occupation. Now when the question came up, I could proudly announce: "I'm in sewerage."

While one of my colleagues, Stan Shelton, took care of the training of manual workers, I was responsible for the training and development of North West Water's staff and managers from graduate recruits to company directors. Between us, we looked after the training needs of about 11,000 people of whom around 5,000 were my responsibility.

The skills required in a water and sewerage business are surprisingly varied. Scientists, engineers, accountants, lawyers, computer operators and a gamut of other specialists need constant training to do their jobs properly. I taught presentation skills to the Authority's scientists, its engineers and its telecommunications staff, mostly ex-RAF, whose work included managing a weather radar chain along the Pennines to monitor rainfall and water levels. I set up courses so that electrical engineers could qualify to switch current from the National Grid to the Authority's plants. I organized the water industry's annual microbiological conference at which experts like Professor Hugh Pennington lectured our bacteriologists, microbiologists and zoologists on legionnaire's disease and the dangers of E.coli. With water quality a constant issue, I arranged training for directors on how to answer public concerns on TV – helped by presenter Geoffrey Wheeler who at the time fronted programmes such as *Songs of Praise* and *Top of the Form*. I even set up training for estate keepers in how to deal with deer and salmon poachers on the land surrounding our rivers and reservoirs.

In the process, I passed the exam to become a corporate member of the Institute of Personnel and Training and was trained in the new science of psychometrics – a technique we mainly used in the recruitment of graduate engineers.

When I first arrived at North West Water, I naturally started looking for other Christians. The first I discovered was Jill White, a librarian in the engineering reference library. She and I agreed we needed a Christian fellowship at head office and invited all the Christians we could find to a preliminary meeting. The event was a revelation, as all kinds of unlikely people turned up, and many who thought they were all alone in their functions or departments found others of like mind. I still recall the reactions as people entered the room: "Didn't expect to see you here… There's a surprise!… You, of all people!"

I believe the fellowship still runs – as does the annual carol service we started holding in the company boardroom.

Another priority for Ethel and myself was to find a church. When we first moved to Runcorn, one of Ethel's friends in Cumbria – a North West Water electrical engineer – had recommended we go to a Brethren church in the town. We did so and were warmly welcomed, but the Pentecostal bit of us still wasn't fully satisfied. Was this really where God wanted us to be? We prayed for some clear direction.

It was almost two years later that the answer came. I was driving home from giving blood, as I recall, when I drove past a van parked outside a house. On the side were the words, "Halton Pentecostal Church".

I braked and peered more closely. Halton Pentecostal Church? I didn't know there was such a thing.

I parked the car and walked back to the house. I knocked and a lady came to the door.

"Excuse me," I said. "Is that your van?"

She said it was. "It isn't normally there but I had to bring it home over lunchtime."

She introduced herself as Margaret, personal assistant to the church pastor. I asked her what time the services were and she gave me the details. "We've got a treat this Sunday," she told me. "Trevor Dearing's coming to speak."

I knew the name. An Anglican vicar from Essex, Trevor Dearing had come to national attention when his own life was transformed by the Holy Spirit and huge crowds started coming to the services of healing at his church in Hainault. Healings of body, mind and spirit had become common. A visit from Trevor

Dearing was not to be missed.

What I most remember about the service at Halton Pentecostal Church that following Sunday was not so much the speaker (I'm sure he was as inspirational as ever), but a prophetic message spoken by one of the congregation as we worshipped. Its content was direct and simple: "God is saying to you that you've arrived home. This is where he wants you to be. Stay in this place until he moves you on."

Ethel gave me a nudge. "I'd say that was guidance, wouldn't you?"

So began fifteen wonderful years at Halton Pentecostal Church in Widnes. The pastor, Benny Finch, was a great fellow whose ministry touched thousands of lives and to whom I owe an enormous debt for his care and guidance. Church services were never dull with Benny. God was active and people came from miles around to see what was happening and to discover Christ for themselves. Thanks to Benny's wide connections, we were fortunate to host a long list of international speakers – Benson Idahosa from Nigeria, German evangelist Reinhard Bonnke, Morris Cerullo, Terry Law and others. It was a time of rapid spiritual growth, both for the church and for Ethel and me as individuals.

We hadn't been there long when I started to feel that God might be calling me to full-time ministry. While some people can testify to hearing God speak directly, I personally find that he speaks more through feelings and intuitions. With experience, I've learned to recognize these promptings when they happen. Over a period of months and after a great deal of prayer, I became convinced that God really was calling me to be ordained.

I shared these thoughts with Benny, his son Mark (the other senior minister) and the church elders. They set themselves to praying and agreed to give me their support. Promoting me from deacon to assistant lay pastor (unpaid), they launched me on a four-year, on-the-job, mature training scheme.

Life was picking up speed. I was still the Staff Training and Development Officer at North West Water, travelling a patch that extended from Stoke in the Midlands to the Scottish borders and from Liverpool in the west to Skipton in Yorkshire in the east. At the same time I was assistant pastor at Halton, undergoing training for the ministry and deeply involved in the running of the church – as was Ethel. I had also started a film unit, initially to record the Sunday services, but the work was now expanding to cover other events as well. And just when it seemed that life couldn't get any more hectic, we decided to rebuild the church.

In the middle of Widnes was a six-acre site that used to be the Widnes Foundry Dressing Shop. Dressing, so I discovered, is the final stage in the finishing of iron and steel components before they're shipped to the customer. In its 100-year history, the Widnes shop had dressed the gates of Waverley Station in Edinburgh, the Mumbles Pier in Swansea and the pipes that carry water from Wales to Liverpool and from the Lake District to Manchester.

By 1980, the building itself was derelict and roofless and the site lay covered in a century's accumulation of chemical ash from the dressing process. Halton Borough Council badly wanted something done with it. Would the church like it? If so, we could have it for a knock-down price.

At the time we were occupying a former Brethren church and straining at the seams on a Sunday. The council's offer was an answer to our prayers. The elders, pastors and deacons trooped down to inspect this gaunt industrial relic and decided unanimously to take on the challenge of turning it into a new church.

The first hurdle was to raise the money. Widnes is not a wealthy place. Our congregation largely consisted of shopkeepers, teachers, airport staff, garage owners, social workers – ordinary people doing ordinary jobs, none of whom had a lot of money to spare. Nonetheless, we decided to ask each working family to give, or pledge to give, £1,000. At enormous sacrifice, most did so. This produced enough for Benny to go to the bank and secure a loan for the £100,000 we needed to buy the site.

We then needed about £250,000 for the construction. We raised some of it by selling our existing building and moving into an old office block on the dressing shop site. But the rest had to be prayed for, and painstakingly gathered in, pound by pound – some in the form of interest-free loans from church members.

On one particular Sunday I preached on the Old Testament story of Elijah and the widow of Zarephath, whose meagre supply of oil and meal miraculously lasted to the end of a lengthy drought. When I'd finished, one of the deacons, Bernie Semourson, came to the front and said that God had revealed to him the previous day that one of the pastors would preach on this very passage. "I didn't know if this *was* from God," he continued, "but now that Stuart has preached, I can see that it was. The thing is, God also told me we should bring our gifts today and lay them at the feet of the pastors."

We had already taken the offering, but Benny agreed that this sounded like God's instruction and we ought to be obedient. So he issued an invitation for anyone with more to give to bring it to the front. He did the same in the evening service and the two offerings together produced an astonishing £30,000. We went home that night humbled by God's goodness and reminded of all those times in the Bible when a simple act of obedience unlocks his supply.

With 100 years' worth of chemical ash beneath our feet, we had to take sample drillings around the site before the planning inspectors would allow us to start construction. Once we had the go-ahead, we built the church ourselves. The congregation included two professional builders and a former pit deputy who offered valuable help and advice. Other members contributed their skills as quantity surveyors or bricklayers. Benny himself became clerk of works, personally supervising the construction. Although I've got no building skills at all, I spent many hours with a shovel digging out the footings. As the church took shape inside the shell of the dressing shop, we brought in a Merseyside construction firm to build thirty-five bungalows alongside. These now provide sheltered care for retired Christian workers and a useful income for the church.

Opened in 1985 and known today as the Foundry Fellowship, the new Pentecostal church at Halton has become a valuable and much-used facility and a centre for new ministries such as training young Christians to become drug counsellors. At the time, however, it was a massive challenge and I never cease to be grateful for the faith and sacrifice that made it possible.

Around the time the new church was opened, someone called my training manager at North West Water and asked to speak to Pastor Stuart. The next day, another call came through to the church office: "Could I speak to the Staff Training Officer, please."

Two misdialled calls in two days were a signal that I could no longer juggle church and my employment at North West Water. Although my bosses were keen to keep me, they understood my decision when I handed in my resignation in the summer of 1985. From now on, my work for God was to be full time.

In the Assemblies of God wing of the Pentecostal Church, ordinations take place once a year in April at the Church's national conference. In 1986, the year I completed my training, the conference took place at Butlin's Holiday Camp at Minehead in Somerset. On the evening of the ordination service, I stood at the front of a packed tent with Ethel and fourteen other newly minted ministers and their wives, pondering my unfamiliar title (the *Reverend* Stuart Windsor – good grief!) and wondering what God was planning for this ex-Barnardo's, ex-RAF, ex-water authority, Pentecostal minister.

The answer was not what I expected.

To explain, I need to back-track. Our pastor, Benny, had once spent time in New Zealand, where he'd met a young Salvation Army officer called Frank Houston. When Frank discovered the transforming power of the Holy Spirit, Benny helped him find his new spiritual home in the Assemblies of God. From New Zealand, Frank had moved to Australia and built up a huge Pentecostal church in Sydney. Later, when his son Brian was called to the ministry, Frank sent him to Sydney's north-west suburbs to plant a new church. They called it Hillsong and the rest is history.

Frank, as it happened, was on the platform in Minehead on the evening of my ordination. A small man with dark hair and glasses, he was on his way to Widnes at Benny's invitation to spend a week at our very own Foundry Fellowship. He didn't know me and I knew him only by reputation. But when the presiding minister invited the dignitaries on the platform to step down, pick an ordinand as they felt led and pray for them, Frank made straight for Ethel and me.

He paused, placed his hand on my head and spent a few moments in prayer. We could hear him speaking quietly in tongues and felt the warmth of God's presence as he waited for the Holy Spirit to guide him in what to say. Finally he spoke.

"God is going to lead you in ways you can't understand at the present time and will use you differently to anything you can imagine. He's calling you to appear before leaders of nations, rulers, presidents and prime ministers. He's going to take you to places you wouldn't normally go. It won't be easy and sometimes it'll be dangerous, but God will be with you and will use you to be a voice."

With a few further words of blessing, Frank moved on.

I was stunned. "How's that going to happen?" I thought. "Presidents and prime ministers? We live in Runcorn, for heaven's sake!"

I heard a lot more from Frank in the week that followed as he spoke at our church in Widnes. And one thing he said has stuck with me ever since. It was about breaking the human logic that says certain things can happen and certain things can't. "The Holy Spirit is speaking to all of us far more than we realize," said Frank at one of his meetings. "And he wants to use us. So if, when you've prayed, you think he wants you to do something – even something crazy like buying a ticket to Australia – just do it. If it's not his will, he's quite capable of stopping you. If we're open, available and obedient, living holy lives and ready to follow him with trust and humility, there's absolutely nothing that he cannot do."

That week changed my life and I committed myself afresh. "You're in charge," I said to God. "I want whatever you've got for me. May your Holy Spirit lead wherever he wishes."

5

A Ministry in Film

As a trainer in the RAF and later at North West Water, I'd often used film to teach presentation skills or to help with distance learning. So when we joined Halton Pentecostal Church, it seemed a natural move to set up a camera to record the talks on a Sunday. With the church growing and services overflowing into the adjacent hall, a TV link meant that everyone could at least see the speaker. We could also put the recordings onto VHS cassettes and send them to people who couldn't get to church.

While it's commonplace now, filming church services was almost unknown at the turn of the 1980s when even the humble video recorder was the latest thing in technology. We were possibly one of the first churches in Britain to try to do it to a professional standard.

To begin with, we simply mounted a black-and-white camera on a tripod and one of our young people kept it trained on the speaker in a head-and-shoulders shot. When people remarked that that was fine but a bit boring, we added a second camera and a switching unit. Then we realized we'd never get decent quality on VHS tape, so we switched to three-quarter-inch Sony U-matic video tape of the kind we were using at North West Water. This greatly improved our picture quality and was better for making VHS copies. Next came a high-tech wide screen for the overflow hall. Then three-tube professional cameras.

At the same time I was building and training a team of fifteen to twenty operators, most of them young church members. Here I had the valuable help of John Rushworth, the pastor's son-in-law and one of the deacons. As others saw what we were doing, we started getting requests to film events elsewhere – weddings, teaching sessions, conferences and so on. That meant we needed a van, so John Leach, owner of the Widnes Car Centre, kindly donated a Ford Transit. The team expanded and we started gaining a reputation beyond the local area.

From those small beginnings grew a business that eventually took the name, Spirit Free Communications. Throughout its life it ran on a shoestring and survived by faith. We made a bit of income in the spring and summer by filming some of the well-known Christian conferences, but finances were always tight and I didn't take a salary. Somehow – and to this day I'm not sure how – God kept it going and met every need until its work was done.

The ministry took a further step when the organizers of Spring Harvest, one of the largest Christian conferences in Europe, phoned us out of the blue and asked if we'd like to film their 1987 event at Skegness in Lincolnshire. This was way bigger than anything we'd attempted so far, especially when we later started filming the Minehead and Pwllheli conferences as well. While it stretched our skills and resources, we must have done a reasonable job because Spring Harvest had us back each year until the early 1990s.

The next to use our services was that other big Christian conference, New Wine. This again was hugely exciting for the team. Like Spring Harvest, New Wine attracts many of the world's best-known Christian speakers – in those days the likes of J. John, David Pytches and Barry Kissell – and being asked to do the filming was a tremendous privilege. Each year from 1989 to 1992 we filmed the New Wine conference at the Royal

Bath Showground near Shepton Mallet and relayed the pictures around the site. It was also our job to edit the tapes, take orders and have video cassettes of the meetings ready for sale before the delegates went home.

New demands meant a major overhaul of our equipment. We moved to professional cameras – Sony 3CCD M7s, just one step down from commercial broadcast standard. We upgraded our mixers and sound kit and traded in our Ford Transit for a fully equipped, outside broadcast truck, a Mercedes previously used for filming speedboat races. In the late 1980s, John Rushworth and I met a young Christian TV engineer called Steve Hale at a broadcasting exhibition in Brighton. Terrific at his job, Steve had installed broadcasting equipment for Sky TV and said he'd love to come and help us. He turned out to be just the person we needed for the big shoots we were then doing. Working with us part time and for no pay, he completely re-rigged our broadcast truck and would oversee the complicated setting up at the start of each event. He was a wonderful addition to the team.

The film ministry took another turn when I met an American called Paul Crawford who ran a similar operation to ours in Seattle. Paul was often asked to film Christian conferences in Europe and agreed to use Spirit Free Communications when such contracts came up. As a result, we found ourselves at frequent intervals driving our truck from Widnes to Sheerness in Kent to catch the Olau Line ferry to Vlissingen in Holland. From there we'd sometimes head north into Scandinavia, sometimes south and east towards the Rhine and the Alps. We filmed Lutheran conventions in Denmark, Sweden and Germany, a Catholic charismatic renewal conference in Bavaria, Pentecostal gatherings on my old turf in Cologne and the first of the worldwide Marches for Jesus led by singer-songwriter Graham Kendrick in Berne, Switzerland.

On one of our first European trips in 1988, the team and

I set off down-country from Merseyside, where I'd been to get our carnet stamped and signed at the Chamber of Commerce. The carnet, as I quickly learned, is a vital document, proving to customs officials at every point of entry and departure that you haven't illegally sold your equipment. While most of the team went by car, I took the truck with Patrick Drake, a young Irish member of our church who drove buses for Halton Transport. Patrick and I spent the best part of a day motoring down to Sheerness. There we caught the evening ferry and arrived in Vlissingen the following morning, ready for another day's drive to Karlsruhe in Germany.

That's when the trouble started. An alert Dutch customs officer pointed out that the carnet had been stamped but not signed. It was therefore invalid. I'd have to go back to the UK and get the necessary signature.

I pleaded that the team had a contract to meet, but he wouldn't be swayed. Sending the car ahead and leaving Patrick to find overnight accommodation in Vlissingen, I had to drive out of the customs shed and back onto the ferry, forking out for another return ticket on the way. When we docked in Sheerness, I drove off, did a short loop round the quayside, found a customs officer to sign the carnet and trundled back on board.

Amazingly, we got to Karlsruhe with exactly the margin we needed to set up our equipment and start filming. This particular conference had been organized by David Hathaway, a Pentecostal minister who for several years had smuggled Bibles into Communist Eastern Europe in his tour bus before being arrested, tortured and thrown into a Czechoslovak prison in 1972. There, he says, God revealed to him the date on which he'd be released. It happened exactly as promised, ten months later, when Prime Minister Harold Wilson travelled to Czechoslovakia to secure his freedom.

The main speaker at the Karlsruhe conference was John Osteen of Houston's Lakewood Church. Along with a wonderful music group called Vinesong, he ministered with great sensitivity to the two or three thousand Eastern European Christians who had travelled from behind the Iron Curtain for much-needed Bible teaching and a brief taste of personal freedom. God was very real for those few days and all of us on the team were deeply blessed just to be there.

Soon after we arrived, John Osteen introduced me to his teenage son, Joel, and asked if we could find a place for him on the filming team. He thought it might help Joel's still tentative faith if he were involved in some way. I agreed, naturally. Today, Joel is the senior pastor at Lakewood where numbers have grown to 20,000 under his ministry. I don't know if the Karlsruhe conference had any effect, but I'd like to think we played some small part in God's plan for Joel.

One of the most eventful of those early filming trips was a visit to the Soviet Union in January 1990. A Northern Irish pastor and close friend called Robert Robinson had asked me to travel with him to Leningrad, Moscow, Minsk and Kiev to help film a mission by the American evangelist, Terry Law. Just as happened on my trip to Nagorno Karabakh three years later, the Russian winter played havoc with our itinerary.

On one of our internal flights from Leningrad to Moscow, the pilot twice had to turn back to Leningrad because of freezing fog at Moscow Airport. As it happened, one of our fellow passengers was the Mayor of Leningrad, Anatoly Sobchak, who lost patience when the pilot announced the second aborted landing. His bodyguard marched down the aisle to the cockpit and banged open the door. From our seats we could hear a scuffle and voices being raised. We later discovered that the bodyguard had pulled a pistol on the pilot and demanded he land because his boss had an important meeting in Moscow.

Now Russian pilots, in my experience, are the best in the world at landing and taking off in extreme conditions. Had the

Cold War erupted into a real war, certainly in winter, I'm sure NATO's pilots would have been outmanoeuvred. But even with a gun to his head, this particular pilot refused to risk it and once again took us back to Leningrad.

By now Robert and I, along with Terry Law and his team, had had enough of Aeroflot and decided we'd get to Moscow more reliably by road. So we hired a bus and drove through the night to get to our next appointment.

In Moscow we stayed at The International, the main tourist hotel and shockingly luxurious compared to the poverty and empty shops and long, hopeless queues in the area round about. As we got into the lift to go to our rooms, we found ourselves surrounded by beautiful Muscovite women hoping to proposition us. Among our party was an American Methodist minister who got talking to one of the girls and found out that her father was dying of cancer. The girl herself was a graduate and a doctor, but the only way she could raise the money for her father's treatment was to become a prostitute. The minister ended up funding the treatment so the girl could resume her medical career.

In the village of Maloyaroslavits a few hours to the south of Moscow, we had the privilege of meeting Pastor Ivan Fedotov, one of the leaders of the underground Pentecostal church who'd spent twenty years in Vorkuta Prison in the Siberian gulag in the 1950s and 60s on account of his faith. A lean, lively, bright-eyed man, he'd survived his ordeal with amazing grace and humour. Two things stick in my memory from the visit. One is the primitive conditions in which he still lived (his toilet was an outside shed with a hole in the ground). The other was his description of looking out from his prison cell towards the nearby railway station and seeing newly freed prisoners collapsing and dying on the platform as they waited to board their trains. Was the prospect of freedom too much for men weakened by years of incarceration, or had the prison guards struck a cruel final blow by poisoning them? He didn't know.

Another leg of the trip took us from Kiev to Minsk. On the way our Antonov AN-24 turbo-prop aircraft flew over the Chernobyl nuclear power station, one of whose reactors had exploded so disastrously four years earlier in 1986. The crew pointed it out to us. (Learning I'd been in the RAF, they also invited me to fly the aircraft, but I declined.) Arriving in Minsk, we toured the dilapidated hospital that was still treating Chernobyl's victims and for which Terry Law was then raising funds. It was heartbreaking to walk the bleak wards and see so many children with thyroid and other cancers caused by radiation from the accident.

Another memory of that eventful trip was my aircraft seat breaking free from its moorings and sliding down the aisle as our Aeroflot TU-134 began its descent into Leningrad. Fortunately, Robert was quick to react and held me back before I slammed into the cockpit. Those Russian pilots might have been superb, but the same could not be said of their aircraft.

In June 1990, an organization called South Asian Outreach invited Mark Finch, my fellow minister and the son of our pastor in Widnes, to go and see the work it was doing in Cambodia. Mark asked if I'd like to go as well and film the trip.

This was just eleven years after the fall of Pol Pot's Khmer Rouge government which had brutalized the country and slaughtered or starved over a million of its citizens. I'd expected the legacy to be grim but wasn't prepared for just how raw and real those terrible years still were for the people of Cambodia. Accompanied by John Hurd, the Director of South Asian Outreach, Mark and I visited the killing fields and the torture chambers and saw the glass cages now stacked high with the bones of Pol Pot's victims. We also visited house churches that had kept the faith alive after Pol Pot abolished religion, most consisting mainly of women and children because very few

Christian men, it seemed, had survived the terror.

Two events from that trip stay deeply lodged in my memory. The first occurred the day we arrived in Phnom Penh. We flew in on a rattling Soviet AN-24 aircraft from Bangkok and caught a taxi to the only hotel in town. Having checked in, we made our way up the stairs to our rooms. As we did so, a small Asian man coming the other way looked me briefly in the eye and uttered one word: "Halleluiah!"

"Do you know him?" asked Mark.

"Never seen him in my life," I replied.

"Well, he seems to know you."

I thought little more about him until the evening, when we happened to be coming down the stairs. The same man was coming up. Again he looked at me. "Amen!" he said.

This time I put a hand out to stop him. "You're a Christian, aren't you?"

"Yes, I am," he said in fluent English. "I'm a pastor from Vietnam. But we can't talk here – I'm being followed. Come to my room later."

He gave me his room number and disappeared.

When we met the following day, he gave his name as Paul Tran Ai and told us his story. "I was once a Buddhist monk in the uplands of Vietnam," he began. "In 1980 some Filipino Christians came to my village to carry out an evangelistic campaign. I warned my people not to go and put a Buddhist curse on their activities. But I went to the meeting anyway to spy on who was there. One of the families in the village had a little girl who was born deaf and dumb, and these Christians prayed for her. To my astonishment, she was healed instantly and began speaking. The Holy Spirit convicted me that Jesus Christ was Lord and I fell on my knees and cried out for forgiveness.

"I'm now the pastor of a church in Ho Chi Minh City and superintendent of the Assemblies of God in Vietnam. I've been imprisoned several times for preaching the gospel and I'm constantly being followed, but God is at work. Some of our people from Vietnam have set up a church in Phnom Penh and I'm here to carry out baptisms. Next I'm catching a bus to Laos, where we have another church plant."

As Paul related his story, the New Testament seemed to live again in the jungles and slums of South-East Asia. The man was dynamite. The hour we spent talking and praying in his hotel bedroom was a time of deep blessing for us all and a memory I'll treasure for the rest of my life.

We handed Paul an English Bible and the little bit of money we could scrape together to help him on his way. Just before we left, Mark asked him why he'd spoken to me as he did when we passed on the stairs.

Paul looked back at me. "I just saw the grace of God in your eyes," he said quietly.

I was not only blessed, but humbled. Though I never saw him again, that was not the last time that Paul Tran Ai made his mark on my life.

The other event I most remember from the visit was a private moment between me and God. One sweltering afternoon towards the end of the trip, I sat on the edge of a field where the Khmer Rouge had bludgeoned thousands of people to death and thrown their bodies into pits. John Hurd of South Asian Outreach was sitting alongside. The poignancy of the place affected us both and we fell silent. John could sense I was troubled and eventually asked me what I was thinking.

"This has happened in our lifetime," I replied. "I really feel the need to repent." And there and then I made a vow to God that never again would I stand by and do nothing while Christians anywhere in the world were being persecuted and killed.

That might have been a foolhardy thing to do. God has a way of calling such vows to account.

6

To Moscow on a Prayer

Scroll forward nearly two years to the Spring Harvest conference at Skegness, Lincolnshire, in March 1992. One of the speakers that year was Josh McDowell of Stanford University. Josh had been converted as a young law student when he set out to disprove the historical basis of Christianity and ended up being convinced by it. Long affiliated with Campus Crusade for Christ, he's renowned as a speaker and apologist and has written extensively on the evidence for Christianity.

On this occasion we found ourselves chatting in the staff lounge of Butlin's holiday camp, Skegness.

"Is that you doing the filming?" he asked.

I said it was.

"Well, look," he continued. "I'm going to be speaking to 700 Russian Orthodox students in Moscow in July. I've been invited by the Moscow University Institute of Biblical Studies and I'm going with Campus Crusade to talk about the validity of the Old and New Testaments. I'm also doing some seminars on 'Why wait for sex?' Would you like to come and do the filming?"

I agreed immediately, put the date in the diary and said I'd be in touch when I'd finished my present round of assignments.

Next stop, direct from Skegness, was Bognor Regis on the south coast, where the Elim Pentecostal Church was holding its national annual conference – the speaker on this occasion being my old friend and mentor, Dr Bob Gordon. Having arrived and checked in, the team and I set up our cameras for the first session and I strolled back to my room to get ready. On the way, I walked past a couple standing outside the reception area.

"Stuart!"

I stopped mid-stride and did a double-take. Even after twenty-seven years, there was no mistaking that Devon voice. I turned and there was Jan Trist, whom I hadn't seen since he'd been invalided out of the RAF with his injured head in the 1960s.

"Jan!" I cried, rushing over and giving him a huge hug. "I've been looking for you all these years!" This was true. Every time I'd been in the West Country, I'd tried looking up "J. Trist" in the local telephone directories, but I'd never been able to track him down.

"What's this?" he teased, pointing to my now-white hair. He introduced me to his wife, Jill, explaining that I once used to be dark haired and a lot thinner – like Jack Charlton, the football player, he said. I only wished that was still the case. In great excitement, I started to tell Jill how Jan and I had been buddies when both of us were boy entrants in the RAF.

"Jan?" she said. "But his name's Malcolm!"

"Malcolm? *Malcolm!*" At once I understood why my quest had been in vain. In all the years I'd known him, he'd gone under his nickname and I hadn't even thought to question if that was his real name. I'd been looking under the wrong initial. As we talked, it became clear that I'd sometimes been very close. Twice I'd been to family funerals at Exeter crematorium, little knowing that Jan – or Malcolm, as I now had to call him – lived less than a mile away.

Our reunion was interrupted by a crisis in the filming team. Helen, one of my camera operators, had been running back to her accommodation when her contact lens dropped out. Without it she was helpless, unable to focus her camera. The first session would be starting within the hour and Helen was in tears.

"Where did you lose it?" I asked.

She waved a hand vaguely. "I don't know. Somewhere on the ground over there."

I looked to where she was pointing. She couldn't have dropped it in a worse place if she'd tried. Between where we were standing and the accommodation block was a ten-metre stretch of sand and chippings, every square centimetre winking and glistening in the late-afternoon sunlight. I shot up a brief prayer. I don't know why, but I then said to Helen: "Don't worry. Malcolm will find it."

"Really?" said Malcolm. "Well, I'll have a go." He wandered over to the area and paced up and down for a few moments. Then he bent down.

"Is this it?"

The evening's filming was saved. And I've never forgotten how Malcolm's re-entry into my life was accompanied by this little miracle, as though God were saying: "Believe me – it's all part of the plan."

Malcolm and I spent many hours that week catching up on old times. I discovered he'd trained as an electrician after leaving the RAF and was now working for a commercial refrigeration business, travelling the country maintaining fridges for big supermarket chains like Tesco and Marks & Spencer. For a long time he'd dropped out of church and had only recently realized how much he missed it. He and Jill had joined an Elim Pentecostal church in Exeter and that had brought them to the conference.

An idea began to form in my mind and towards the end of

the week I voiced it.

"Malcolm," I said, "Josh McDowell has invited me to Moscow in July to film some sessions at the university. If you're free, I'd like you to come with me."

"Absolutely. I've never flown there before."

"We're not flying, Malcolm. We're going to drive."

Once he'd come round to the idea, Malcolm booked two weeks' holiday in July and came to join me in Widnes. As there was only room for two of us in the truck, I sent the rest of the team to Moscow by air and Malcolm and I set off from Liverpool down the M6, stopping off in Watford to pick up a mixing station from a friend. Along the way I remember saying casually to Malcolm, "That Holts Radweld is good stuff, isn't it?"

"What do you mean?" he asked nervously.

"Well, I had a leak in the radiator, but I put some Radweld on the hole and it seems fine."

Malcolm was horrified. "You mean we're going to Moscow – 4,000 kilometres – and we're setting off with a radiator plugged with Radweld?"

"Well… yes," I said, sensing we maybe had different ideas about what constituted being ready. "Also, I should tell you we're missing a jack. I tried to find one but didn't have time."

"Have you got *any* tools on this thing?" he asked.

I thought about it, then opened up the glove compartment and pulled out a small cross-head screwdriver. "I've got this," I said. "But don't worry. I'm sure God will look after us."

I wouldn't have been surprised if Malcolm had changed his mind there and then. But he didn't. He took a deep breath, gave me a look and carried on driving.

We caught the Olau ship *Hollandia* at Sheerness (having toured the town in a last vain attempt to find a jack), crossed to Vlissingen and pointed the truck towards Germany. Just three years after the fall of the Berlin Wall, the contrast as we left the former West Germany and entered what had been the Communist East was startling. Drab, slab-like tenements replaced the trim houses of the West and people looked sadder. The roads deteriorated. Familiar names like Shell and BP disappeared. Eventually the filling stations became little more than shacks, manned (or womanned) by fearsome ladies who looked like Ena Sharples in *Coronation Street*. The quality of the diesel grew worse, clipping our top speed by a good fifteen kilometres per hour. The sense of gloom increased when our headlights picked out a sign with the chilling name: *Treblinka*.

By now, Malcolm's fears about the reliability of the truck were proving all too real. The indicators had stopped working somewhere near Berlin. Then, on the E30 autobahn in Poland, the very thing we didn't want to happen did. One of the tyres blew. I pulled over to the side, wishing I hadn't been so blasé about not having a jack.

What to do? As usual in a fix, we started by praying. Then we sat back and looked at each other, clueless as to what to do next.

"Maybe he could help," said Malcolm, pointing across the carriageway at a forty-tonne truck that had just pulled up on the other side.

It was our only chance. Dodging across four lanes of traffic, we knocked on the window of the cab. The driver looked up from his cup of tea, then wound down his window and spoke in what we assumed was Polish (the magnificent Lech Walesa moustache providing something of a clue). Using sign language and sound effects, we tried to explain our predicament. With a sigh that obviously translated as "What a pair of Charlies!", he clambered down and found his jack. The three of us scuttled back to the other side of the motorway, where he jacked us up and we took off the wheel. Malcolm climbed onto the roof of the truck to get the spare and found the tyre completely flat. I don't think he swore, but I'd certainly have excused him if he had. Another flit across the motorway produced a foot pump with which the Polish driver finally got us roadworthy.

But the crisis wasn't over. The man then clutched his chest, gave a little moan and collapsed onto the ground. "What's this, Lord?" I muttered. "You send this wonderful, brave man to help us and he dies in the attempt. That's surely not the plan."

Having little knowledge of first aid, Malcolm and I again did the only thing we could. We knelt down next to the man and prayed for his recovery. After a few moments he opened his eyes and seemed to come round. A little later he signalled that he was well enough to go back to his truck. We helped him over and left him with a tray of juice cartons that Ethel had given us before we left.

Before we parted company, he asked us in halting English where we'd come from.

"Liverpool," we replied.

"And going to…?"

"Moscow."

For a moment he looked to be having another seizure. "Moscow!" he gasped with such a splutter we wondered if we'd have to start praying again. "Too dangerous! Bandits on road from Brest to Moscow. Go back Liverpool now!"

With that warning, he crunched into gear and pulled out into the carriageway. There was no question of turning round. We had to go on. We continued to pray for our rescuer as we went on our way, thanking God that he'd stopped where and when he did and vowing that next time we'd be better equipped.

We also promised ourselves we'd be on our guard against whatever perils the road to Moscow might present. From then on, when we stopped to refuel from the tin cans we had on board, we made sure we kept the engine running.

We groaned in unison as we approached Brest, the border town where route E30 crosses from Poland into the former Soviet republic of Belarus. Ahead was a stationary line of traffic that stretched as far as we could see. We joined the queue, switched off the engine and settled down to wait. The hours ticked by. From time to time there was movement and drivers who'd been lying out in the sun by the roadside hurried back to their vehicles to creep a few metres forward. Others simply pushed, to avoid restarting their engines and using up precious fuel.

We discovered later that the Polish border guards were staging some kind of protest and only letting a few drivers through at a time. In all, it took us twenty-two hours to cover the last twelve kilometres to the border. During that time we slept fitfully in the cab and – when we really had to – relieved ourselves in whatever semi-private spot we could find alongside the road.

When we finally made it through into Belarus, a bright young Russian border guard decided he'd like to examine the truck. I explained that we were part of a film crew and opened up the back to reveal our three Sony cameras, forty Telefunken and Grundig video recorders, several camera control units, racks of sound gear and mixers, and hundreds of metres of cabling.

"Good God!" he exclaimed, slamming the doors shut again.

I wondered if he thought we were spies, but that didn't appear to be his problem. "Don't let anyone see what you've got," he said. "Let's hope no one did. Where are you going?"

"Moscow," I replied.

He rolled his eyes. "Don't go. There are bad people who'll follow you and rob you and probably kill you. A load like this – it's too dangerous. Take my advice. Go back to England at once."

Two warnings in as many days. What was it about the road to Moscow?

Needless to say, we ignored the advice again. We had a job to complete and as long as we were doing what God wanted – well, experience had taught me there was no safer place to be.

Eight hours later we arrived in Minsk, the Belarusian capital. We found the New Minsk Hotel where we'd booked a room and then discovered that the hotel would only accept payment in Russian roubles. We had Deutschmarks and US dollars, but not a single rouble. Worse, it was now early evening and anywhere that might have changed our money was closed.

"I am sorry," explained the concierge. "I cannot let you into room without roubles. If you cannot take it, I give to someone else."

"Can I help you?"

We turned round and a casually dressed young man introduced himself. "My name is Nikolas. I heard you speaking English. I am a student of English. What is the difficulty?"

We explained and he seemed to think this was not a problem. If I waited at the hotel and made sure the room was kept, he would take Malcolm and his wad of dollars and Deutschmarks and find us some roubles.

Was this a con or another of God's interventions? Like tourists in strange places the world over, we had no choice but to trust the local man.

Malcolm describes the next hour as one of the scariest of the trip. Nikolas led him to an apartment in a bleak, Eastern-Bloc tenement, told him to wait and disappeared out into the streets. Malcolm paced anxiously up and down the tiny room for the next forty-five minutes, wondering if some branch of the Minsk mafia was about to turn up and mug him – or worse. But eventually Nikolas returned with a fistful of roubles, enough for the hotel bill and for all the fuel stops we'd need to make between Minsk and Moscow. Even better, he'd somehow secured a more favourable rate of exchange than we'd have found in any bank.

Once again, the right man was in the right place to help us on our way. And that night, the first in a proper bed since leaving home, we slept like babies.

The Moscow conference was being held in the vast Izmaelova Hotel, a Moscow landmark where the world chess championships had taken place the year before. We parked the van at the foot of one of its tower blocks (having arrived, again, with just enough time) and ran our cables up the side of the building and in through a window. This made it very obvious we were filming and during the week we were constantly interrupted by shifty-looking Muscovites who assumed we were making blue movies and wanted to watch the action. It gave us great pleasure to explain who we were and what we were really doing.

The filming itself ran mostly by prayer, both to keep the truck safe (the warnings of the Polish truck driver and the Russian border guard were never far from our thoughts) and to keep the equipment running on Moscow's uncertain power supply. Sometimes the voltage dropped so low, we had to switch off some of our monitors in order to conserve enough power for the cameras.

Confirmation that our efforts were all worthwhile came at the end of the conference when Josh McDowell noticed an old lady on the front row. "This dear lady has been to every session," he said though his interpreter. "I'm curious to know why she came. Could you ask her?"

The lady replied: "When I heard we had a foreigner coming to teach our young people about religion, I was very suspicious. But what I've heard has changed my mind. I know our country needs food and medicine, but what it needs most of all is what this man has been talking about. I am glad he came."

The response, not just of the old lady but of all 700 delegates, was heartfelt and humbling. Before we left, a student called Olga, whom Malcolm and I had helped to become a Christian during the conference, presented Malcolm with a Russian Bible and made a moving speech about how her life had changed. On the final evening, the delegates prayed for Malcolm and me that we wouldn't be held up for twenty-two hours as we had on the way over.

God had other ideas. He held us up for twenty-five hours.

As so often, our troubles on the return journey centred on our carnet. On the Friday afternoon before our departure on the Saturday, Malcolm took the document to the Moscow Chamber of Commerce to get it stamped and signed. Having waited in the queue with his forms ready, he was alarmed to see the lady at the desk pulling down her shutter and announcing it was five o'clock. He pleaded with her to wait a few more minutes and stamp the carnet, but she wouldn't listen. It was now the weekend, she explained in English. He could come back on Monday.

"But we're leaving tomorrow!"

"Monday!"

Slam.

We now couldn't officially leave Russia. At the same time we had no choice. We had to chance it.

Our efforts to get clear of Moscow before the Saturday-morning rush came to nothing when we got lost, went round in circles and found ourselves back at the Izmaelova Hotel an hour and a half later. We eventually extricated ourselves from the city and drove ten hours with barely a stop to the Belarusian–Polish border and the same bleak, barbed-wire crossing near Brest where we'd been delayed on the journey over.

When a granite-faced border guard demanded our exit papers, we handed them over with a silent prayer that somehow we'd be able to get through. It didn't work.

"This paper, no stamp," he said in broken English, pointing to the empty box on the carnet.

We smiled politely and explained that we'd tried very hard to get it stamped, but there had been a slight problem – *problemochka* – and we hadn't quite managed to get it done. He was unyielding and said we'd have to drive the thousand kilometres back to Moscow and complete the paperwork. We were equally determined we wouldn't. Having prayed, we decided to sit it out until something, anything at all, should turn up and break the deadlock.

We waited and prayed, and prayed and waited. We could see the border just 100 metres ahead beyond a line of barbed wire and a strip of no-man's-land, but it remained tantalizingly out of reach. Border guards came and border guards went. As each new detachment came on duty, we tried again to see if they'd allow us through, but each time the answer was the same: "No stamp. Go back to Moscow."

A full twenty-four hours after we'd arrived, a lady we hadn't seen before came on duty. I remember her being small, dark and attractive with a smile on her face and a twinkle in her eye – not the kind of border guard we were used to dealing with. Curiously, she wasn't in uniform but wore a plain, olive-green summer dress. We explained to her that we'd been in Moscow filming at a Christian conference and that now we were held up because someone there had refused to stamp our carnet.

She took us aside. "I, too, am a believer," she whispered. "My name is Tanya. Maybe I can help you. Wait here."

We assured her we weren't going anywhere. That was the problem. She disappeared into one of the buildings and we burst into praise that God had finally provided someone who could help. Amid the barbed wire and barriers and indifferent border guards, we began to think our prayers were being answered.

Tanya returned a few minutes later. "I understand my superior officer is on his way to his *dacha* right now," she said. "I will phone him in ten minutes when he arrives and ask if he will allow you through."

We thanked her profusely and I said to Malcolm, "Now you know why Olga gave you that Russian Bible." Malcolm pulled it from his luggage and presented it to Tanya. Her eyes filled with tears and she clutched it to her chest as though it were infinitely precious.

"Thank you," she murmured. "Thank you."

While we waited, we took the opportunity to photograph each other with our new friend. Unlike any border guard I've ever met, she was happy to pose with us. After a few minutes she went to make the phone call and came back to announce that her commanding officer had indeed given permission for Malcolm and me to be allowed through.

Before we left Moscow, we'd bought and fitted a new tyre to replace the one that had punctured on the way over. But because Russian specifications were different to ours, the new tyre had stood a centimetre or two clear of the ground when we placed it next to its partner as one of a pair. To bring it back into contact with the road, we'd released some of the air from the adjoining tyre.

Four thousand kilometres later, as we rolled off the ferry at Sheerness, we thought we should have our tyres checked. A sign for Sheerness Tyre Fitters was our cue, and we pulled in. The fitter had a look.

"Do you realize one of your tyres has blown?" He pointed to the tyre we'd partially deflated in Moscow. We should have known this was likely to happen, driving so far on a soft tyre. "So that means you've been travelling on this one," he added. He whistled in surprise at the state of the week-old Russian tyre. Not only had it lost all its tread and gone completely bald, the rubber itself was no more than a millimetre thick on the canvas lining.

"I've never seen anything like it," he said. "Where have you come from?"

"Moscow."

He whistled again. "Well all I can say is, someone up there loves you."

In the following months, we tried to keep in contact with some of the people we'd met on the trip. We wrote to Nikolas in Minsk and Olga in Moscow and both responded. I was also keen to get in touch with Tanya. While we'd been stuck at Brest I'd made a note of the phone number at the border post. I called a few days after we got back and managed to find someone who spoke English. I asked if Tanya was available.

"We have no one of that name," said the voice at the other end.

"But we met her last week. She phoned your superior officer to allow us into Poland."

"I'm sorry, I don't know who you mean."

"Tanya. You know. Small... dark..."

"There is no one of that description in this unit."

I thought there must be some mistake and phoned repeatedly over the next few days. Each time I got the same reply until someone said firmly: "This woman is a figment of your imagination." Eventually they asked me to stop ringing, clearly thinking I was deranged.

Make of that what you will. If anyone reading this book can identify the lady I'm with on the seventh page of the photographs, I'd love to trace her. Failing that... well, I do recall we never saw her interacting directly with any of the other border guards. All she'd done, apparently, was make a phone call to her absent boss. Which makes me wonder if I'm one of the few people in the world to have been photographed with an angel.

Moscow was one of the last assignments for Spirit Free Communications. We'd had a good run, but we needed new equipment and didn't have the money to buy it. Also most of the work was in the summer conference season and I didn't see us staying viable through another winter. With a heavy heart, therefore, I made the decision to close the unit down.

Almost the last call I took before doing so was from Sam

Yeghnazar, pastor of the Iranian Christian Fellowship in London and founder of Elam Ministries, which trains Iranian Christians to reach their countrymen for Christ. I'd met Sam and his family some years previously at Spring Harvest in Skegness and knew of his work. In a further connection, Sam's brother-in-law – an Iraqi Jew by the name of Elias Zaidifard – had been a friend of mine in Widnes where he ran a company manufacturing fire engines.

When I explained to Sam that I was shutting down the unit, he asked if I'd kept back any equipment. I told him I had one camera pack left.

"That would be enough," he said. "The thing is, I'm taking fifty tonnes of aid to Armenian Orthodox Christians in Nagorno Karabakh. I wonder… would you bring your camera and make a film?"

7

Down from the Mountain

"Just leave me, please. I can't go any further."

The relay station at Zange Zhor – "The Place of Bells" – still looked an impossible distance away. Below us I could see our broken-down Lada Niva and several other stranded cars, all completely covered in snow after the previous night's blizzard. Only the red bus poked above the drifts with no sign of movement from those on board.

"Stop that talk!" said Mike Sookias. "You've got to keep going. Here. Lean on me."

Mike wrapped his arm around me and hauled me forward through the snow. "Come on, Stuart!" he kept saying. "You can't give up now."

An hour or so later, we staggered onto the concrete apron of the relay station and collapsed through the door. Two Armenian operators sat warming themselves before a brightly blazing, wood-burning stove and looked up in surprise as we tumbled in. I lunged towards the stove, desperate for warmth, but one of the men shouted a warning and held me back. He'd assessed my condition in a flash. By the blackening of my ears, he realized I was suffering from frostbite and knew that sudden heat could cause even more damage. Gently but insistently, he pushed his arms up my anorak sleeves and held me for about forty minutes, gradually thawing me with the warmth of his own body.

When we'd all started to recover, the two Armenians gave us coffee and soup. Never has a simple hot drink been such a godsend. It was then we learned that the temperature the previous night had fallen to minus fifty. Our hosts were surprised we'd survived.

Tempting as it was to stay in the warmth, we knew we had to get back to the car and try to resume our journey. After about an hour at the relay station, we wished our new friends a happy Orthodox Christmas Day and struck off down the mountainside towards the road and the row of white hummocks that marked where the traffic had stopped. By now there was movement. It seemed that people in the other cars had taken refuge in the bus, whose driver had run his engine all night to keep the heating going. Stiff-looking figures were now emerging from the bus and digging their way back into their cars.

We located the Lada beneath its mound of snow and crammed back inside. The driver tried the ignition but the engine was dead. There was nothing to do but pray, huddle together for warmth and wait for rescue.

At about midday we saw a line of snowploughs crawling up the mountainside from Goris, clearing the road of the worst of the snow. An hour or so later, we were delighted to see our friends from Spitak Rescue arriving from the same direction in a six-wheeled Uri. They'd driven from Yerevan the previous day to collect their two colleagues injured in the crash that Frank and I had so narrowly avoided and were now bringing them back. They stopped, examined the Lada and informed us that the head gasket had gone.

Resourceful as all Armenians seem to be, the Spitak crew hitched a rope to the Lada and pulled it clear. For the first time in nearly eighteen hours we were on the move. As the Uri towed us down the road towards Yerevan, I remembered my reason for being there and recorded the scene on film – the red bus, the huddled figures, the blinding white landscape.

I didn't know it, but those few seconds of film were to change my life.

Between Goris and Yerevan lies the mountain town of Yeghegnadzor. We arrived in the central square in the late afternoon and the Spitak men set about repairing the Lada. With little we could do to help, Sam, Frank, Mike and I got out and discussed plans. We'd missed our flight from Yerevan to Paris by several hours and the next one wasn't for another week. The question was what to do now.

The immediate decision was made for us. A door opened in the house opposite and a man stepped out. He paused long enough to listen to us talking and disappeared back inside. A moment later he re-emerged with an old man who appeared to be his father and came over to talk to Sam and Mike, the two Armenian-speakers among us.

"He heard us talking English," translated Sam. "He says we shouldn't be out here in the cold on Christmas Day. He insists we come in and share Christmas dinner with his family. It's all prepared."

We didn't take much persuading and the Spitak men agreed to join us once they'd finished working on the Lada. Speaking a little English, the man and his father (one an optician, the other a brain surgeon, we later discovered) showed us into the house where a family of about ten was waiting to begin the feast. And a feast it was, despite the shortages caused by the war with Azerbaijan. The table overflowed with cuts of lamb and salads and sweets and cheese and nuts and apricots and plums. Having barely eaten since leaving Stepanakert on the morning of Christmas Eve, we were overwhelmed by God's provision and the generosity of this family of strangers – hospitable as only Armenians can be.

Glasses were passed around and quickly filled with the sweet, local, semi-fermented wine. As the feasting began, the younger man took the traditional Armenian role of *tamador* – party host and organizer of toasts.

After the day or so we'd spent in Stepanakert, I knew that every Armenian feast involves more toasts than you could ever hope to count. In fact, I think it's the idea that you *should* lose count. Under the direction of our *tamador*, we took it in turns to pay fulsome compliments to other people at the table – and, once complimented, each of us had to compliment someone else and propose a toast. Fuelled by large amounts of Armenian brandy and vodka, the toasts took on a British theme.

"England!" roared the host.

"*England!*" echoed the family, raising their glasses and quaffing deeply.

"Shakespeare!"

"*Shakespeare!*"

"Arsenal!"

"*Arsenal!*"

The home team also had its quota with toasts to Armenia, Yerevan and Nagorno Karabakh. It was hard to believe that twenty-four hours previously we'd been trapped in a blizzard in fear of our lives. God was certainly springing surprise upon surprise. As the evening wore on and the party continued, the family urged us to stay overnight. Reluctantly, we had to decline. There was business to be done in Yerevan and by midnight we were back on the road for the two-hour drive to the capital.

With no scheduled flight out of Yerevan for another week, we still had to figure out what to do next. But that was a question for the morning. First stop once we'd arrived was the Hotel Armenia, where we checked in and collapsed into bed. It had been an unforgettable Christmas Day.

The following morning I noticed a young Russian airman

in uniform in the hotel restaurant. The question of how to get home was now becoming urgent and the sight of this airman, toying with his breakfast porridge, gave me an idea. I walked over and asked if he spoke English. He did – a little. I asked where he was headed and he told me he was flying to Moscow that evening.

"Listen," I said. "There are four of us here and we've missed the Armenian Aeroflot flight to Paris. Is there any chance of a lift to Moscow?"

The airman said I'd better speak to the captain and gave me his room number. I went and introduced myself. The captain spoke excellent English and I was able to explain the situation. He seemed delighted at the prospect of some extra company. "We're an ex-Soviet Air Force crew," he told me. "But now there's no Soviet Air Force, we're earning a living flying stuff around the Caucasus. Today we've got a cargo of cars that we're taking to Moscow Vnukovo Airport in an Ilyushin IL-76. You're welcome to come along."

I asked what he'd like for payment and he brushed the question aside. "Just one problem," he said. *Problemochka* – that word again! "The weather's bad over the Caucasus and we might get delayed. I'll have to let you know."

In the event, the flight was delayed to the following day. We used the time, however, to get out into Yerevan and visit a number of churches linked to Sam's aid effort. We eventually took off on the afternoon of 8 January. Once in the air with the captain and his buccaneering crew of ex-Soviet airmen, we settled down in the cavernous interior of the IL-76 to think about the next leg of the journey from Moscow to London.

It wasn't going to be easy. All we had were tickets from Yerevan to Paris on Armenian Aeroflot. We had no visas to allow us to land in Russia and no carnet to get the filming equipment through customs. What's more, our destination – the military base at Vnukovo – was two hours' drive from Moscow's main international airport at Sheremetevo, the departure point for flights to London. By now, though, we'd seen enough of God's miraculous interventions to be reasonably sure he wouldn't let us down at this point. We were content to pray and see what happened.

What happened was a weather alert that all Moscow airports were closed, and we'd have to divert to Krasnodar military base in southern Russia.

With a sigh, the captain swung the giant aircraft around and headed west. By the time we landed at Krasnodar, the daylight had gone and it was clear we'd be there for the night. For the crew, that meant checking into Krasnodar barracks. For the rest of us, it wasn't as simple. As a bunch of foreigners arriving in Russia without visas, we had no choice but to spend the night on board.

"Stuarto! You sleep there," said the captain, pointing to the pilot's seat. "You can lean your feet on the joystick. And the rest of you… make yourselves comfortable there, there and there." Then he wished us good night and locked us in.

On a trip that had taken many surprise turns, I hadn't expected to spend a night in an IL-76 on a Russian military base. But by now I was reaching a point where almost nothing would surprise me. The experience was marginally more comfortable than a night in a Lada Niva in a blizzard, but not one I'd care to repeat. I was glad when morning broke and the crew came filing back on board for the two-and-a-half hour flight to Vnukovo.

Before parting company with the captain and his crew, we were determined to repay them in some way. Although they still refused payment for the flight, we pooled whatever cash we had – it came to about US$100 – and forcibly stuffed it into the captain's pocket once the IL-76 had taxied to a stop at Vnukovo. Split between eight airmen, it was little enough, but at least it was a token of the gratitude we felt.

But the captain hadn't finished yet. "Wait here," he said as he trotted down the steps onto the tarmac. We clustered round the doorway of the IL-76 and watched him stride away into the terminal. A few minutes later an airport bus appeared from behind the building and glided to a stop next to the aircraft. The captain stepped out and beckoned us down.

"Your transport to Sheremetevo!" he called. "Come aboard! Bring all your stuff."

With a final instruction to the driver, he shook us all by the hand and waved us away – a Russian hero if ever there was one. The driver set course across the tarmac and left the base through a back gate, completely avoiding any customs, visa or equipment checks. Two hours later, we stepped through the doors at Sheremetevo and headed for the British Airways check-in desk.

As we did so, the information board behind the desk flicked over to announce that BA 873, the last flight to London that evening, had just departed.

The routine at times like this was well rehearsed. So often in the last few days we'd been forced to rely on God to get us out of trouble and now we were having to do it again. The four of us gathered in a huddle in the middle of the concourse and we prayed. "Lord, you know our need. You know how we need to get back home. You've kept and protected us so wonderfully, but please... what do we do now?"

"English, *ja*?"

We looked up to see a passenger standing a couple of metres away. He smiled and continued in his heavy German accent: "Would I be right in thinking you have missed your flight to London?"

We confirmed that yes, we had. Did he have any suggestions?

"Oh, *ja*. If you go down that way to the Lufthansa desk, you can catch a flight to London via Frankfurt. But I think you will have to hurry."

We thanked him profusely, scooped up our belongings and sped towards the Lufthansa check-in. "Please," said Sam as we skidded to a stop at the desk. "Do you have four tickets for London on this evening's flight?"

The man at the check-in scrutinized his screen. The furrow on his brow did not look promising. "No, I'm sorry," he said. "We appear to be fully booked. No, wait a minute. We have just four. But only in First Class. Do you wish to take them?"

"How much?" asked Sam.

The man named a price in roubles that we mentally translated into pounds. It was an eye-watering figure. "However," he continued, "as these are the only four left, I can let you have them at Economy price."

"Thank you, Lord!" I breathed.

Sam reached for his wallet. "We'll take them." Then he paused. "Excuse me one moment. I just need to consult with my colleagues."

Sam stepped away from the desk and beckoned us closer. "I've just realized," he whispered. "I've got no credit left on my Visa card. I used it all to buy the aid for Nagorno Karabakh. I don't suppose any of you have got any money?"

The last of our cash had gone to pay our friend the captain and neither Mike, Frank nor I had any other means of paying. We closed our eyes and shot out another prayer. "Dear God, please sort something out here. You've given us these wonderful seats and don't think we're not grateful, but have you perhaps overlooked one little detail – like how to pay for them?"

"I'll just try," said Sam. "There's no choice."

He turned back to the desk and handed over his card. The man swiped it. "That's odd," he said. "The computer link appears to be down."

"What does that mean?" asked Sam nervously.

"It means we can't check the credit on your card. But we

can't reject it either. We'll just have to do it manually." He placed Sam's card on the Visa hand terminal and slid the handle across and back. "Sign here, please."

Sam did so and the deal was done.

"There you are," smiled the man. "Four First Class tickets for Heathrow. I'll take your baggage and your flight boards in thirty minutes."

As I sank into the luxury of Lufthansa's First Class seats, I marvelled at the series of miracles we'd just experienced. At the same time my thoughts flew back to the people of Nagorno Karabakh, especially our friends in Stepanakert enduring another night of Azeri shelling. I knew that my first priority in England, even before going home, was to edit the week's filming into something Sam could use to help raise more funds for the enclave.

The flight produced one more surprise when the stewardess invited us into the cockpit. Being an aircraft enthusiast (as you may have noticed), I couldn't resist the opportunity and spent a happy half hour quizzing the pilots about the Airbus A319. I was interested to learn that the Moscow to Frankfurt flight required just two and a half tonnes of fuel, including reserves for diversions and stacking, and I thought back to the ten tonnes an hour that the Ilyushin IL-76 devoured. While my admiration for Russian pilots is immense, there's no doubt that Soviet aero-engine technology had fallen way behind that of the West by the end of the Cold War.

Back in London, Sam and I said goodbye to Frank and Mike and went almost immediately to Reuters' Park Royal office in north London, where we had the use of an editing suite. After Sam had sorted out his finances (which mainly meant clearing his Visa bill before the Lufthansa payment came through), he and I got to work to condense the trip into five minutes of film. The result later helped him raise about US$250,000 for Nagorno Karabakh as he showed it at churches and events around Europe.

When the editing was done, I contacted one of the news researchers at Sky TV to say I was sending them the film in case they wanted to use it. Only then did I catch the train and rejoin my long-suffering family in Widnes.

A day or two later I had a call from Sky. Yes, they'd like to use the film, they said. There wasn't much other news happening and Nagorno Karabakh was an area they hadn't previously covered. Could Sam and I come to London to be interviewed alongside the film? And by the way, they were also going to interview Baroness Caroline Cox, Deputy Speaker of the House of Lords, who'd just come back from visiting the enclave on behalf of an organization called Christian Solidarity International.

I didn't know who Baroness Cox was, but I was pleased that Nagorno Karabakh was finally getting some air time. On 14 January 1993, Sam and I met up again at the Sky TV studios in Isleworth, west London, and were sent upstairs to the waiting room to get ready for our appearance in front of the cameras.

"We've hit a bit of a problem," explained the programme assistant, riffling through the papers on her clipboard. (At least she didn't say *"Problemochka"!*) "There's breaking news about Miss Whiplash and we may have to bump you off the running order."

Miss Whiplash was Britain's most famous prostitute. Otherwise known as Lindi St Clair, she ran a high-class brothel whose clients were rumoured to include Members of Parliament and other senior public figures. With the Inland Revenue pursuing her through the courts for non-payment of income tax, she'd sensationally disappeared near the notorious suicide leap at Beachy Head.

"Apparently she's just turned up again," explained the assistant. "We hope to have an interview. Wait here and we'll let you know if we can fit you in."

With the clock ticking by, we sat in the waiting room and watched as Miss Whiplash came on air to answer questions about her disappearance and imminent bankruptcy case. She'd been away resting, she said, and didn't know what all the fuss was about. (In researching what happened to her since, I find she discovered God after a serious road accident in 2009. But that's another story.) As the interview went on, Sam and I prayed fervently that the story we so badly wanted to tell would make it onto air.

Finally, to our great relief, the news turned to Nagorno Karabakh. In the adjoining studio with the presenter was Baroness Cox, an energetic, eagle-eyed lady in her fifties with a no-nonsense manner and a clipped, upper-class accent unlike anything I'd heard in Runcorn and Widnes. She explained that she'd wanted to show solidarity with the Armenian Christians by spending the Orthodox Christmas with them. She spoke movingly about the suffering of the Karabakhis and the atrocities inflicted by the Azeris – the beheading of Armenian villagers, the gouging out of people's eyes, cluster bombs dropped on Stepanakert and the surrounding villages. After a few minutes of Caroline Cox's graphic reporting, the presenter paused the interview to run our film.

Through the glass we could see Caroline watching our footage with intense interest. When the scene cut to the blizzard at Zange Zhor, she nearly leaped out of her chair.

"That bus! I was on it in that same blizzard! Who filmed that?"

The presenter told her it was Sam Yeghnazar and Stuart Windsor, who'd also just returned from the enclave.

"Well, where are they? I've got to meet them!"

"They're right next door."

As soon as she'd done her piece, Caroline Cox came scuttling through to the waiting room. "Are you Sam and Stuart?"

We said we were.

"And were you in that blizzard?"

"Yes," I replied. "About 100 metres away from you."

"How extraordinary! Thank you so much for going to the aid of the Karabakhis. Very few people even know where Nagorno Karabakh is, let alone go there. They need all the help we can give them."

We still had a few minutes before Sam and I were due to go on air, so we hastily swapped notes on what we'd been doing and who we'd met on our respective visits to the enclave. I asked Caroline if she'd be willing to do a further interview for us to add to our film and she said she'd be delighted. Finally, as Sam and I were being ushered into the studio, she made a suggestion.

"I'm going back to Nagorno Karabakh in a few weeks. Why don't we all go together?"

8

Christian Solidarity

With the film ministry now closed, Ethel and I had been praying about our next move and whether our future lay in Widnes or somewhere else. One or two churches had invited me to join as pastor, but we didn't feel drawn in that direction. In the absence of any clear guidance, Caroline's suggestion that Sam and I join her on another trip to Nagorno Karabakh was the only clue I had as to what I should do next.

I had long ago learned that when all other doors are closed, God probably wants you to take the one that's open. So I agreed to go.

Our mission was again to take aid, but also – just as importantly – to gather information about what was happening on the ground in Nagorno Karabakh. So this time there was no Ilyushin IL-76 to transport vast amounts of food and medicines. The plan was to fly to Yerevan via Paris, carrying our supplies as baggage, and then take the overland route into the enclave. My task, as before, was to film Sam's relief effort, helped by the plucky Frank Walsh who, despite several near-death experiences on the previous trip, had agreed to come again as my sound man. He and I were to go on ahead and Sam and Caroline would take a later flight and join us in Yerevan.

So it was that Frank and I found ourselves one Saturday

evening in March 1993 queuing at the departure gate to board an Armenian Aeroflot TU-154 aircraft at Charles de Gaulle Airport in Paris. We were near the back of the line with a straggle of passengers in front of us preparing to board. As we waited, we noticed two middle-aged ladies working their way along the queue from the front, stopping to talk to each group of passengers.

As they got closer, we could hear what they were saying. "Excuse me… Excuse me… Do you mind us asking…? You see, God has told us that there are two Christians on this flight going to Yerevan to deliver aid, and we wondered if you're them."

As you might expect, the queuing passengers were shifting uncomfortably and trying to avoid eye contact with these two strange ladies. We could almost read the thought bubbles floating above their heads: "That's all we need. A couple of crazies! Let's hope they're not going on the same flight as us!"

As they came closer I said to Frank, "Come on. We can have some fun here. Let's give people something to think about."

The passengers in front of us shrugged the two ladies off and they turned to us. "Excuse me," they began. "God has told us…"

"God has told you?" I boomed. "What do you mean, God has told you? Don't be ridiculous!"

"But really, he has! He's told us there are two Christians…"

"That's nonsense," I continued at the top of my voice. "God doesn't speak to people!" By now most of the people nearby were paying attention, some out of interest, some in alarm that the two religious nutters had apparently been joined by a shouty nutter. Again the thought bubbles: "Looks like we picked the wrong flight tonight!"

The ladies held their ground. "Oh, yes! God speaks to us all the time, quite clearly."

"You're sure? How do you know?" After that I couldn't keep a straight face and began to laugh. "You're quite right," I said.

"You've found us. What can we do for you?"

After telling me off for being so mean, the ladies explained that they knew someone in Yerevan, an Armenian pastor by the name of Ashot, and that they had some Bibles and teaching materials to give him. Would we be willing to take them?

I'd known Ashot as a young student at the International Bible Training Institute at Burgess Hill in Sussex where a friend of mine had been the principal. Breaking all the rules about taking packages from strangers at airports, I agreed to help and managed to get the parcel to Ashot when we arrived. The two brave ladies, Zilla Harrod and her friend Esther, later became committed supporters of Christian Solidarity.

Two days later we met up with Caroline and Sam at the Hotel Armenia in Yerevan, an establishment that was now becoming very familiar. Since meeting her at Sky TV, I'd found out more about the so-called Battling Baroness and why she was so passionate about Nagorno Karabakh.

The first time Caroline heard mention of Nagorno Karabakh was at the First International Andrei Sakharov Memorial Congress that took place in Moscow in May 1991 during the period of *glasnost* or "openness" in the final years of the Soviet Union. Attended at its opening by both Mikhail Gorbachev and Boris Yeltsin, the Congress was held to commemorate the Soviet nuclear physicist turned human rights campaigner, Andrei Sakharov. Caroline was there at the invitation of his widow, Elena Bonner Sakharov. During the proceedings, the delegate from Nagorno Karabakh – a grizzled, fiery-eyed mountain of a man called Zori Balayan – spoke powerfully about the brutal deportation of entire Armenian villages by Azeri and Soviet forces. "Please will you send someone to see the situation at first hand," he pleaded.

The Congress took note and asked Caroline to lead a delegation. Never one to refuse a challenge, Caroline arrived in

Armenia two months later with a group that included Elena Bonner Sakharov – herself of Armenian descent. The first stop was Goris where Caroline spoke to peasant farmers driven from their homes in Nagorno Karabakh by troops using helicopters, tanks and armoured personnel carriers. People had been beaten, tortured and shot. She later visited a village where hours earlier the Azeris had sawn the heads off twenty-two Armenian men in front of the church altar. The blood-stained implement still lay where it had been dropped.

At great personal risk, she and her delegation continued gathering information from both sides of the conflict. In her report, sent to Mikhail Gorbachev among others, she wrote: "Here were Christians fighting, not only for life but for their families, for the right to live in their historic land, and also for their Christian heritage – and their struggle was largely unknown to the rest of Christendom."

Now fiercely committed to Nagorno Karabakh, Caroline approached the leadership of Christian Solidarity International in October 1991 and asked that as a human rights organization they do something to help. CSI had been set up in 1979 to campaign for persecuted Christians and Caroline had become a trustee in 1990. The result was a programme of aid for the enclave. By the time we travelled there in March 1993, Caroline had already made numerous trips to Nagorno Karabakh on CSI's behalf. She has since taken her tally of visits to more than fifty.[3]

It was clear, even then, that Baroness Cox – the *Baronoohi*, as the Armenians call her – was a legend in the land. The people of Armenia and Nagorno Karabakh were extravagantly grateful for her stand, for her willingness to share their suffering, for her weeping with them over ruined villages and dead sons and husbands. Wherever we went on that first tour together, crowds gathered and people would press in to shake her hand and ply her with gifts and flowers. "Thank you for not forgetting us," was the constant greeting. On one occasion a peasant woman flung her arms around the *Baronoohi* and exclaimed, "She is our own. She is our guardian angel. We love her."

To many in Armenia and Nagorno Karabakh, Caroline Cox is their own version of Evita (I mean, of course, the original and much-loved woman of the people, not the stage version). The Armenian parliament has honoured her. Roads and buildings have been named after her. When her sixth grandchild was born, the announcement was carried on Armenian radio.

By the same token, Caroline Cox was public enemy number one in Azerbaijan. Many on the opposing side would have liked to see her eliminated and her frequent narrow escapes from death (including having her helicopter raked by gunfire) simply added to the legend. She sat equally lightly to the adulation and the hatred – embarrassed by the one and fired by the other to seek lasting justice for the Karabakhis.

For me, that first trip with Caroline was one long series of eye-openers. I saw more of the suffering of the Karabakhis and came to appreciate the magnificent work of CSI in exposing the truth of what was happening. Together we met Nagorno Karabakh's President Kocharian and Prime Minister Petrossian, unrecognized by any country apart from Armenia but running a de facto state and striving to hold it together under the onslaught from Azerbaijan. These visits to the country's leadership became a feature of every trip we made and we found ourselves feted as heroes for daring to make the journey. Both Caroline and I were made honorary citizens of the enclave and I believe I'm one of the few foreigners to hold a Karabakhi visa.

The prophecy given by Frank Houston at my ordination began to take on new meaning. "God is calling you to appear before presidents and prime ministers." They might have been the president and prime minister of a weak, embattled territory no bigger than an English county, but I could sense a momentum in my life, as though God were changing the gears in preparation for something new.

One day, as Caroline and I bucketed over the mountains between Yerevan and Stepanakert in an ageing Russian MIL-8 helicopter, she happened to mention that there might soon be a vacancy for the post of UK National Director of CSI. In an instant I pictured myself in the killing fields of Cambodia, vowing that I'd never again stand by if Christians were being persecuted anywhere in the world. It seemed God had taken me at my word. As clear as could be, short of hearing an audible voice, I knew God was saying to me: "Stuart, that job is yours."

While I was away, Ethel had spent an evening at a Pentecostal meeting in Sankey Bridges on the outskirts of Warrington near our home in Widnes. At the end, a lady called Dorcas Willows approached her and said she had something to say to her that she thought was from God.

"God is telling you this," she continued. "You're on the verge of entering a new ministry. You're going to mix with lords and ladies, senators and government ministers. The Lord is going to take you to new places all around the world. You can't imagine what he has in store!"

Ethel's reaction was typical of her trusting acceptance of God's power. "Well, I don't know how that's going to happen, but God is God, and I suppose he can do anything."

She told me what Dorcas had said as soon as I arrived home and before I'd had a chance to mention my conversation with Caroline. I was astounded and humbled at the same time. Not only had God spoken to me in Nagorno Karabakh about the vacant CSI post, he had underlined the promise with a separate word for Ethel. When he chooses to speak, he certainly has a way of ramming home the message.

I decided it wasn't for me to approach CSI. If God wanted me as UK National Director, he was quite capable of making it happen with no interference from me.

At the time I was on the Broadcasting Council of the Assemblies of God in the UK – this being the body that oversees the church's radio and TV ministries. One of my fellow council members was a Pentecostal pastor called Terry Hanford who also happened to be a trustee of Christian Solidarity International. Unknown to me, Terry had telephoned Mervyn Thomas, Chairman of the CSI Board, and suggested that I might be a suitable candidate for the soon-to-be-vacant post.

A few days after getting back from Nagorno Karabakh, I received a call from Mervyn himself. I'd met him once when I'd filmed him giving a presentation on CSI at our church in Widnes in 1989, but his call to me in March 1993 came completely out of the blue.

"What are you doing at the moment?" he asked.

I told him I was praying about my future.

"Are you interested in a job at CSI?"

I almost burst out laughing. After what God had said both to Ethel and to me, I knew it would only be a matter of time before events started to move. "Actually," I said, "I've already met Caroline Cox and seen the work you're doing."

"Oh? So where did your paths happen to cross?"

"Strictly speaking," I said, "it was in a blizzard on a mountain in Armenia."

I later discovered that Mervyn had taken a similar attitude to mine concerning the appointment. When the post became vacant, CSI's administrator, Susanna Hodgson, had wanted to advertise. And for good reason. She'd been working on her own for a number of months and desperately needed a new National Director to share the workload. Mervyn had resisted, believing that God would supply the right person at the right time.

"We'll know," he'd said to Susanna. "Let's wait and see who he brings along."

Mervyn's call was just the first step in my selection. Having sent in my qualifications, I was called to London to meet the board and trustees. Given that several of the trustees were MPs, the interview took place in the august surroundings of one of the committee rooms in the Houses of Parliament. I already knew some of the interviewing panel – Mervyn, slightly, and Caroline and Terry Hanford rather better – but I couldn't help being apprehensive as they tested me on my credentials and sense of calling. In reply, I spoke of the promise I'd made to God in Cambodia and what I'd seen of the suffering church in Russia, Armenia and Nagorno Karabakh.

At one point the Deputy Chairman, a barrister called Franklin Evans, looked at my details and noted that I'd been the Staff Training and Development Officer at North West Water. He asked if I'd known David Large and Mike Stimpson QC. Most certainly, I said. David had been the principal engineer and I'd worked with him on graduate engineering programmes. As for Mike, he'd come to Warrington every year to lecture our engineers on contracts and other legal topics and I had organized his visits. It turned out that Franklin had taken over Mike's role after I'd left and knew several of my former colleagues. I joked that my work at North West Water had given me a good working knowledge of reinforced concrete and water-retaining structures. If that was what they wanted, I was definitely their man.

With or without my knowledge of concrete, the board appointed me National Director in April 1993 and asked if I could start work the following month. When he called to break the news, Mervyn Thomas apologized for the size of the salary. That didn't worry me. Since leaving North West Water, I'd lived on practically nothing. The film ministry had been a venture of faith and my only regular income came from a small amount of personnel work – mainly psychometric testing of potential recruits – for an industrial design outfit called DATS Holdings. It was almost enough to live on, but not quite. There were some months when I couldn't pay the mortgage and we got by only because anonymous well-wishers posted money through the door or left groceries on the doorstep. To have a salary at all was a bonus.

The appointment with CSI was provisional on my sorting out the residual finances of Spirit Free Communications. In order to buy filming equipment, I'd taken out a £3,000 business development loan from NatWest Bank and named myself as guarantor. Once the business had been wound up, the loan had to be repaid and I didn't have the means to do it. The situation was saved when a letter arrived at the CSI office from a friend who'd previously quizzed me on the state of my finances. Inside were six words from Genesis chapter 22 – "Jehovah-jireh: the Lord will provide" – and a cheque that exactly paid off the outstanding amount.

God continued to meet our needs in wonderful ways, not least in the matter of a car. As CSI National Director, I inherited an old Vauxhall Astra in which I commuted every week from our home in Widnes to the CSI office at Witney near Oxford. One day, shortly after I joined, the car was stolen from the car park at Oxford Station. Over the following few days, quite unexpectedly, I kept seeing a particular face in my mind's eye. It belonged to a man called Paul Heffer whom I'd met several years previously when he'd brought an elderly lady to look round one of the homes we'd built alongside the church in Widnes. I remembered that Paul owned a Ford garage somewhere in the East of England but had no idea where.

The feeling persisted that Paul Heffer was somehow important to my present circumstances and that I really ought to contact him. With nothing much to go on, I phoned the main Ford dealership in Cambridge and asked if they knew another dealer in the area who happened to be a Christian. They said they did. His name was Paul Heffer and he ran the dealership in nearby Newmarket.

I phoned Paul immediately and was delighted to find he remembered me from his visit to Widnes. I explained that the charity's Vauxhall Astra had been stolen. "This is all a bit strange," I said. "Ever since the theft I haven't been able to get your face out of my mind. It's as though God has been telling me to call you. Even stranger is the fact that I don't really like Ford cars!"

He was gracious enough to laugh and started asking me more about CSI – including the address and phone number of our Chairman, Mervyn Thomas. As I gave him the details, I noticed that Mervyn's area code was the same as Paul's.

"Just leave it to me," he said. "I'll see what I can do about getting you a replacement. Call back this afternoon and I'll let you know how I've got on."

When I did so, I was surprised to find Mervyn himself answering the phone. "Oh, sorry, Mervyn," I said. "I must have dialled the wrong number."

"No, you haven't," replied Mervyn. "You want Paul Heffer, don't you? I'm sitting with Paul right now in his office."

It turned out that Paul and Mervyn had known of each other's existence for some time. They had always wanted to meet but had never succeeded in making contact. After my call that morning, Paul had at last been able to telephone Mervyn, who lived not far away, and Mervyn had gone straight round to the showroom to introduce himself. As a result of that meeting, the two became prayer partners and close friends, and Paul himself became a CSI supporter. By following the hunch to telephone Paul, it seemed I'd been instrumental in God's plans for him as well as vice-versa.

As for the car, Paul was as good as his word. A second-hand Ford Sierra was delivered to the office in Witney the following week – ours free of charge for as long as we needed it.

These signs of God's goodness provided much-needed reassurance as I took up my post at CSI in May 1993. I seriously wondered what I'd let myself in for. There were just two of us in the office – Susanna and myself – and the work had been piling up for months in the absence of a fully functioning National Director. Just to get to my desk, I had to step over 5,000 copies of the CSI supporters' magazine that hadn't been distributed. Future editions were waiting to be compiled and edited. A database of 7,000 supporters urgently needed overhauling. There were churches to visit, meetings to organize, exhibitions to attend. And before I could even begin raising the profile of CSI around the country, I needed to get familiar with the charity's work and mission.

All that in addition to the real work of CSI, namely fighting for the cause of persecuted Christians around the world.

Was I up to it? – a Barnardo's boy with half a degree from the Open University, now moving among so many qualified and eminent people. It was surely just a matter of time before they rumbled me and realized I was out of my depth.

But I couldn't argue with the extraordinary sequence of events that had brought me to this overflowing desk in a cluttered office in Witney, Oxfordshire. Where had it started? Sam's request to go with him to Nagorno Karabakh? The blizzard at Zange Zhor that had pinned me down on the same mountainside as Caroline? The encounter at Sky TV? Or did God's leading go further back to a hot day in the killing fields of Cambodia when the voices of the dead had so haunted me? Or even to the RAF and the start of my work in film? And if the RAF, maybe it began with Commander Luxton at Barnardo's suggesting I join the services. Or did it start with my mother leaving home?

I pondered on the way God knits together the often chaotic threads of life to make things happen his way. Convinced he'd brought me here for a reason, and trusting he'd continue to guide, I surveyed my bulging in-tray and pleaded to know where to begin.

My prayer was interrupted by Susanna, bringing in a message

that had just arrived on the fax machine. I took it from her and ran my eye down the page. It came from a Christian press organization. "The following Vietnamese house church leaders have been released from prison," it read. Underneath were three names. The third was Paul Tran Ai, the irrepressible pastor I'd last seen in Phnom Penh preparing to travel to his new church plant in Laos.

"Thank you, Lord," I breathed – not just for the release of Paul and his Vietnamese brothers, but for God's impeccable timing. Having called in my promise never to rest while Christians were being persecuted, here he was, a few minutes in, bringing me news of captives freed.

"I get the message," I said. I bowed my head and prayed we'd see many more.

9

Return to Nagorno Karabakh

Thanks to Caroline Cox's tireless campaigning, the plight of Nagorno Karabakh was now widely known among Christian Solidarity's supporters around the world – especially in countries like Britain, the USA, France and Argentina that have sizeable Armenian populations. The challenge for Christian Solidarity was to find a way of transferring large amounts of aid into what was still a war zone and extremely dangerous to get to.

With typical directness, Caroline contacted the UK Government's Department for International Development (DfID for short). Why, she demanded to know, was DfID supplying aid to the Azeri capital, Baku, and none to Nagorno Karabakh? Surely it was time to redress the balance.

The department investigated and found about ten aid agencies active in Baku. Stepanakert had just a handful. Médecins Sans Frontières was there. So was the Red Cross, mainly arranging prisoner-of-war exchanges. The British medical charity, Merlin – of which Caroline was a trustee – had done some vaccinations in the enclave. And then there was Christian Solidarity. Apart from these, Nagorno Karabakh was more or less abandoned by the outside world.

DfID decided it had to be seen to be even-handed. If Christian Solidarity could provide the aid, the department would fund the air transport to get it as far as Yerevan. At about £35,000 per round trip on an Ilyushin IL-76, this was not cheap. They agreed to try it for one trip with a DfID representative on board and to fund a further seven flights if they thought we were doing a useful job.

So to add to my other tasks, I now became an aircraft loadmaster. After we passed DfID's initial scrutiny, the flights continued every eight weeks during 1994 and early 1995. On each occasion I had to buy or purloin fifty tonnes of aid, get it to Manston Airport in Kent and arrange for Hanover Aviation, the company handling DfID's aid flights, to produce an IL-76 ready for loading. Hanover gave me a telephone handset with a number they thought would suit me – 585007 – and from then on I was "007" to the crews and ground staff.

At the time, a lot of Karabakhi fighters were losing limbs from gangrene, so one of our first flights carried 50,000 units of anti-gas gangrene toxin. Specially manufactured in Switzerland, it couldn't be stored and had to be rushed to the front to help save the lives of amputees. Almost as urgent were the fifteen to twenty tonnes of milk powder we loaded onto each flight. With so many cattle being killed, the enclave faced a serious shortage of milk. Thanks to regular donations from the St Ivel dairy company in Trowbridge, Wiltshire, we were able, at least partially, to restore supplies.

Other flights carried food, clothing, blankets and beds for field operating theatres. Shortly before Christmas 1994, we took a consignment of 50,000 shoeboxes donated by the Christmas Child organization. These contained pencils, mirrors and other goodies so that every child in the enclave could at least have a Christmas gift from the outside world. On this occasion, the regional control centre ordered the pilot not to land at Yerevan because the temperature was minus twenty and the runway was 100 per cent fog-bound. To the dismay of the Radio Kent reporter who had hitched a ride to report on who was flying where out of Manston, the pilot ignored the order, told us to strap in tight and put the huge aircraft straight down the centre of the runway. I could only admire his skill, especially when we opened the cabin door and I couldn't see my own arm for fog.

In the space we had left after we'd loaded our cargoes, we packed in up to twenty passengers per trip – doctors, nurses, builders, journalists, Christian Solidarity supporters, human rights activists and anyone else who could either help the aid effort or raise the profile of what was happening in the enclave.

One trip included a party of pilgrims braving the fighting to visit Nagorno Karabakh's ancient monasteries – led, needless to say, by Caroline herself. Passengers at other times included Congressman Frank Wolf (now an energetic advocate of our work in the USA) and Lieutenant Colonel Colin Mitchell of the anti-landmine organization, the Halo Trust. Caroline and I had previously met Colonel Mitchell's wife to ask if he'd be willing to come to the enclave to advise the Karabakhis on mine clearance. It was only after he'd agreed that I realized our contact was the legendary Mad Mitch of Aden fame. Back in 1967, he'd become a national hero when he defied his superiors and led his Argyll and Sutherland Highlanders into Aden's Crater district – kilts swirling, pipes blaring "Scotland the Brave" – to reimpose order in the area.

At the time we met him, Mad Mitch had left his military career behind and was now an authority on landmines and a deacon in the Church of Scotland – not a combination you often find. His trip with us was an early reconnaissance, but it opened the way to the Halo Trust sending further teams to the enclave.

Yet another flight carried a crew of Lancashire firemen, en route to Nagorno Karabakh to take part in safety training with the Spitak mountain rescue service. They travelled with a good supply of Foster's lager, which proved extremely useful on the way back. Because Yerevan had no fuel on account of the blockades by Azerbaijan and Turkey, we had to make the short hop to Min Vody in southern Russia to take on enough fuel for the flight back to Manston Airport. But Manston had a curfew – no arrivals or departures after 10 p.m. On this occasion it was vital we were refuelled quickly or we'd miss our return slot.

"Mr Stuart," said the captain as we sat on the runway at Min Vody, "there are fifty aircraft ahead of us waiting to refuel. There's no way we'll make it back to Manston tonight."

This was bad news. Staying overnight at Min Vody was not part of the plan.

"Unless…" continued the captain.

"Unless what?"

He stared meaningfully at the crates of Foster's piled up behind our seats. "Unless there is something we can offer the ground crew to persuade them to refuel us ahead of the queue."

I followed his gaze and realized what he had in mind. The Lancashire firemen nobly agreed to make the sacrifice, the pilot made a call in Russian on his radio and minutes later a fuel truck was speeding across the tarmac in our direction.

It was while we were refuelling that Russian immigration came aboard in one of their random checks to count the number of people in transit. We were officially listed as having twenty passengers and crew but had somehow ended up with twenty-one. To compound the sin of bribing the ground crew, I had to ask everyone on board to keep moving about and to make sure there was always someone in the toilet. Not one of our finest hours, I'm sorry to say – but we did make it back to Manston before the curfew.

Of the eight flights I loaded at Manston, I travelled on four. We would cruise down over Europe, Romania and Ukraine, flying parallel to the Black Sea and turning right to cross the Caucasus.

At times the skies were brilliant with stars and, like the psalmist, I'd sit and contemplate God's amazing handiwork – such a poignant introduction to the horrors I knew would be waiting in Nagorno Karabakh. At other times, as with the Christmas Child flight, the conditions on arrival would be atrocious and my admiration would turn to our Russian pilots. I've seen them execute perfect landings in conditions of ice and fog that would terrify the average RAF pilot.

If the weather was bad on arrival, there was no option but to reload our cargoes onto trucks and make the slow crawl over the mountains to Stepanakert – a journey of eight to ten hours, assuming we didn't break down or get stuck in snow on the way. To make matters worse, a slow-moving convoy would always be a target for Azeri gunners. While we ourselves were never attacked, others were.

When the weather allowed, it was quicker and safer to go by helicopter. Yerevan Airport had its own small fleet of Russian MIL-8s, piloted by Armenian veterans who'd gained their combat experience flying attack helicopters during Russia's invasion of Afghanistan. These same pilots now made a living by ferrying passengers and freight along the Lachin corridor to Nagorno Karabakh.

Each MIL-8 carried thirty people. I remember that fact because we sometimes tried to cram in thirty-one or thirty-two, some of them standing between the seats. The pilot would typically get a few feet off the ground, drop to earth with a bump and kick one or two people off to wait for the next flight.

The shortest, most direct route would get us from Yerevan to Stepanakert in about seventy-five minutes. It was also the safest route. But because there was no radar over the mountains, the smallest amount of cloud cover meant we had to make a detour out over Azeri territory and back in again. Which was clearly more dangerous.

On one of my first flights over the war zone, the helicopter lurched without warning and continued to turn and twist for another couple of minutes. As my fingers tightened on the armrests and my stomach heaved, Caroline calmly announced that we'd just been hit. The pilot had taken evasive action but hadn't quite been quick enough. We landed in Stepanakert with a bullet hole in the fuselage.

Monty Melkonian was an American Armenian who'd given up his law practice in California to come and fight for his homeland. A portly, talkative, humorous man, he took his nickname from his hero, General Montgomery, and now commanded the Karabakh Defence Forces in Martuni in the southern part of the enclave. On one of our trips, Caroline and I travelled down to see him in the company of Andrew, a BBC journalist whom I'd persuaded to make a short documentary for Breakfast TV back in Britain. As part of the deal, I'd agreed to do his filming.

Andrew had already had me filming bombed-out villages and fleeing refugees but was eager for some serious action. British breakfast-time viewers would want to see live firing at the front, he explained.

We discussed his requirements with Monty.

"You've got two options for getting some action," said Monty. "There's an Azeri observation post nineteen kilometres to our north, manned by a gunner who couldn't hit a barn door and will probably miss if we go that route. Or we can take the road to the south past another observation post. But I warn you, there's a mortar gunner there who's pretty sharp. We'll get some real firing there. We'll drive as fast as we can, but we might get hit."

He turned to Caroline. "Which is it to be?"

Caroline immediately suggested the more dangerous route. Monty then looked at me. Given that Caroline was in charge, I had no option but to agree.

That left Andrew, who by now had gone a strange, greenish

colour. "On second thoughts," he stammered, "I think I'll make do with the footage we've got."

It's possible that Andrew saved our lives. A week later, Monty Melkonian was killed by that same Azeri gunner. His funeral in Yerevan brought thousands onto the streets, some from as far away as America. This brave, patriotic lawyer-turned-soldier ended up giving everything for the country he loved. His death was a serious blow to Armenia's war effort.

One of the villages that suffered most in the conflict was Maraghar in the north-east of the enclave. In 1992 it was the scene of an Azeri attack in which forty-five Armenians had been butchered in the village church. A hundred women and children had been taken hostage and the village set alight. Unable to return to their ruined homes, the people had resurrected Maraghar in a new location closer to Stepanakert.

Having visited the original village the day after the killings, Caroline was eager to see the progress at New Maraghar and she and I travelled there together. The speech of welcome was given by a lady who revealed afterwards that she'd lost four sons and a daughter-in-law in the massacre and was now left looking after her grandchildren. "We have nothing," she told us. "We didn't only lose our families, we also lost all our cattle. Our children have forgotten the taste of milk."

We decided that the least that Christian Solidarity could do for New Maraghar was to replace the dairy herd. We managed to procure about fifty cows and a bull from Armenia and had them transported to the site. We later learned that the villagers had begun naming them after Christian Solidarity personnel. A particularly beautiful cow was christened Joanna after one of our country officers for the Caucasus. A stupid cow that kept running away was teasingly called Carolina. And the bull took the name Stuarto.

Later still, the news came back that Stuarto had died,

possibly from exhaustion, having impregnated an entire field of cows. Grateful as they were, the villagers couldn't waste a good bull and had eaten him. Despite his ignominious end, I believe my namesake deserves honourable mention for his services to his country.

On another occasion, I took a call from Caroline on her satellite phone somewhere in Nagorno Karabakh to say she'd got up very early to pray and been bitten by a rabid dog. She was having the treatment, but wanted all of us in the Christian Solidarity office to pray for her. We did so and were much relieved, shortly afterwards, to hear that she'd recovered. Oddly, though, the dog was found dead – an event that Caroline has found very hard to live down.

In all their suffering, the people of Nagorno Karabakh never lost their sense of humour. I have vivid memories of the day they reopened the theatre in Stepanakert. The inaugural play was an Armenian farce and Caroline and I were guests of honour. With so many men away at the front, most of the parts were taken by women. Although I couldn't understand a word, I've rarely guffawed so much in my life or felt such a shared sense of solidarity through the medium of laughter. In that darkened, wartime theatre, I knew the spirit of this remarkable race would never be broken.

In 1993, my colleague Gunnar Wiebalck of Christian Solidarity in Switzerland paid a visit to the Armenian city of Gyumri, badly damaged in the great Armenian earthquake of December 1988. While he was there, he happened to drive past a large, steel container lying in a field, apparently abandoned and surrounded by grazing cows. He stopped to investigate. It turned out to contain an operating theatre and prosthetic workshop, fully kitted out with the latest equipment for making artificial limbs. A gift from Germany following the earthquake, it had somehow been dumped in the field, unused, and had lain there ever since.

Faced with this unusual find, Gunnar approached the Armenian government to see if they needed it. They didn't, so he asked if he could have it. The government agreed and gave him permission to load it onto a truck and drive it over the mountains to Stepanakert. There, under the direction of a German-trained prosthesis specialist called Howannes Tschugurian, it became the centrepiece of a new unit for treating amputees and fitting prostheses.

As the fighting raged on, more and more Karabakhis were losing arms and legs from landmines and cluster bombs, and Tschugurian and his team were kept extremely busy. In the unit's first three months, they fitted forty artificial limbs.

Although they could operate and fit prostheses, the team still couldn't provide the physiotherapy that amputees have to have if they're going to get full benefit from their new limbs. One day, as Caroline and I were holding one of our regular meetings with the Karabakhi President and Prime Minister, they made a proposal. "We've got this empty building in Stepanakert," they told us. "It's been hit by a Grad missile so it's gutted. We want to turn it into a physiotherapy centre for treating amputees. Could your organization do the repairs?"

Caroline, who says yes to everything, assured them we could. We went to take a look and found what had been a large, elegant, two-storey townhouse, now roofless with all its windows blown out. Turning it into a clinic was going to be a massive job – Halton Pentecostal Church all over again, this time in a war zone more than 3,000 kilometres from home.

In the following months we raised the necessary money, much of it from Armenians in Argentina, and put together a team from England to carry out the task. My old friend Malcolm Trist took time off work to help with the electrics. He was joined by a bricklayer called Bob who'd worked on our church in Widnes. Also in the team were our Widnes project co-ordinator, Jimmy

Ogden, and a roof tiler by the name of Dave Dowling. Dave had worked for the Marley tile company before setting up a roofing business of his own and ploughing much of his profits into a British-sponsored school in Armenia. His contribution was to prove invaluable.

So as well as aid, our cargoes from Manston now included bricks, piping, timber, concrete, electrical equipment and, on one flight, a complete Marley tile roof supplied by Dave's company. And all the time we were praying desperately that this madcap project might somehow end up as a finished and functioning building.

The project was not without its crises. On one occasion, Bob the bricklayer informed me that our quantity surveyor had got his sums wrong and that as a result we were short of materials to the value of £20,000. I put a call through to Caroline to break the news. Our first response was to pray together down the phone, inform God of the problem and ask him what we should do next.

Later that evening, Caroline called me back. "You won't believe it, Stuart," she said. "One of our supporters in Argentina has just been in touch out of the blue. He wants to donate a large amount of money to the project. Would you like to know how much?"

I somehow knew the answer. "I think you're about to tell me," I said.

"Exactly. When you translate the currency, it comes to £20,000!"

Although I've seen it happen so many times, I've never ceased to be amazed by God's provision at precisely the right moment as people with no idea of our needs, sometimes on the other side of the world, are moved to take action. As we often say in Christian Solidarity, we don't believe in miracles, we rely on them.

Against all the odds, the project was eventually complete. Opened in 1995, the new centre was named the Cox Physiotherapy Clinic by decree of the Armenian parliament.

Although a valuable addition to the care of the injured, the centre still fell short of the original vision in one important respect. The team at the new clinic had always wanted a hydrotherapy pool. We'd allowed for one in our plans and had even laid the foundations, but various experts had then told us it was impossible to keep a hydrotherapy pool running in such difficult conditions without a full-time hydrotherapy professional. Not having such a person, we abandoned the project and the pool lay half built and empty.

God, it seemed, had other plans.

After the clinic was opened, Ethel and I spent a few days in Northern Ireland, staying with our friends Robert and Lorna Robinson and helping to man a stand at the Christian Resources Exhibition. Before we left, my assistant Michelle had asked me which flight she should book us back on. There was one leaving soon after the close of the exhibition and another two hours later. I said we'd go for the later flight.

When the exhibition ended, we took down our stand and Lorna dropped us off at Belfast City Airport. As we walked in I noticed a lady sitting by the fountain in the foyer and felt one of those promptings from the Holy Spirit that I knew so well. Ethel could tell immediately what was going through my mind. She despairs of my habit of accosting strangers and usually pretends I'm not with her!

"Oh no, Stuart," she sighed. "Not again. Please don't."

"I'm sorry, Ethel, I can't help it. I just know God wants me to talk to that lady."

"Stuart, you're impossible!"

I went over and struck up a conversation. The lady was Australian and I asked her what she did. She told me she was a physiotherapist working for Wiltshire County Council. (You can tell where this is going. By now I was also starting to sense that God was up to something.)

"A physiotherapist?" I said. "That's interesting. I'm looking for an expert in hydrotherapy."

"That's what I am," she replied. "Why do you want one of those?"

"Well, in this little country called Nagorno Karabakh which you won't have heard of, I've just been helping to build a rehabilitation clinic for amputees and people with spinal injuries. We've got the foundations for a hydrotherapy pool, but we need an expert to run it."

My new acquaintance became intensely interested. "You're absolutely right. You do. Where is this place? Who are you? What's your work?"

The lady was on the same flight back to London, so we were able to talk further. Her name was Helen Whitelaw. She was a Christian and eager to do something new for God before going home to Australia. As a result of that meeting in Belfast, she ended up travelling to Stepanakert at her own expense to get the pool ready and operating. Hundreds of war victims have since had cause to be thankful for Helen's expertise and her willingness to follow God's leading.

One day Caroline phoned me from Nagorno Karabakh, and her words were heavy with despair. "You know, Stuart," she said, "They're bringing so many dead and injured back from the front, I don't think the Karabakhis will be able to carry on much longer. I fear they're about to be overrun and the entire population will have to flee the enclave. And that'll be the end of Nagorno Karabakh."

Then, quite suddenly, the situation changed. At the height of the fighting, as the Azeris were recapturing many of the villages they'd previously lost, Azerbaijan agreed to a temporary, Russian-mediated ceasefire in May 1994. To Christian Solidarity and many other observers, this was totally unexpected and the reasons are still not clear. Possibly the Azeris failed to realize how bad things were in the enclave and how close they were to outright victory. Whatever the reasons, the enclave's survival was a miracle.

Although clashes continued well into 1995, an uneasy peace eventually returned and the enclave has been able to make a slow recovery. While Nagorno Karabakh no longer heads our list of concerns at Christian Solidarity, I see it as one of our crucial missions – not just for the aid but for the hope and solidarity we were able to share with the suffering population. In their darkest hours, faced with destruction as a country, they knew they were not forgotten.

10

The Martyrs of Iran

On Christmas Day 1990, two and a half years before I joined Christian Solidarity, my friend Elias Zaidifard – the man who made fire engines in Widnes – made an announcement in our church in Halton. Elias had close links to Iran and was a constant source of information on the plight of Iranian Christians.

His message was stark. "The authorities in Iran have murdered Hossein Soodmand, a pastor in the Assemblies of God. Hossein was bold in his witness and a faithful shepherd to the church in Iran. They hanged him in prison in the city of Mashhad as an example to others thinking of leaving Islam. They didn't even allow his family to see his body."

Pastor Soodmand was the third Christian leader to be martyred in Iran since the Islamic revolution of 1979. In 1980 Arastoo Sayyah, the priest in Shiraz, had his throat cut when he opened the door to two men claiming they wanted to know more about Christianity. In the same year, gunmen burst into the Isfahan apartment of the Anglican bishop, Hassan Dehqani-Tafti, and fired five bullets at his head as he and his wife lay in bed. They missed. Shortly afterwards, however, the couple's 24-year-old son, Bahram, was kidnapped, driven to the city outskirts and shot dead. The pressure continued in the years that followed. By the time I joined Christian Solidarity in 1993, Iran was a cause of increasing concern.

One of the first names that came across my desk as National Director was that of Mehdi Dibaj. A convert from Islam (that fact alone would put his life in danger), Mehdi had joined Pastor Soodmand's Assemblies of God fellowship and become an evangelist. In 1983 he was arrested and imprisoned in the city of Sari in north-eastern Iran. There he'd been tortured and abused, subjected to mock executions and kept for three years in solitary confinement in an unlit cell just one metre square. While he was in prison, his wife left him and reverted to Islam after being threatened with death by stoning. During this period, Mehdi was twice sentenced to death for apostasy. But although both sentences were overturned by Iran's Supreme Court, he'd never been released.

Ever since his incarceration, Christian Solidarity had been publicizing Mehdi's story and urging its supporters to write to the Iranian authorities on his behalf. His cause was also championed by two fellow Iranian Christians.

One was my old friend Sam Yeghnazar, brother-in-law of Elias Zaidifard and my companion on two trips to Nagorno Karabakh. Growing up in Tehran, Sam had been a close friend of the now martyred Pastor Soodmand and regarded Mehdi Dibaj almost as a brother. Having left Iran, Sam now ran the Iranian Christian Fellowship in London and was Chief Executive of Elam Ministries, whose college in Surrey trains Farsi-speaking pastors and evangelists to take the gospel to their Iranian countrymen around the world.

The second of Mehdi's leading Iranian advocates was Bishop Haik Hovsepian Mehr. A poet, a singer and a Christian pastor since his teens, Haik moved to Tehran in 1981 to take up the post of Superintendent of the Assemblies of God churches. Five years later, his election as President of the Council of Protestant Ministers made him leader of the country's evangelical Christians and set him on a collision course with the Islamic authorities. He refused to bar Muslims or Muslim converts from his churches, as the law required. He refused to sign a statement that Christians enjoyed full rights in Iran. He angered the government by inviting the UN rapporteur for religious freedom to visit Iran and investigate discrimination against Christians. And he used every opportunity to draw the world's attention to the plight of his imprisoned friend, Mehdi Dibaj.

On 3 December 1993, Mehdi went on trial yet again before the Islamic court in Sari and was found guilty of apostasy. The court informed him that sentence would be passed later in the month, after which the decision would go to the Iranian Supreme Court for ratification. When Bishop Haik visited him in prison shortly afterwards, Mehdi told him he was too weary at the age of sixty to fight the case any longer. He was ready to die for his faith and all he wanted now was to write his final testimony.

A few days later the phone rang in my office in Witney. It was a frantically busy time at Christian Solidarity and I hoped the call was not another crisis.

"Stuart," said Sam Yeghnazar, "please would you come down to Elam straight away. There's something I have to show you."

"But can you tell me what...?"

"I'll show you when you get here. Please come as soon as you can."

I have too much respect for Sam to ignore that kind of request, so I got in my car and drove to Shackleford in Surrey to the former Barnardo's home that is now the Elam Ministries training college. I had no sooner walked into Sam's office than he thrust some sheets of paper into my hand.

"Brother Stuart, read this."

"What is it?"

"It's Mehdi's testimony. It's what he said in court, but now he's written it down. He gave it to Haik who faxed it straight to me. You and I are the only people outside Iran who've seen it."

I sat down to read the three-page document. As I did so I felt a surge of excitement, an inner quickening as I recognized the touch of the Holy Spirit on Mehdi's simple words. Here was the voice of a joyful, courageous martyr, utterly confident in his Lord and ready to give his life. Like Stephen in the New Testament, he seemed already to be glimpsing heaven as he prepared for death. Reading on, I struggled to hold back the tears.

I am a Christian, a sinner who believes Jesus has died for my sins on the cross and who, by his resurrection and victory over death, has made me righteous in the presence of the holy God...

In response to this kindness, he has asked me to deny myself and be his fully surrendered follower, and not to fear people even if they kill my body, but rather rely on the creator of life who has crowned me with the crown of mercy and compassion...

People say, "You were a Muslim from your birth." God says, "You were a Christian from the beginning." He states that he chose us thousands of years ago, even before the creation of the universe, so that through the sacrifice of Jesus Christ we may be his...

I would rather have the whole world against me but know that the almighty God is with me, be called an apostate but know that I have the approval of the God of glory, because man looks at the outward appearance but God looks at the heart, and for him who is God for all eternity nothing is impossible. All power in heaven and on earth is in his hands...

They tell me, "Return!" But from the arms of my God whom can I return to? Is it right to accept what

people are saying instead of obeying the Word of God?
It is now 45 years that I am walking with the God of
miracles, and his kindness upon me is like a shadow and
I owe him much for his fatherly love and concern...

The good and kind God reproves and punishes all
those whom he loves. He tests them in preparation for
heaven. The God of Daniel, who protected his friends
in the fiery furnace, has protected me for nine years in
prison and all the bad happenings have turned out for
our good and gain, so that I am filled to overflowing
with joy and thankfulness...

I have committed my life into his hands. Life for
me is an opportunity to serve him, and death is a better
opportunity to be with Christ. Therefore, I am not only
satisfied to be in prison for the honour of his holy name,
but am ready to give my life for the sake of Jesus my
Lord...[4]

"Sam!" I said as I reached the end. "This is like the final chapter of the Acts of the Apostles. The world has got to read it. We must get this out to the press."

"I agree," said Sam. "Let's publish."

The call, when it came, was as I expected. "Stuart," said Sam, "I've just heard from Haik. The court in Sari has sentenced Mehdi to death – public hanging from a crane."

Though the sentence still had to be ratified, the Supreme Court was due to make its decision in January and there was no time to lose. I prepared a press release explaining that the Iranian authorities were intent on hanging a Christian minister for apostasy. I attached Mehdi's testimony in full and faxed it to BBC radio and television and the main national newspapers.

Twenty minutes later, Susanna our administrator took a call. Through the door of my office I could see her talking on the phone. She looked shocked and surprised.

"What's wrong?" I mouthed.

"It's Bernard Levin from *The Times*. He'd like to talk to you."

I knew Bernard Levin by repute as one of Fleet Street's sharpest and most respected commentators. I also knew he was a big fan of Caroline Cox. Long before joining Christian Solidarity, Caroline had co-written a book called *Rape of Reason*, based on her struggles as Head of Sociology in the stridently Marxist Polytechnic of North London. Bernard Levin had spoken highly of the book and of Caroline's contribution to education in his column in *The Times*. As a result, Prime Minister Margaret Thatcher had read some of Caroline's work, including *Rape of Reason*, and had given her a peerage on the strength of it.

I picked up the phone. "Good morning, Mr Levin."

"Good morning, Mr Windsor. I wanted to say I'm deeply moved by this press release you've just sent. It's a wonderful, wonderful testimony. Do I have your permission to print it verbatim in my feature in *The Times*?"

This was better publicity than I'd dared to hope for. "Absolutely," I said.

Bernard Levin then asked if I had any other suggestions for the piece. As well as appealing for Mehdi Dibaj to be released, what else might he ask of the Iranian authorities?

Knowing he came from a Jewish background, I mentioned another of our concerns at Christian Solidarity – the fact that Bible House, the Bible Society's bookshop in Tehran, had been closed down by the government in 1990. The loss was felt not only by Iranian Christians but also by the Jewish population who now had nowhere to buy copies of the Old Testament. He agreed to raise the issue and I understand he later had a letter from the Board of Deputies of British Jews thanking him for doing so.

Mehdi Dibaj's testimony appeared in Bernard Levin's column

on 13 January 1994 and triggered a worldwide clamour for his release. Our own campaign moved up several notches as we urged people to pray and keep protesting. Western governments became involved with representations to Iran from the USA and the European Union. According to Bernard Levin himself, some 50 million people eventually read Mehdi's remarkable testimony and hundreds of thousands added their voices to the international outcry.

The government in Tehran was obviously listening. On 16 January, with no warning or explanation, the Supreme Court, instead of ratifying the death sentence, ordered Mehdi to be released. I heard the news from Sam just after Mehdi had called him to say he was free. I remember punching the air in elation. According to Sam, Mehdi had gone immediately to Tehran to see Bishop Haik and the young people from Haik's congregation had lined the path to his front door singing, "In the name of Jesus, we have the victory!"

The mood in the churches in Iran and among Mehdi's supporters was jubilant. But it was not to last.

A few days later, Haik left home to drive to Tehran Airport and meet some friends who were flying in from another part of Iran. He never arrived. No one knew what had happened to him, only that he'd gone missing between his home and the airport.

At Christian Solidarity we were certain he'd been picked up and detained by state security and began an international campaign on his behalf. I phoned Bernard Levin to explain this new twist and he responded with an article demanding to know what the authorities had done with Haik Hovsepian Mehr, Iranian patriot and man of God.

On 31 January 1994, ten days after he'd disappeared, the authorities announced that they'd found Haik's car. Inside was his body, horribly butchered. The police, who denied all knowledge of his abduction, photographed the mutilated corpse and showed the pictures to his son, Joseph, for identification. By then the authorities had already buried Haik, but they reluctantly agreed to exhume his body and return it to his family for Christian burial.

The funeral at Haik's church in Tehran on 3 February attracted friends and supporters from all over the world. Mehdi Dibaj paid tribute. "It should have been me," he declared. "I should have died, not Brother Haik."

After the funeral had taken place, the international organizations with whom Haik had worked – Elam Ministries, the Evangelical Alliance, the Assemblies of God, Brother Andrew's Open Doors, ourselves and a number of others – held a memorial service for Haik at Westminster Central Hall in London. As in Tehran, the building was packed.

To this day, no one has ever been charged with Haik's abduction and murder.

Later that year, on 24 June, Sam called me again. "Brother Stuart," he said, "Mehdi Dibaj has gone missing. He was going to visit one of his daughters and he's disappeared."

I was shocked, though not surprised. Along with most of Mehdi's supporters, I had never believed the Iranian authorities would relinquish such a high-profile prisoner without striking back in some way. Once again we issued press releases and launched a campaign for his release.

Five days later there was more bad news. Tateos Michaelian, the 62-year-old leader of Iran's Presbyterian evangelicals, had also gone missing. A former general secretary of the Iranian Bible Society, Tateos had taken over as President of the Council of Protestant Ministers after Haik was murdered. As well as being a much-loved pastor, Tateos was an eminent poet and a translator of Persian literature.

On 2 July, police looking for Tateos discovered the body of Mehdi Dibaj in the University Park in Tehran. He'd been tortured and murdered. Shortly afterwards, the son of Tateos Michaelian was summoned by the authorities to identify a second body. Tateos had been found shot in the head.

The church in Iran had paid a heavy price with the martyrdom of three of its leaders in the space of six months. More persecution was to follow, particularly against churches that were seen to be attracting and converting Muslims.

Early one morning in September 1996, Bagher Yusefi, an Assemblies of God pastor, left his home in Sari to pray. A convert from Islam, Pastor Yusefi and his wife had helped to raise the two sons of Mehdi Dibaj during his years in prison in the same city. They had also been a great support to the family of Hossein Soodmand after his execution. Later that same day, the authorities contacted Bagher's family to say his body had been discovered hanging from a tree. After Arastoo Sayyah, Bahram Dehqani-Tafti, Hossein Soodmand, Haik Hovsepian Mehr, Mehdi Dibaj and Tateos Michaelian, he became the seventh Christian leader to be murdered in Iran since the 1979 revolution.

In addition to the killings, the Iranian church has suffered years of harassment and hostility from the authorities. In September 2004, more than eighty pastors and elders were arrested at a Christian conference in Tehran and held for questioning. All were released apart from Hamid Pourmand, an Assemblies of God lay preacher and an officer in the Iranian navy. Hamid was charged with converting to Christianity without telling the navy (under Iranian law, it's illegal for a Christian to hold a commission in the forces) and with attempting to convert Muslims. Christian Solidarity and other agencies ran a campaign on his behalf. When he came to court, the judge declared: "I don't know who you are, but the rest of the world does." Our campaigning had evidently worked. Hamid was cleared of apostasy and proselytizing and convicted simply of deceiving the Iranian navy.

Back in Mashhad, the pastor who succeeded Hossein Soodmand was ordered to report to the local police station every week for three years. On each occasion, an officer would put a gun to his head and pull the trigger in a mock execution. The experience affected him mentally and he's since had to leave Iran. The current pastors in Mashhad are Mehdi Dibaj's daughter, Fereshteh, and her husband, Amir Montazami, both of whom have been detained and questioned about their Christian activities. Although they've been released, they remain under surveillance – as do many other Iranian Christian leaders.

One of our recent campaigns centred on Marzieh Amirizadeh and Maryam Rustampoor, two young converts from Islam who were arrested in March 2009 and held in the women's section of Tehran's notorious Evin prison. The chief warden reportedly said they should both hang for apostasy and for blaspheming the Prophet Mohammed. When they appeared before the state prosecutor in August 2009, he demanded they recant as the price of their freedom. They refused, claiming they could do nothing else than follow the Lord Jesus. After 259 days in prison, they were released on bail in November 2009 and finally acquitted the following March.

On that freezing night in January 1993 when we stood on a mountain road in Armenia waiting for the Spitak rescue crew to retrieve our broken-down trucks, Sam Yeghnazar had made a cryptic remark. Nodding towards the Iranian border some seventy kilometres to the south, he commented: "We're close to the domain of the Prince of Persia. We must be on our guard."

His words were a reference to chapter 10 of the book of Daniel and the hints in Scripture that the regions of the world have their own spiritual princes opposed to the work of God.

In the case of Daniel, a messenger from God comes to him in a vision and speaks of being "resisted" in his mission by the Prince of Persia.

Little did Sam know in 1993 that the following year would see the martyrdom of three of his Iranian friends – Haik, Mehdi and Tateos. His warning was prophetic. And given the longstanding opposition to the church in Persia – modern-day Iran – it's not unrealistic to think of malign spiritual forces brooding over the nation and still seeking to frustrate the kingdom of God.

The present situation in Iran presents conflicting trends. From some of the evidence, we might conclude that the Prince of Persia remains a force in the land. Pressure on Christians continues, with church leaders and Muslim converts particularly singled out for surveillance, harassment and persecution. It's common for government spies to attend Sunday services and for phone lines of church leaders to be tapped. In the cradle of the Islamic revolution, the penalties for converting to Christianity remain harsh. With many Christians leaving Iran to escape the restrictions on their freedom, there have been fears that the Iranian church will eventually wither.

On the other hand, Iran is a country in desperate spiritual need. It has massive economic and social problems including high rates of unemployment and drug addiction. Two thirds of its population are under twenty-five and young Iranians are restless, disillusioned with the Islamic revolution and searching for answers to life's deepest questions. The growth of satellite TV and its use by Christian broadcasters such as SAT-7 have opened a door to new ways of thinking. Church leaders in Iran report an extraordinary openness to the gospel and an explosion in the number of underground house fellowships. It's said that more Iranians have become Christians since the Islamic revolution than during the previous 1,300 years.

God is also working directly. We hear reports that growing numbers of Iranians are turning up at churches and asking for information or Bibles. When asked why they've come, it's common to hear that they've seen Jesus in a dream or vision and that he has sent them.

God has clearly not given up on the ancient land of Persia.

11

The Lost Children of Russia

In September 1990, Caroline Cox – then a Christian Solidarity trustee – was invited to a human rights conference in Leningrad organized by Leningrad City Council and the Solidarity Human Rights Commission in Poland.

Shortly before the conference opened, two newly elected deputies on Leningrad City Council wrote to the Commission with an appeal. Thanks to their new positions, they'd been able to gain access to Russian institutions normally closed to the public. Their letter revealed that thousands of orphans were being wrongly diagnosed as mentally deficient, shut away in appalling conditions and deprived of normal human rights for the rest of their lives. Please would some of the conference delegates come and assess the situation. "Unless we draw attention to the system," the deputies added, "it's never going to change."

Responding to the appeal, the conference organizers quickly arranged for a group of experts, Caroline among them, to take time out from the conference to visit some of Leningrad's orphanages and the adolescent wing of a psychiatric hospital.

What Caroline and her colleagues discovered was to lead Christian Solidarity into a new area of activity and bring about a revolution in childcare in the Russian Federation.

Russia, at the time, was emerging from seventy years of a Communist system that had constantly told its citizens that the state was supreme and that individuals were of value only to the extent that they were useful to society. In Soviet thinking, a human being was a means, not an end. Under the guidance of the state, declared the Communists, humanity was evolving towards a perfect society populated by perfect citizens.

Which meant that anyone regarded as "imperfect" was by definition inferior. If you were mentally handicapped, for example, the state felt little obligation to care for you. You might have value as cheap labour but not for much else.

These attitudes made life particularly harsh for Russia's orphans. The Soviet Union wreaked enormous damage on the family unit as poverty, alcoholism and drug addiction forced many parents to hand over their children to the care of the state. In some cases a criminal record or evidence of "fanatical" religious belief was enough for the government to break up a family and forcibly remove the children. And while struggling parents in other countries might have benefited from a system of foster care and adoption, Russia had no such thing. Seven decades of Communism had eroded the concept of charity, stifling voluntary organizations and leaving the state as the sole provider for parentless children.

The Communist system drew little distinction between genuine orphans and those whose parents might still be alive but unable to care for them. Bizarrely, it also equated being an orphan with being mentally handicapped. Any sign of emotional disturbance – the kind of behaviour you'd expect in children torn from their parents – was enough to brand them subnormal. I'm sure most of the children I knew in my Barnardo's home would have been labelled in this way had they lived in Russia. I expect I would have been.

The common diagnosis applied to orphans was "oligophrenic", the Greek word for "small brained". The diagnosis was usually perfunctory and was almost never reviewed. As a result, hundreds of thousands of Russian children were misdiagnosed, shut away from society in grim Soviet institutions and given just enough education to turn them into useful manual labourers.

Clearly, there were many children in the system who knew their lives were being blighted and expressed their frustration by making trouble or trying to run away. The treatment was often powerful doses of drugs. Magnesium sulphate was particularly common. The line between therapy and punishment was a fine one, as was evident in the way the Soviets treated political or religious dissidents. Here, too, many healthy individuals were misdiagnosed as mentally ill and pumped with drugs in ways that would never have been tolerated in a non-totalitarian society.

Life for these children was no better when they left their orphanages. If they didn't escape to the streets and a life of crime, they were normally channelled into unskilled manual jobs and forced to live in single-sex factory hostels with no opportunity for a normal family life. Anyone diagnosed as oligophrenic was not allowed to vote or drive a car.

Almost the only other option was to go into the army. After a lifetime of emotional deprivation and lack of normal human contact, orphan soldiers could be trained to carry out orders that would sicken their comrades. There's evidence that the troops who beat a group of protesters to death with shovels in the Georgian capital, Tbilisi, in April 1989 were a detachment of orphans. The Romanian dictator, Nicolae Ceausescu, certainly knew the value of emotionally stunted orphan soldiers and recruited them into his personal bodyguard.

This was the legacy that Caroline and her colleagues encountered when they slipped out of the Leningrad conference in September 1990 in the company of their city deputy hosts to visit an institution for "oligophrenics".

After walking past the posters with quotations from Marx

and Lenin extolling the virtues of work, Caroline found herself in a clean, functional building with staff who seemed concerned to do their best for the children in their care. That said, there was no attempt to encourage individuality or to make the surroundings at all homely. Caroline speaks of dormitories with twenty beds and absolutely nothing else – no pictures, no lockers, nowhere to keep even the smallest personal possessions. Children were described in their own hearing as half-wits, as though the staff genuinely believed they were sub-human.

In these homes for the so-called handicapped, the group met lively, articulate children who were eager to talk and showed no obvious signs of being subnormal. Some were even playing chess. To an outside observer, the questions were urgent and obvious. How was it possible for so many apparently normal children to be diagnosed as handicapped? Where was the systematic, ongoing assessment of the children in care?

The answers from the deputies accompanying the tour were disturbing. The initial diagnosis of these children was casual in the extreme (it was not unknown for psychologists to conduct the tests in the car on the way to the orphanage) and it usually stuck for life. As for why it was so seldom reviewed – well, the Soviet Union needed a good supply of unthinking, unskilled, manual workers.

Worse was to come the following day when the group visited Leningrad's secure psychiatric hospital – brutal, Soviet-style brick and concrete on the outside; bare, dingy wards and corridors on the inside. The adolescent wing was a bleak room with rows of beds and piles of soiled mattresses. It was occupied by twenty or so listless, shaven-headed boys, many of whom seemed to be drugged.

"Please will you find me a mother," said a wan-faced boy called Ilya[5] who'd been certified insane and sent to the psychiatric ward for trying to run away from the orphanage where he was being bullied. "Please. I want to get out of here."

Out in the courtyard, Caroline wept in despair at these young, ruined lives.

Back home in the UK and deeply troubled by what they'd seen, Caroline and her colleagues decided to carry out a more systematic assessment to put facts and figures to the initial impressions. Encouraged by members of Leningrad City Council who were equally determined to see the system changed, they brought together a team consisting of a paediatrician, an educational psychologist, a clinical psychologist, a nurse (Caroline herself), a Soviet expert and a TV cameraman and returned to the city in September 1991. In a sign of the changes afoot in Russian society, the trip coincided with the city's change of name from Leningrad to St Petersburg.

The aim this time was to apply recognized scientific techniques to assess orphans in St Petersburg and Moscow and discover the extent to which normal children were being misclassified as mentally handicapped. The group conducted tests on 171 children in 15 institutions and found that most of those labelled "oligophrenic" had no disability at all. Indeed, many were assessed as having above-average intelligence.

A bright 14-year-old called Vladimir complained that his school work was undemanding and told the group he wanted to learn a foreign language and become a marine architect. The team's educational psychologist believed he had the intellectual capacity to pursue his ambition. Tragically, the odds were stacked against his ever doing so. Education in the homes took second place to "work therapy" which consisted of mindless tasks like folding egg boxes or sticking price labels on bottles and was really a front for free labour. Even the brightest, by the time they left their institutions, would have fallen so far behind their peers in Russia's education system that any hope of catching up would have long since gone.

The group also confirmed that only one in a thousand of the

children in these institutions was ever reassessed. As a result, the 19,000 so-called oligophrenics in St Petersburg, not to mention the million or so others in Moscow and elsewhere, were doomed to live forgotten, locked-away lives with no opportunity to fulfil their potential.

Moving on to the juvenile wing of a St Petersburg prison, Caroline and her team discovered that almost a third of the inmates were from children's homes. Here they saw boys in their early and mid teens incarcerated in cells originally designed for three but now accommodating fifteen. Each cell had a stinking, overflowing toilet in the corner, and the boys were allowed just one hour's exercise per day in a concrete yard measuring three metres by five. Many were there for minor offences such as stealing food when they were hungry.

The issue was stark. How could Russia's blighted orphans be rescued from their orphanages, psychiatric wards, prisons and hostels and given the chance of a normal, productive life?

The team's findings were published in 1991 in a report entitled *Trajectories of Despair*. "There needs to be a complete revolution in the approach to the mentally retarded," the report stated. Among its many recommendations on diagnosis, the use of drugs, education and government policy, it called for greater use of fostering and adoption. "With proper procedures for selecting prospective parents, this should prove an effective method for reducing the numbers of children in orphanages and promote more healthy development of those children."

The report went on: "International experts with experience of adoption procedures may be required to teach these procedures and safeguards as the Soviet system has barely allowed adoption up till now and experience of selection and training of prospective parents is non-existent in many areas."

For all its measured, scientific tones, the report proved explosive in showing what was really going on behind the closed

The Windsors.
L to R, back row: Uncle Arthur and my father. Front row:
Grandma, Uncle Ken and Grandad.

My mother, Irene. Though she lived until 1994, I last saw
her in 1954 when I was ten.

With my Dr
Barnardo's
"family", soon
after arriving
at High Broom,
Crowborough, in
1953. I'm second
from the top on
the far right.

Escorting Princess Margaret on her visit to Dr Barnardo's in 1958.

With my Windsor siblings in 2003. L to R: Brian, Reg (who died in 2008), me, Maureen and Janet.

A giant Russian Ilyushin IL-76 carrying aid for Nagorno Karabakh is greeted at Yerevan Airport.

Iranian-born Sam Yeghnazar, my companion on two trips to Nagorno Karabakh.

January 1993: aid for Nagorno Karabakh is loaded onto dilapidated Soviet trucks, all of which later came to a stop with punctures.

Aslan Krikorian, former Olympic skier and head of Spitak Rescue in Nagorno Karabakh, who saved hundreds of lives in the Armenian-Azeri conflict.

The Spitak rescue vehicle after it slid off a mountain pass in Armenia. Had Frank Walsh and I not followed a hunch to get out, we would certainly have been killed.

The results of a Grad missile strike in Stepanakert. The pregnant wife and two children of the man on the left lie dead under the rubble. He and his brother have worn the tops off their fingers trying to reach them.

An Azeri Russian tank, destroyed in the fighting in Nagorno Karabakh.

One of the ageing MIL-8s that ferried us between Yerevan and Nagorno Karabakh. We landed on one occasion with a bullet hole in the fuselage.

The gutted building in Stepanakert before we started work to turn it into a physiotherapy clinic.

My RAF buddy, Malcolm Trist, joins an aid flight to Yerevan.

Seen as we waited at the border between Belarus and Poland in 1992 – a Russian jet engine that someone had tried, and failed, to smuggle across.

With Tanya, a border guard unlike any I've ever met. Later enquiries failed to find her. Was she more than a border guard?

"Someone up there loves you." The worn tyres that had just taken us 4,000 kilometres from Moscow to the UK.

Martyred in Iran (L to R): Pastor Hossein Soodmand, hanged in December 1990; Bishop Haik Hovsepian Mehr, murdered in January 1994; and Revd Mehdi Dibaj, tortured and murdered in June 1994.

Caroline Cox (L) and Maria Ternovskaya, driving forces behind the *Nasha Semya* project in Moscow.

Helping to entertain Russian orphans at *Nasha Semya* with Christian Solidarity's Chairman, Mervyn Thomas.

The boy in the dream: Dimitri, abandoned in a dustbin as a baby, later became an accomplished violin player.

The team battling for religious freedom in Mongolia outside the Parliament building in Ulan Bator. L to R: Wilfred Wong, John and Altaa Gibbens, Alan Johnston and Robin Brodie.

Dr Martin Panter, champion of Burma's suffering minorities, with Karen refugees on the Thai-Burma border in 2007.

Christian Solidarity President, the MP David Atkinson, visits Rehmat Masih (L) and Salamat Masih in their safe house in Pakistan as they await trial for blasphemy in 1993.

Group Captain (Retd) Cecil Chaudhry, air force hero and a leader in the struggle for religious freedom in Pakistan.

Manzoor Masih's widow mourns at his funeral with thousands of other Christians after he was shot outside the High Court in Lahore in April 1994.

John Joseph, bearded to look like a mullah, arrives at court in November 1995 to give evidence against the killers of Manzoor Masih.

With Tina Lambert (L), Ethel and I lay flowers on the graves of martyrs
Manzoor Masih and Tariq Iqbal in the Christian cemetery in Lahore.

The response of the people of Shanti Nagar after their village was attacked by a mob in 1997.
The questions remain valid.

Vladimir Lankin, the Russian embassy official who became a Christian in Dhaka jail, with his wife, Natasha.

With Caroline Cox in Southern Sudan, handing over medicines in Wun Rok, Bahr El-Ghazal, shortly after the 1998 massacre.

The De Havilland Buffalo that God provided at an hour's notice to get us to the slave encampment in Abyei County, Southern Sudan.

LIST OF SLAVES REDEEMED - DATE_____ PLACE_____ PAGE___5

#	Name of Slave	Age	Sex	Abducted From	Date	Abducted To	Owner's Name	Comments
1	Awut Deng	29	F	Mabior dit	10/6/98	majitel-	Abdulai	
2	Yai Mabok	20	F	malual Aleu	15/6/98	celap	Ahmed	
3	Matet Aduum	13	m	Mabior dit	10/6/98	mujitel-	Abdul	
4	Maileck gui	4	m	malual Aleu	15/6/98	majitel-	Ahmed	
5	Alor Pap	21	F	malual Aleu	" "	Garangcak	Abdulai	
6	Ajok Deng	13	F	dier	2/5/98	celap	Abdulai	
7	Atak wek	16	m	malual Aleu	15/6/98	celap	mahamed	
8	Tiem Then	14	F	malual Aleu	" "	celap	Abdul	
9	Ador malual	28	F	" "	" "	" "		
10	Deng Deng	6	m	" "	15/6/98	Abuteleer	malimed	
11	Biar Mayeng	7	m	" "	29/2/98	dcongker-pars	Adam	
12	Aliar malual	10	m	" "	" "	cetap	Hussan	
13	Rek mayeng	5	m	majak	11/6/98			
14	Achol yuel	5	F	" "	11/6/98			
15	Marop yuel	18	m	malual/dleu	15/6/98	mujital-	Adam	
16	Mangok panu	16	m	" "	11/6/98	celap	Hassan	
17	Ring mayar	17	m	dino	2/5/98	Garangcak	Abdulal	
18	Mangok malual	9	m	" "	" "			s
19	Abiel majile	9	F	Ngong	7/5/98	Abuzet	Abu Adam	

One of the lists of captured villagers, meticulously drawn up by the SPLA after every slave raid.

With Caroline Cox and Andy Jacobson, negotiating for slaves with Arab middlemen.

Nine-year-old Joseph, freed after two years as a slave and not knowing if his parents are still alive.

Miracle in the Nigerian bush: Godwin (R) and his friends who produced a brand new set of Honda wheel bearings from a nearby hut (below).

The lads jack up the car and replace the bearings like seasoned mechanics.

doors of Russia's orphanages. Caroline expected serious flak from the Russian authorities for presuming to criticize their childcare provision, but the response was quite the opposite. Officials at national and local level welcomed her conclusions. It was as though the lies and distortions of seventy years of Communism had been stripped away and those running the system were finally able to see it for the perversion it was.

"Now you've given us the evidence," said one orphanage director, "we have the ammunition to change the system from within."

The upshot was a request from the Russian Federation Ministry of Education and the Moscow Education Department for Caroline and Christian Solidarity to help find a solution. They admitted that they themselves knew nothing of modern practices in fostering and adoption. The country had no laws to govern how these things should be done and the system as it stood was run by government administrators rather than childcare professionals. There was no process for preparing foster or adoptive parents and no concept of post-placement support. The task was therefore immense. New legislation would have to be drafted and passed. Childcare professionals would need to be trained and potential foster parents recruited. An entire new system would have to be developed, tested and implemented.

The centre of Moscow alone had 5,000 abandoned or orphaned children living either in shelters or in the city's orphanages. These now became the focus of a new and ground-breaking project to change the nation's childcare system.

Independently of Caroline's work, a Moscow University physics lecturer by the name of Maria Ternovskaya was deeply disturbed by the plight of Russia's orphans. She wanted to do something to help and was looking at the possibility of setting up homes for small family groups. In 1992 she met Caroline at a childcare conference in Moscow. Caroline, by now, was well known in

Russia for *Trajectories of Despair* and the two women recognized in each other a mutual passion for changing the system. For her part, Caroline saw Maria as a vital link in a possible solution. She realized, though, that Maria's plans would need considerable support from Western agencies – not least Christian Solidarity.

Although it was now involved through Caroline, Christian Solidarity was not a childcare organization. It therefore needed specialist partners. Over time we were joined in the project by the Bridge Child Care Development Service (the consultancy that helped set up the Childline service in the UK), by the National Foster Care Association (now called the Fostering Network) and by the UK Department of Health. Each became involved in the training and planning that were now taking place in partnership with the Russian and Muscovite education departments.

When I joined Christian Solidarity as UK National Director in 1993, the Russian childcare issue was top of the agenda in my briefings with Caroline. For the first time I found someone who was genuinely delighted I'd been brought up in a children's home. "Excellent!" she said. "You'll know how it feels." From then on, whenever I visited our Russian projects, I was introduced as the man from the children's home. It broke the barriers immediately!

In 1993, Maria Ternovskaya won a scholarship from an educational charity to visit the UK and study the ways that other countries provided childcare. This brought her to Ruskin College, Oxford, on a three-month placement. It was here that I met the sparky, energetic lady who would prove so influential in Russia's new system of foster care. When the Zurich office decided that the Russian childcare project would be run by Christian Solidarity UK (and therefore by me), it was clear that Maria and I would be working closely together.

On our many visits to Moscow between 1993 and 1996, Caroline and I heard frequent promises from the authorities that they'd find us a building in Moscow suitable for the pilot project we had in mind. Having been somewhat sceptical, we were delighted to be offered a substantial, five-storey house close to Red Square. Maria was installed as manager and gave it the name *Nasha Semya* (meaning "Our Family") – the sense of family being the thing most seriously missing in the lives of the orphans we wanted to help.

Nasha Semya was to be a half-way house between the existing orphanages and the foster families to which the children would eventually be transferred. Among its many innovations was a special therapeutic programme to help children removed from their parents to make the transition to a new family. It was also a centre for training childcare specialists and would-be foster parents and supporting foster families post-placement. With its emphasis on rehabilitation, *Nasha Semya* was unlike anything previously seen in the Russian Federation. It was new even within Europe in dealing with child protection, family support, family placements and after-placement support under one roof and bringing together all the necessary childcare professionals. If it worked, the intention was that the *Nasha Semya* model would be replicated throughout the country.

The home was first registered in 1994 and opened its doors to the initial intake of twenty orphans in May 1996.

At the heart of *Nasha Semya* was a real family – Leonid and Luda and their six-year-old son, Andrei. We felt it important that the children joining the home should encounter a loving, functioning family unit to counterbalance the fraught and chaotic memories of family life that many carried with them. Leonid and Luda quickly established an atmosphere of trust and laughter with a strong emphasis on celebrations and family rituals and doing things together. Underlying everything at *Nasha Semya* was a deep respect for the dignity and individuality of each child, something most of them had never experienced. Even an act as simple as a birthday party was a novelty for children previously treated as dumb animals. In the gentle, supportive environment that Leonid and Luda created, brutalized lives began to be healed. Along with Maria, this devoted couple deserve much of the credit for *Nasha Semya*'s success.

As *Nasha Semya* was getting started, we thought we might have trouble recruiting suitable foster parents. It turned out to be easier than we expected. We started by advertising in churches and the Moscow papers and were overwhelmed by the response. We could afford to be selective in those we invited for training and were then even more selective when it came to matching children to families. Leonid and Luda were particularly picky about the quality of parents suitable for "their" children. But when a good home was found, they were overjoyed.

One of our foster mothers had lost her own son in his late teens – the victim of muggers who'd attacked him for his mobile phone. But he told her before he died that he thought she had plenty of love to give to another child and that he'd always wanted a younger brother. Shortly after his death, she watched a television programme about a boy called Sergei who'd suffered from a botched throat operation as a toddler and spent ten years in hospital with apparently incurable paralysis of the lungs. He had the same name as her deceased son – a sign, she felt, that she should give him the little brother he'd always wanted, even though he wasn't there to see him. Through *Nasha Semya*, she ended up fostering the child, who recovered amazingly quickly once he was part of a real family.

Another child had been taken to hospital by his mother at the age of four months and wrongly diagnosed as having a severe form of rheumatic fever. Unable to cope with a child she believed would never walk or be able to do anything for himself, his mother had abandoned him there and then. Little Maxim spent the next eight years in a hospital bed and a home for disabled children. Even though the doctors eventually realized the initial diagnosis had been wrong, he'd spent so long lying on his back that the muscles in his arms and legs had never developed. In all that time he'd received none of the treatment or surgery that might have helped. Nor had it occurred to anyone to teach him to speak. It was only when a charity worker discovered his plight and referred him to *Nasha Semya* that Maxim's recovery could begin.

The staff at *Nasha Semya* found and trained a suitable foster mother and helped to provide the necessary treatment. In a matter of months, Maxim had learned to talk and his arms and legs were growing stronger. Before long he was able to walk and he grew up to become a cheerful and confident teenager. By then, despite the damage inflicted on him by incompetent medical staff, he'd set his heart on becoming a doctor.

His story then took an unexpected twist. When Maxim was fifteen, his foster mother became seriously ill and he faced the risk of being sent permanently to a home for the handicapped. To avoid this happening, Maria Ternovskaya was desperate to find a new family to take him in. Her quest was successful. Within six months, Maxim had been adopted by a family in America where, in a first step towards his childhood dream, he now works in a hospital.

Every child came with an extraordinary personal story, but few were more amazing than that of Dimitri, a little red-haired boy who was found half-starved in a dustbin and handed in to the police. After he'd been treated in hospital, the police contacted *Nasha Semya* to see if they could find a foster family for him.

In the meantime a man called Igor, a computer scientist at Moscow University, had had a dream in which he and his wife, Natasha, had been standing in a field gazing up at the stars. As they did so, two smiling boys dropped from the sky and landed at their feet. The smaller of the boys seemed to be trying to tell them something, but his speech was slurred and he couldn't get it out. The dream was unusually vivid and Igor remembered every detail.

About a year later, Igor and Natasha were in church – both were devout Orthodox Christians – and saw an advertisement to become foster parents. They went forward for training and became one of the first couples to qualify. When *Nasha Semya* invited them to meet a possible foster child about to be discharged from hospital, Igor immediately recognized the younger boy in the dream. Dimitri, the boy discovered in the dustbin, was then four years old. The only voices he'd heard in his early years had been those of his drunken parents, so his own speech was slurred and indistinct.

Igor and Natasha took Dimitri home and he quickly learned to communicate. He then started talking about an older brother whom he'd never seen but had heard about from his mother. Maria Ternovskaya and her staff set about trying to trace this child, if indeed he existed, and eventually found him in an orphanage for oligophrenics. His name was Semyon and he was then aged eleven. As soon as Igor saw him, he knew he was looking at the second boy in the dream and that he, too, was a gift from God. The brothers had been miraculously reunited and Igor and Natasha now had two new sons to add to their existing family.[6]

Dimitri has since become a talented violin player, as I heard for myself on one of my visits to *Nasha Semya*. On that occasion I had a persistent cough and felt privileged when this serious, delicate-looking child whose own life had been so infused with miracles, put down his violin and came over to pray for me.

Although the Moscow authorities provided the premises and met the main running costs of *Nasha Semya*, it was up to Christian Solidarity UK to cover other expenses such as staff training. The money could only come from our supporters who, as always, responded magnificently. All the same, *Nasha Semya* was a heavy financial burden alongside the many other projects we were supporting at the time.

Again we discovered that unfailing truth that when things are desperate, God acts.

On one of the many flights that Caroline and I took to Moscow (it's remarkable how many key events in my life involve aircraft), the pilot announced soon after take-off that we'd have to return to Heathrow because the landing gear was failing to retract. A buzz of conversation broke out among the passengers as we banked steeply and joined the stack of aircraft waiting to land. I got talking to the man across the aisle who asked what I'd be doing in Moscow if we ever got there. I told him about *Nasha Semya*, then asked what he did.

He turned out to be a director of an oil exploration company. "As it happens," he said, "we've got some spare budget in our charity fund. I think we may be able to help you."

"I know just the person you need to speak to," I replied. I darted back to fetch Caroline who was sitting a few rows behind. An oil company executive with his hand already half in his pocket stood little chance against Caroline's persuasive powers and his company ended up making a grant to support our foster families.

Another channel of funding opened up when Caroline received the 1995 Wilberforce Award for her contribution to human rights. The award is given each year by Charles Colson of Prison Fellowship International and involves a presentation ceremony at the National Prayer Breakfast in Washington. On the day Caroline collected her award and gave her speech of acceptance, there were three ladies from Casper, Wyoming, in the audience. Betsy Vigneri and Lisa Scaling were the wives of hospital surgeons in Casper (Joe and Sam respectively) and Dr Anne Zimmerman was married to Wyoming senator, Gail Zimmerman. All three went back to their husbands and enthused about this English baroness they'd heard talking about orphans in Russia and the work of Christian Solidarity. As a result, we started getting letters and gifts from Wyoming at the Christian Solidarity office.

I later called our Wyoming benefactors to express our appreciation and they told me they'd love to attend our annual October conference. I was only too pleased to invite them. They began to come regularly and became so involved that they acquired their own nickname: "the trinamic trio". At the 1998 conference, we took a collection as we always do and were pleased to raise a little over £3,000. It was only later that our treasurer, Andy Philips, discovered a folded piece of paper among the gifts. It came from Anne and Gail Zimmerman and pledged generous additional support for the work in Moscow.

That's when we discovered that Anne Zimmerman was the daughter of Sir John Templeton – Wall Street legend, millionaire philanthropist and founder of The Templeton Foundation that awards an annual prize for "progress in religion". Designed to acknowledge the religious dimension overlooked by the Nobel Prize, the Templeton has gone to names such as Mother Teresa, Alexander Solzhenitsyn and Billy Graham. Anne was one of the award judges and came to London every year for the presentation by the Foundation's patron, the Duke of Edinburgh. She died, sadly, in her fifties, but Gail took her place on the Templeton board while her brother, Jack, succeeded Sir John as chairman.

Anne's pledge proved invaluable and a few years ago I had the pleasure of taking Jack and his wife to Moscow to see the work of *Nasha Semya* for themselves. Lisa Scaling has also visited *Nasha Semya*, while Betsy and Joe Vigneri have worked with us in Nagorno Karabakh. The Wyoming link continues with Lisa now the chairperson of Christian Solidarity USA.

By the time *Nasha Semya* ceased operating in its original form in 2009, it had found safe, loving homes for over 300 children.

Our own involvement wound down between 1997 and

2000 when we handed over to HART, a separate charity set up by Caroline Cox to supplement the work of Christian Solidarity. In a parallel project, we also worked with the Russian Federation Ministry of Education to help change public policy and redraft Russia's regional legislation to support fostering and adoption. By 2008, over forty regions had approved these laws and set up their own pilot projects to replicate the work of *Nasha Semya*. As a result, about 6,000 Russian children have been taken out of the orphanage system and placed with foster families.

Although the Russian project was outside our usual remit of speaking up for persecuted Christians, it was central to our mission of being a voice for the voiceless and we're grateful to God for what it was able to achieve. As Caroline has noted, the results are more than we could have hoped. "When I came out of that psychiatric hospital in Leningrad," she comments, "I never thought such a thing would be possible. It's a triumph of the human spirit."

Just one example of that triumph is Vladimir, the so-called oligophrenic who wanted to be a marine architect and whom we doubted would ever have the chance. A film of the 1991 study by Caroline and her team was shown on US television and prompted an American family to come to Russia to adopt him. He now lives in the States with every opportunity to overcome his appalling start in life and achieve his ambition.

By pioneering a new and enlightened approach, Maria Ternovskaya and her staff helped to change the face of Russian childcare. I'd like to think that we at Christian Solidarity also contributed by challenging the destructive effects of Communist atheism, exposing the plight of Russia's suffering children and marshalling the support and resources to do something about it – all in the course of trying to bring God's love to a dark and hopeless situation. Today, techniques and training materials developed at *Nasha Semya* are widely used across the country and a new generation of childcare professionals is continuing the work.

This progress comes despite a recent hardening of attitudes on the part of the Russian authorities, possibly linked to a trend towards totalitarianism in the country as a whole. There's worrying evidence that some of the bad old ways are returning and that childcare professionals are once again being excluded from decisions affecting vulnerable children.

I pray – and I ask for your prayers – that God will protect the gains already made and that the work begun at *Nasha Semya* will continue to transform the lives of Russia's lost children.

12

A Plea from Mongolia

The dying days of 1993 were one of those times when everything crashes in at once. I had an Ilyushin IL-76 to load in preparation for our first aid flight to Nagorno Karabakh, and the fifty tonnes it takes to fill one of those beasts is a frightening amount of cargo to have to organize. The Mehdi Dibaj crisis was unfolding in Iran and I was up to my eyes producing our bi-monthly magazine, raising funds and speaking at churches around the UK.

The office was winding down for Christmas when my fax machine clattered into life and delivered a message from John Gibbens. A pastor and a Christian Solidarity supporter, John had lived for a number of years in Mongolia. He'd felt called to the country as a young man, had studied Russian and Mongolian at Leeds University and had ended up at university in the Mongolian capital, Ulan Bator. There he met a Mongolian lady called Altaa who later became his wife. During the period of Soviet control, John and Altaa were briefly imprisoned for their Christian activities. After the country's independence and the restoration of religious freedom in 1990, the two had founded an evangelical church. John himself had recently translated the New Testament into Mongolian and was now working on the Old Testament.

His fax, sent to Christian Solidarity and the Jubilee Campaign for human rights, was an appeal for help. Despite Mongolia's post-1990 constitution which guaranteed freedom of religion, the country's parliament had just passed a law promoting Buddhism at the expense of Christianity. It was, said John, a dangerous and unconstitutional assault on the small Christian community – then numbering about 2,000, with most of its members converted in the previous two years.

John's message went on to explain that Altaa, now Executive Secretary of the Mongolian Bible Society, would be petitioning against the new law in Mongolia's Constitutional Court in the second week of January. The case could be decisive in determining the future of Christianity in the country. To avoid another slide into Soviet-style restrictions, would Jubilee and Christian Solidarity please send lawyers to support the case.

"John," I thought, "you don't know what you're asking! In the week before Christmas, where am I going to find a lawyer who just happens to be free and who won't mind going all the way to Mongolia in the depths of winter at two weeks' notice? It'll need a miracle."

Mindful that Christian Solidarity was no stranger to miracles, I telephoned our Chairman, Mervyn Thomas, and told him of John's request. Mervyn pointed out that just the presence of Western lawyers in cases like this could have a major influence on the outcome. It was very important, he said, that we find someone.

"Thanks!" I said. "But who?"

"You might try a chap called Robin Brodie," replied Mervyn. "He's one of our supporters. Works for a law firm somewhere in Scotland. I believe he's been helpful in the past."

I did some research in our database and found that Robin Brodie worked for Ledingham Chalmers, an international law firm based in Aberdeen and Edinburgh. The firm's senior partner, David Laing, was a Christian Solidarity supporter and Robin himself had done legal battle on behalf of persecuted Christians in countries such as Romania, Czechoslovakia and Malaysia. I wondered how he'd feel about Mongolia.

I telephoned Robin first thing the following morning and caught him just as he was getting up. I apologized for the early hour and introduced myself.

"Robin," I said, "what are you doing in the new year?"

"What had you in mind?" asked a distinctly Scottish voice.

I took a deep breath and explained. I couldn't really believe that a busy professional would be free at such short notice, even if he was willing. I prayed as he considered my request. In that brief moment, I think Robin was also praying.

To my great surprise he said yes. He had just one proviso. Experience of other cases abroad had taught him that it's always best to go with someone else, both for moral support and to have someone to pray with. Would we be willing to find and fund a companion?

I said we would, of course, and promised to look for someone.

My next call was to the Jubilee Campaign where I spoke to its parliamentary officer, Wilfred Wong. A lawyer and parliamentary research assistant to the MP, David Alton, Wilfred had also received John's fax and was ready to go to Mongolia himself. I asked if he'd be able to accompany our man, Robin Brodie, but Wilfred, for reasons of his own, was planning to travel via Beijing, so couldn't oblige. He said he'd meet Robin there.

Robin, meanwhile, had been asking a number of his lawyer friends if they fancied a winter break in Ulan Bator. Not surprisingly, there was little enthusiasm. But he did find one of his neighbours, a retired consultant physician called Dr Alan Johnston who loved travelling and who said he'd be delighted to go with him.

So far so good. All I had to do now was get the two of them from Aberdeen to Ulan Bator before the case began.

Dedicated lawyer that he is, Robin was quickly at work mastering his brief. He located an academic called David Ott, a member of the Department of Constitutional Law at Aberdeen University, and asked him to prepare a paper on Mongolia's obligations towards religious minorities under its own constitution and the various international treaties by which it was bound. Working at great speed, David analysed the constitution, a US-style document drawn up when Mongolia emerged from Soviet domination, and highlighted a number of ways in which the new law contradicted its terms.

The constitution, he noted, provides that "all persons lawfully residing within Mongolia are equal before the law and the courts". It also prohibits discrimination on the basis of ethnic origin, language, race, age, sex, social origin and status, property, occupation and education. The new law seemed to violate both those provisions. By embodying in law a preference for traditional and indigenous Mongolian customs and religion, it appeared to discriminate against non-Buddhists and groups not regarded as part of Mongolia's culture.

The constitution also guarantees freedom of conscience and religion to all Mongolian citizens. In contrast, the new law forbade Christians to carry out "religious preaching, teaching or propaganda outside the church" while explicitly allowing Buddhists, Muslims and Shamanists to conduct their activities in public. It also contravened the human rights provisions of the UN Charter which Mongolia, as a UN member, was obliged to uphold – not to mention the International Covenant on Civil and Political Rights and the International Covenant on Economic, Social and Cultural Rights which Mongolia had also signed.

The Mongolians, in other words, had fallen foul of the high ideals of their own constitution. It now fell to Altaa Gibbens and the British delegation to remind the court of that fact and persuade the authorities to back down.

Robin and Alan flew out from Aberdeen on 8 January 1994. David Ott was waiting at the airport with a translation of the Mongolian constitution and his own hastily finished but meticulous analysis which he handed over almost at the run as Robin and Alan scurried to catch their flight to Heathrow.

Getting two passengers from Scotland to Mongolia was complicated, to say the least. To obtain their Mongolian visas, Robin and Alan had had to send their passports to London and there wasn't time to return them before they left home. So they left Aberdeen with only their tickets to London, trusting that passports, visas, money and onward tickets would be ready and waiting as they passed through. As a self-confessed "belt and braces" man, Alan admits that winging it like this was an unnerving experience. Even from London, the journey was far from sorted. The best I could manage was to book them on a British Airways flight to Moscow and arrange for them to collect and pay for their onward tickets at the office of MIAT Mongolian Airways at Moscow's Sheremetevo Airport once they'd arrived. We'd given Robin £2,000 for the purpose. With four hours in transit, I reckoned they'd have enough time to get themselves booked on the Ulan Bator flight.

What I hadn't foreseen was that MIAT's office was in the far reaches of the airport building and that Robin and Alan would be effectively imprisoned in the transit lounge. Despite all their attempts at persuasion, the rules were inflexible: the rest of the airport was out of bounds to anyone not holding a Russian visa. As Robin tells the story, they rushed from one official to another to try to get help. With the court case due to begin in less than twelve hours and the fate of Mongolian Christianity hanging in the balance, it seemed the outcome depended on somehow getting access to room 35 on the sixth floor, where the MIAT tickets were being held.

Minutes before the flight was called, Robin was finally able to contact MIAT on the phone. He'd be the first to admit that his Mongolian is not great – indeed it's non-existent – but he managed to convey the situation to a MIAT clerk who agreed to come down to the transit lounge and hand the tickets over.

They made it on board by a whisker. There followed a six-hour, overnight flight to Ulan Bator where the snow lay hard as concrete and the freezing air (minus twenty-five degrees even by day) hit them like a truck as they emerged from the terminal. Without having slept and with no further time to prepare, they were met by two members of John Gibbens' church and taken immediately to the Constitutional Court. They walked in at 11 a.m. on 10 January, ninety minutes after the start of the proceedings.

Presiding over the court were five judges who sat on a dais at the front. Also present were various politicians and other interested parties along with the British chargé d'affaires and a representative of the American embassy. Altaa Gibbens sat with Wilfred Wong who'd arrived a couple of days previously and had spent the weekend helping her to prepare (it's obviously quicker to get to Ulan Bator via Beijing than it is via Moscow). John Gibbens was on hand to translate for Wilfred, Robin and Alan.

There was one other person present – a silent individual who arrived each morning with a large Bible which he placed prominently in front of him. John and Altaa knew him to be a Christian from one of Mongolia's smaller ethnic groups. He didn't speak, but he listened intently. According to Alan, the man's faith shone like a beacon and his still, silent presence made a deep impression on the visitors, if not the judges.

The intention was that Wilfred would present Altaa's case. The first act of the court, however, was to rule that he was not allowed to speak (the same applied to Robin) and that Altaa could not be legally represented. Deprived of this constitutional right and obliged to speak for herself, she was frequently cut short by the judges while those defending the law were given as much time as they liked. As the proceedings went on, however, Altaa was allowed more time (possibly because the Western contingent was now more obvious) and vigorously pressed the case that the law was unconstitutional.

It soon became clear to Robin that the best contribution he could make was to get a copy of David Ott's analysis into the hands of the judges and as many government officials as possible. But that meant cutting it down to a digestible length. Seated on the front row of the court on the second morning, he riffled through David's ten-page document and hacked out an abbreviated version. This he handed to Alan to take away and retype at the offices of the Mongolian Bible Society. Despite being delayed by a power cut and having to wrestle with a Japanese-style word processor, Alan had it typed and printed in time to hand to the judges on the third and final morning.

In the meantime, conversations with John Gibbens had thrown new light on the reasons behind the law. After so many years in the country, John was well tuned to Mongolian sensitivities and the right and wrong ways of presenting the gospel. He found himself increasingly frustrated by hit-and-run missionaries from the USA or Singapore who saw ex-Communist Mongolia as a prime target and were rushing in with evangelistic programmes that were often culturally unsuitable or even offensive. He cited one group that distributed 300,000 yellow tracts in Ulan Bator. Yellow being the colour of Buddhism, these caused enormous anger when they ended up littering the streets and getting trampled underfoot. There was more annoyance when another group showed Campus Crusade's *Jesus Film* in cinemas throughout Ulan Bator. Although it's a great evangelistic tool in the right context, it just wasn't appropriate for the time and place.

As a result of these activities, the authorities had become alarmed by what they saw as a foreign invasion by Christian groups – not to mention the Mormons and Seventh Day

Adventists who had joined the rush to convert Mongolia. The law was partly designed to counter these new, aggressive and insensitive forms of evangelism.

The President of the Court explained the country's point of view to Robin at the end of the second day when they had a chance to speak. He thanked Robin for coming all the way from Scotland and said he sympathized with his quest. He pointed out, however, that Mongolia had a difficult line to tread between allowing religious freedom and recognizing the traditional role of Buddhism within the country. As a small country squeezed between Russia and China, it was understandably sensitive about protecting its national identity.

The judgment, delivered on day three, was a partial victory for Altaa Gibbens. The court ruled that three aspects of the new law breached Mongolia's constitution. These were the ban on foreigners spreading religious propaganda, the requirement that religious organizations should register with the government and the article allowing Buddhists, Muslims and Shamanists to preach outside the places of worship of other religions. But other clauses were left unchanged, not least the pre-eminent position of Buddhism and the state's right to control the number of clergy and the location of places of worship of any religion. The law would now be sent back to parliament to be redrafted.

In summing up, the President of the Court asked John to translate a special message for the three British visitors. He was, he said, extremely grateful that they'd come all this way and had taken the trouble to point out the contradictions between the new law and the constitution. He hoped they were satisfied with the result.

They were, to a point. The view of John and Robin was that Christian freedom in Mongolia might still depend on the way the remaining clauses were applied. To try to influence any future interpretation of the law, they decided there was one more thing they could do before Robin and Alan left – that was, to tour the government ministries in Ulan Bator and hand over copies of David Ott's abbreviated statement to as many officials as possible. "To kick up a bit of dust while we could," was the way Robin put it.

They started at the Ministry of the Interior. Thanks to John's long experience of how to go about things in Mongolia, they were able to see the minister himself and make a polite protest that Christianity could still be disadvantaged. They did the same at the Foreign Ministry where they had a long discussion with the first deputy foreign minister. Finally they met ex-Vice President Gonchigdorj who said there was some hope that parliament might reconsider the whole law and not just the three articles now declared unconstitutional. He also agreed to meet John again so that John could keep him informed of the views of Mongolia's Christians.

The reception at each of the ministries was courteous, indeed welcoming. Ministers and officials seemed genuinely surprised that the outside world had taken such an interest in Mongolia's religious affairs, even to the point of sending a couple of lawyers all the way to Ulan Bator to appear in court. Although they barely spoke, the presence of Robin and Wilfred had clearly made an impression and had helped to swing the verdict in favour of Christianity. It also challenged the Mongolian perception that Christianity was just for poor people: if lawyers and academics could be Christians, perhaps the faith deserved greater respect. It's probably true to say that the rapid response of Christian Solidarity and the Jubilee Campaign, together with the prayers of our supporters, prevented Christianity being outlawed and forced underground.

John's hope had always been that making Mongolia more aware of international concerns would ensure a fairer deal for Christians in the future. Since 1994 the authorities have, by and large, stayed true to their constitution in their treatment of religious minorities. In a country first reached by Catholic missionaries in the Middle Ages (even before the arrival of Buddhism), Christians today enjoy a large measure of freedom. The re-born Mongolian church is growing vigorously and now numbers about 180,000 – a dramatic increase on the 2,000 or so at the time of the court case and equivalent to about 6 per cent of the population. With John's translation of the Old Testament now complete, the country's Christians are better equipped to grow both in faith and in numbers.

God answered more prayers on the return trip. At Moscow Airport, Robin and Alan endured a seven-hour delay as Aeroflot, amazingly, held up the flight to London in order to pack more passengers onto the plane. (Apparently this was common practice, with delays sometimes lasting a day or more.) While infuriated ticket-holders besieged the Aeroflot desk demanding to be transferred to the British Airways flight, a harassed official led Robin and Alan to a quiet corner and, like an old-time Soviet spy handing over secrets, slipped them two coveted BA boarding cards on condition they didn't tell the other stranded passengers. As far as they knew, they were the only passengers who managed to get transferred.

They also calculated that out of their seven-day trip, one complete day had been spent in the transit lounge at Moscow Airport. In comparison, said Alan afterwards, "Heathrow was bliss!" But it was, they both agreed, a price worth paying for Mongolia's religious freedom.

13

A Prayer for Burma

At Christian Solidarity, we try to be alert to instances of persecution anywhere in the world. But before we can act, we need to be sure of the facts. That means identifying and making contact with people who have reliable information.

Burma is a case in point. Today we're one of the main agencies working on behalf of the country's persecuted Christians, especially those from ethnic minority tribes such as the Karen, the Karenni, the Chin and the Mon. But our involvement started when God answered a one-sentence prayer back in 1993.

I was just a few weeks into the job at Christian Solidarity when we started to pick up reports of ethnic cleansing in Burma. A military junta had seized power five years earlier in 1988 and had changed the country's name to Myanmar. The pro-democracy campaigner, Aung San Suu Kyi, had been placed under house arrest and barred from standing in the 1990 elections. That didn't stop her National League for Democracy winning a landslide victory with over 80 per cent of the parliamentary seats. Burma's ruling generals ignored the result, imprisoned thousands of pro-democracy activists and began cracking down on religious and ethnic minorities.

Most of these groups live in seven mountainous states along the country's borders and include the largely Christian Karen and Karenni peoples. The Karenni are best known in the West for their "giraffe" women who lengthen their necks with brass bangles and feature prominently in holiday brochures and tourist snaps. For their part, the Karen have been Christian since the nineteenth century when an American Baptist missionary called Adoniram Judson arrived in Burma and fulfilled an ancient legend that a white man from far away would come with a golden book and teach the truth about the gods.

It was widely known by the 1990s that the Burmese regime was one of the most vicious in the world. But now news was filtering back from the country's remote border regions that the generals had embarked on a course of genocide. We started to hear of the widespread and systematic use of rape, torture and slave labour, of the conscription of child soldiers, the use of children as human minesweepers and the forced relocation of villages. Thousands of Karen and Karenni were apparently being forced from their homes, some to face death in the jungles, some escaping to refugee camps on the Thai border. But here they were trapped. They risked death if they tried to return, but were forcibly prevented from finding work and bettering their lives in Thailand. Confined to their border camps, they lived in poverty and despair.

It was hard in those early days to separate rumour from fact. We decided we had to find out more.

One morning in June 1993, our administrator, Susanna Hodgson, said to me that she'd heard of a British doctor working with the Karen and Karenni on the Thai–Burma border. His name was Martin Panter, but that was all the information she had.

Martin was potentially an important link – someone on the ground who could tell us what was really going on. Frustratingly, we couldn't discover any more about him. We tried tracing him through our normal connections, but he didn't appear to be working for any recognized agency. For all our efforts, the mysterious Dr Panter remained a phantom presence like one of those elusive jungle beasts that are heard about but never seen.

So I did what we always do when we're stuck. I suggested to Susanna that we pray. We pulled up a chair each in the office and asked God very simply: "Lord, please would you help us to find Martin Panter. Amen."

At the time, Ethel and I were still living in Widnes. My routine was to stay with Ethel's sister and brother-in-law in Gloucestershire during the week (their home was about forty minutes from the office in Witney) and to travel back to Cheshire for the weekends. But not on this particular weekend – the weekend after we'd prayed to find Dr Panter. Friday saw me pointing the car down the M5 towards Bridgewater in Somerset where I'd agreed to speak at a series of meetings at the United Reformed Church.

It was a packed weekend with engagements on the Friday night, twice on Saturday and again on Sunday and Monday. After I'd finished speaking at the first meeting, a slight-looking man called Lenny Carroll came up and asked in his West Country accent if he could have a word.

Lenny had had an unusual career. An orphan from Somerset, he had no formal qualifications but had once answered an advertisement in the *Daily Express* to become a footman at the British Embassy in Moscow. One of his duties was to take care of the coats of embassy visitors who included a fair number of world leaders. Lenny's personal mission was to slip a Christian tract into the pocket of every coat. I would love to have seen how presidents and prime ministers reacted when they pulled these leaflets out and wondered how they'd got there. Clearly no one ever complained, because the ambassador retained Lenny's services when he later moved to Washington.

Lenny was interested in what I'd been saying in the meeting about Saudi Arabia. Back in the early 1990s, we were campaigning on behalf of expatriates from India, Pakistan, Sri Lanka, South Africa and South Korea who were serving time in Saudi jails for their Christian activities. As well as describing their situation, I'd also spoken about the large Christian fellowships in the US, British and other embassies – these being the only legal Christian gatherings in the country.

"There's someone you should meet," said Lenny. "He's a friend of mine called Harry Jacobson, working in Saudi installing fire extinguishers in offices. He helps to run the fellowship at the British embassy."

Harry was due back on leave in a few weeks' time. I said I'd be pleased to meet him. Lenny promised to find out when he'd be arriving and to let me know.

My Monday evening talk was to the Full Gospel Businessmen's Fellowship in Bridgewater. On the Monday morning the people I was staying with had gone out and I found myself sitting at the kitchen table pondering what to speak on. I felt myself drawn to the story of Caleb in the book of Numbers. Caleb and Joshua were two of the twelve spies that Moses sent ahead into Canaan before the Israelites moved in. Whereas the other ten described it as a land of giants and fortified cities too strong to be attacked, Joshua and Caleb urged the people to move forward. "If the Lord is pleased with us," they said, "he will lead us into that land, a land flowing with milk and honey, and will give it to us" (Numbers 14:8).

For this attitude of trust, God speaks of Caleb as having "a different spirit" and promises to bring him and his family safely into the Promised Land. It's a story full of meaning for Christian Solidarity, where we often feel inadequate against the giants we have to face and are forced to trust that God will see us through.

As I sat thinking about Caleb, the phone rang. It was Lenny. "First thing," he said, "I know what you're going to talk about tonight."

"Oh? What's that?"

"You're going to speak on Caleb."

"How did you know?" (I'd only just decided myself.)

"God told me," said Lenny matter-of-factly.

This was interesting, I thought. Clearly Lenny was a man walking closely with God and deserved a careful hearing, whatever he had to say. His reason for calling was to confirm when Harry Jacobson would be back from Riyadh and to say again that he'd like me to meet him. Indeed, he emphasized how important it was that I *should* meet him. I didn't fully understand why at the time. However, if God was at work, I knew I should take Lenny's suggestion seriously.

The meeting with Harry occurred a couple of months later. Once again I drove down to the West Country to the village of West Coker, not far from my childhood home in Yeovil. Harry was briefly back on holiday and we met at his home. He turned out to be a Scouser with a wonderfully cheerful personality. Given that Widnes, where we lived, was not far from his home patch in Merseyside, we found we had a lot to talk about.

After a conversational detour into the Saudi fire-extinguisher market (not a subject I often find myself discussing), I asked Harry to update me on the situation for Christians in Saudi Arabia. He told me what he knew of the underground church (it appeared to be growing: the official line that there were no Saudi Christians was plainly wrong) and went on to describe the fellowships in the various embassy compounds. He also knew of Indian, Pakistani and South Korean Christian groups that met covertly in and around Riyadh.

"There are three of us leading these embassy fellowships," he told me. "There's me. Then there's Colonel Chris Mineau, a consultant to the Saudi Air Force who used to fly F15s in the US Air Force and was badly injured when he bailed out over Norfolk and shattered nearly every bone in his body. He became a Christian in hospital. These days he's more or less bolted together. He carried on flying afterwards, using a special crane to crank him into the cockpit."

"And the third?" I asked.

"The third is someone you won't have heard of. He's called Dr Martin Panter."

I bolted upright. "Martin Panter! *The* Martin Panter? The one who works in Burma?"

"That's the one," continued Harry. "He came to Saudi as consultant physician to King Fahd's brother. When he visits the Burma–Thai border, he brings back plants that the Karen and Karenni use to treat their ailments and has them analysed to find out more about their medicinal properties."

I breathed a silent prayer of thanks. Through Susanna, Lenny and now Harry, the trail was leading inexorably towards the elusive doctor. God must have something in store, I thought. I told Harry I was keen to get in touch with this Martin Panter and scribbled a note for Harry to pass on when he next saw him. "Please call me as soon as you can," I wrote. "We'd like to talk to you about helping Christians in Burma and along the Thai border."

Months went by and nothing happened. It came to the last week before Christmas 1993 and those frenetic few days when every crisis in the Christian Solidarity casebook seemed to erupt at once. We were gearing up for our inaugural aid flight to Nagorno Karabakh. Mehdi Dibaj was facing execution in Iran. John Gibbens in Mongolia needed a lawyer to challenge the government in the constitutional court. Feeling shredded after eighteen-hour days and one emergency after another, I sighed with relief as I switched off my computer, set the answering machine and prepared to head home for Christmas. Susanna had gone. The office was deserted. All I had to do was lock up and leave.

I froze in the doorway as the phone rang. "Should I? Shouldn't I?" I thought. "Perhaps I'd better, in case it's urgent."

I picked up the receiver. "Stuart Windsor here."

"Stuart! Hullo. It's Martin Panter. I got your letter. I'm in the UK. Can I meet you?"

In the week between Christmas and New Year, I dropped Ethel off at her sister's in Gloucestershire and carried on to Uffcombe in Devon where Martin Panter had a house on a farm belonging to a local minister. On the lane leading down to the farm, I passed a lady on a bicycle and stopped to check the way. She turned out to be Martin's wife, Sally, and she pointed me to the gate. I arrived and was greeted at the door by a lean, rangy, alert-looking man in his fifties whose weather-beaten features betrayed long, active years in deserts and jungles. After all these months, we were finally face to face.

I shook his hand like Stanley greeting the long-lost Livingstone: "Dr Panter, I presume."

He showed me in – every inch the English gentleman – and we began talking. Martin, I learned, was a specialist in tropical medicine. He'd had a medical practice in Cairns in northern Australia, but had leased it out to go and work in Saudi Arabia. His real passion, however, was for the Karen and Karenni in the squalid camps along the Thai–Burma border. The money he earned in Saudi Arabia helped to fund his frequent visits back to Burma to bring medical aid to the refugees.

His tale was one of daring and adventure in the midst of the fighting. On one of his numerous trips, he discovered from a member of Karen intelligence that the area he was planning to visit the following morning with his medical team was going to be the target of an air and infantry attack the same day. Given that his three young children were with him, he agonized over whether to abandon his mission. But after praying and finding himself drawn to Psalm 27 ("Though an army besiege me, my heart will not fear; though war break out against me, even then will I be confident"), he decided to go ahead.

The mission passed without incident. It was only on a later visit to Burma that Martin discovered why. The air strike was scheduled to take place as soon as the morning mists evaporated, as they inevitably did at that time of year. But on this particular day, a freak bank of cloud had billowed up from the river and formed a thick blanket over the entire area, making it impossible for the government aircraft to attack. All they could do was circle uselessly until their fuel ran low, then jettison their bombs and return to Rangoon.[7]

Having heard his remarkable story, I then talked to Martin about Christian Solidarity and our concern for the Karen and Karenni peoples. I also explained how finding him had been an answer to prayer. I told him we were desperate for hard news out of Burma, that the Holy Spirit must have engineered our meeting and that maybe there were opportunities to do something together.

Martin stopped me. "The fact is, I've been looking for you, too," he said. Although he was busy on the ground in Burma, he was concerned that the outside world didn't seem to care and that no one was speaking out for Burma's persecuted minorities and the large Christian elements within them. He believed Christian Solidarity could fill that role.

But his ideas went further.

"My time in Saudi is done," he explained. "After my next trip to Burma, I'm going back to Cairns to take up my medical practice again. But what I'd like to do is set up Christian Solidarity in Australia."

Now it was my turn to interrupt. I knew exactly the person he should speak to and broke off excitedly to put in a call to Caroline Cox. Once I had her on the line, I passed the phone to Martin to introduce himself and explain what he had in mind. The two hit it off at once and we all agreed to meet the following week at Heathrow Airport before Martin and his team flew out on their next Burmese mission.

The consequences of that simple prayer to find Martin Panter continued to ripple out for years to come.

I was busy with other projects in 1994, so wasn't in a position myself to do much more with the Burma link. But Caroline and Martin took on the task together. In October 1994, Martin spoke at a Christian Solidarity human rights conference at London's Westminster Chapel and painted a grim picture of conditions in Burma. "Successive authoritarian governments in Rangoon have harassed, brutalized, tortured and killed countless thousands of Karen villagers," he told the conference. "They're liable to be murdered, raped, enslaved and pressed into forced labour. It's a terror regime. Even if they flee to the refugee camps on the border, the conditions are severe and they may still be subject to attack."

The following month, Caroline and Martin travelled to Burma together on a fact-finding trip. The aim, as with most of our missions to a new country, was to gather first-hand evidence of violations of human rights, to assess the need for aid and to show solidarity with the suffering. The reports were harrowing. Caroline came back with stories of appalling cruelty; of people burned alive or killed by having stakes forced through their ears. The exodus into Thailand was continuing. By now the ramshackle camps along the border were home to around 150,000 displaced and desperate people. Children were growing up who had never seen the world outside the camp perimeter.

Burma joined our list of target countries and we started campaigning for the Karen and Karenni. Caroline and Martin returned to the Burmese border in December 1996 and met Plyar Reh, the exiled president of the Karenni state of Kayah. Martin recorded the president's appeal to the outside world: "We need more help and prayer. Ask the governments of England

and Australia to help regain our independence." To this Martin added his own comment: "This is a small Christian nation suffering tremendous persecution. We fail in our Christian duty to be a voice for the oppressed and the voiceless if we do not heed their cry."

Caroline and Martin made a further visit in April 1998 and found the plight of the Karen and Karenni even worse. Present-day evidence suggests that a third of the Karen have been displaced since 1996, with over 3,500 villages in eastern Burma destroyed by the military. Government offensives continue. Although Aung San Suu Kyi has just been released from house arrest at the time of writing, the future for democracy remains uncertain. Along with other bodies like the Burma Campaign UK, Christian Solidarity continues to speak out for Burma's minorities and to urge governments to put pressure on the generals to bring about change. We regularly brief the British Foreign Office, Members of the European Parliament and Congressmen and Senators in Washington to keep the fate of Burma's minorities on the international agenda.

Today, this work is headed by our Burma country officer, the journalist Benedict Rogers.[8] Ben, as he's known, is a leading authority on Burma and the human rights abuses of the regime and he regularly takes Members of Parliament and others to visit the Burma–Thai border. One of these groups has included John Bercow, currently Speaker of the House of Commons. John was extremely moved by seeing the plight of the Karen and Karenni refugees in the border camps and has become something of a spokesman for victims of the regime.

We've come a long way from Martin's comment in Uffcombe, Devon, back in 1993 that no one seemed to care about the Karen and Karenni. And much of the credit for the widespread international concern we see today must go to Martin himself for his long-term commitment to Burma's suffering minorities.

Martin was also true to his promise to me. In November

1995, Caroline, Ethel and I, along with Christian Solidarity's International President, Hans Stuckelburger, travelled to Australia to mark the setting up of Christian Solidarity Australia under Martin's chairmanship. The Australian office has continued to lead missions to the region and to keep the Australian government up to date on the evils of the Burmese regime.

One further consequence of the prayer to find Martin was a link with Colonel Chris Mineau, the bolted-together American airman who became a very effective speaker for Christian Solidarity. On one occasion we took him to a meeting at the House of Lords and the alarms went berserk as he walked through security. As guards came running and Caroline and I wondered what was happening, the half-metal fighter pilot smiled nonchalantly.

"I'm used to it," he said. "I'm bionic!"

14

Death in Lahore

Early in 1993, shortly before I joined Christian Solidarity, a 12-year-old boy called Salamat Masih and a farmer by the name of Rehmat Masih were arrested in the Punjabi village of Gjnanawala near Lahore.

"Masih" means "messiah" in Urdu, so the name is commonly used by Pakistani Christians to denote their religion. Salamat and Rehmat, both Catholics, faced the same charge of scribbling blasphemies against the Prophet Mohammed on the wall of the local mosque. The offence violated Pakistan's penal code, as revised between 1979 and 1986 when President Zia ul-Haq abandoned the country's constitution and introduced elements of Sharia law. The changes made life extremely difficult for Christians who found themselves constantly falling foul of two of the code's clauses: 295B – three to ten years for desecrating a holy book; and 295C – a mandatory death sentence for blaspheming (or even criticizing) the Prophet Mohammed.

Salamat and Rehmat were charged under 295C and so faced the real possibility of execution. Even the fact that Salamat was just a boy made no difference to the sentence he might expect.

In the same village lived Salamat's uncle, Manzoor Masih. Also a Catholic and then in his late forties, Manzoor was illiterate but had nevertheless learned the book of Psalms and the book of Revelation off by heart. Outraged at the arrests, he turned up at the local police station to try to get his nephew released. Not only did he fail, he found himself charged with the same offence and thrown into prison.

By the time the news of the arrests reached Christian Solidarity, Salamat, Rehmat and Manzoor were making weekly appearances in court in Gjnanawala while the charges were clarified. At each hearing, the two village mullahs who had brought the original accusation would pack the room with supporters baying for the death sentences to be carried out. The tirade of insults and abuse was intended not only to frighten the defendants but also to terrorize the judge and the defence lawyers and was a common tactic in Pakistani blasphemy trials. In between times, the three were kept in prison and refused bail.

The Gjnanawala case was one of the first issues I had to deal with when I joined Christian Solidarity. We decided we'd start by sending our President, the MP David Atkinson, to assess the situation. An excellent man for the job, David had worked with the Council of Europe in Strasbourg and been its rapporteur for several Eastern European countries seeking to prove they met mandatory standards of democracy and freedom before being admitted to the EU. David travelled to the Punjab in the summer of 1993 and was able to meet the three prisoners, who by then had been released on bail but remained in hiding for their own safety. He returned to the UK determined to publicize their case and see Christian Solidarity campaigning on their behalf.

At the same time, supporters within Pakistan were taking up the cause. One was the lawyer, Asma Jehangir. Although a Muslim herself, Asma was, and still is, a passionate opponent of the country's blasphemy laws and was much involved with the Human Rights Commission of Pakistan. Along with the men's parish priest and other church leaders, Asma was worried that Salamat, Rehmat and Manzoor would not get a fair trial in their home village in the face of such vehement local opposition.

Another to raise concerns was Group Captain Cecil Chaudhry, a towering figure in the struggle for religious and civil rights in Pakistan. Cecil's own story is remarkable. As a fighter pilot in the Pakistani Air Force, he was much decorated and would have risen to Marshal of the Air Force had President Zia not blocked his promotion for the sole reason that he was a Christian. During a long and illustrious career, Cecil acted as consultant to the Jordanian Air Force under King Hussein, taught the Iraqis to fly MiG fighters and advised the Saudis on aircraft procurement. He was later nominated as military attaché to the Pakistan High Commission in London. Once again, though, President Zia cancelled the move after Muslim extremists said they wouldn't tolerate a *kaffir* – an unbeliever – in such a sensitive position.

When a Muslim pilot junior to Cecil was promoted above him, Cecil resigned his commission on principle. Leaving the Air Force, he was appointed head of St Anthony's High School in Lahore, one of the largest Christian schools in the country. He also became involved in human rights, even to the point of working incognito in a brick kiln to expose the use of child slave labour. At a more official level, he's been a member of the Human Rights Commission of Pakistan (where he's worked with Asma Jehangir) and Secretary of the Catholic Bishops' Justice and Peace Conference. Friend of presidents and prime ministers, known and respected throughout the services and a man of total integrity, Cecil has been the lynchpin of our work in Pakistan for many years. We have been through much together. I regard him as a brother and would trust him with my life.

With help from Pakistani church leaders, Cecil and Asma persuaded the authorities to transfer the trial of Salamat, Rehmat and Manzoor from Gjnanawala to Lahore. The three appeared in the trial court in Lahore in April 1994.

Supporting the accused in court was a Christian prison visitor and human rights activist called John Joseph. John was already well known to the authorities. In 1986 he'd formed a group called the Christian Organisation for Human Rights to support the families of people arrested for blasphemy and to visit the accused in prison. A year before the Salamat, Rehmat and Manzoor case, he had taken part in protests against Pakistan's Muslim League government which had wanted to issue Christians with separate identity cards and compel them to wear a uniform. He and his fellow protesters had burned copies of the proposed law along with effigies of the mullah responsible outside the assembly hall in Lahore. Now they were back in Lahore to support the Gjnanawala three and provide physical protection for their Christian solicitor, Naeem Shakir (the extremists having threatened to kill anyone who took up their case).

Naeem Shakir began by asking for a copy of the allegation against his clients. The trial judge refused. Not only that, he refused to allow the charges to be read out on the grounds that this would repeat the blasphemy against the Prophet and so contravene clause 295C. So Naeem started making notes. At this the mullahs in the courtroom kicked up a protest, claiming he was blaspheming by writing down the offending words. With the alleged crime not able to be described for fear of more accusations of blasphemy, the case reached a shambolic impasse.

Which possibly suited the judge. It was common knowledge that this was a trumped-up charge – not least because all three defendants were illiterate and could not possibly have written insults on a mosque wall. Several judges had already declined the case or conveniently booked holidays so as not to have to face down the militants in court. The judge who eventually found himself in charge was also unwilling to risk the militants' wrath and wound up proceedings as quickly as he could. He released the prisoners on bail and told the lawyers on each side to sort the matter out in private. He should, at that point, have made sure the defendants had police protection, but failed to do so.

Faced with this unexpected turn of events, the three accused, along with Naeem Shakir and John Joseph, left the High Court and crossed the road to Naeem's offices to decide what to do next. After a brief consultation, Salamat, Rehmat, Manzoor and John left to catch a bus to the nearby Catholic centre where they were staying.

John later described to me what happened next.

"We came out of Naeem's office onto a busy street alongside the High Court. As usual, the front of the court was lined with armed police. As we waited at the bus stop, three guys in robes and turbans rode up on a motorbike. They stopped a couple of metres away and opened fire with Kalashnikovs. I was facing the other way, talking to the other three. A bullet hit me in the back. Another singed my hair and hit Manzoor in the forehead, killing him instantly. I swung round and grabbed the hand of the man firing. Another bullet grazed my wrist and then we were fighting face to face. I knew my attacker from seeing him in court. And I knew his name – Fazi al-Haq.

"As we struggled, the other two mullahs jumped off the bike and continued firing. Salamat and Rehmat were both injured. The street had emptied in seconds. Even the police guarding the High Court had fled when the shooting began.

"I continued grappling with al-Haq with three or four bullets in my body. But I was feeling weak. He wrenched his Kalashnikov free and fired point-blank into my face. The bullet hit me in the chin and came out at the side of my neck. I lost consciousness. As I lay on the ground, two of the attackers escaped on the motorbike and al-Haq ran to a seven-seater minibus that was waiting nearby. It was packed with mullahs. The bus ran over me, crushing my arm and ribs, and roared away down the street.

"Once they'd gone, people started coming forward to help. I regained consciousness to find someone helping me into a car. Salamat was put in the same car and someone stopped a rickshaw to pick up Rehmat. We were taken to hospital. But even then we were not out of danger. Fazi al-Haq was spotted in a corridor, trying to find out where we were. Fortunately, the hospital's security was enough to prevent him finishing the job.

"God gave me the chance of another life," adds John Joseph. "The mullahs were not very good shots and the three of us were spared, even though poor Manzoor was killed – his only crime being to ask for his nephew to be released."

The UK press had been following the story for some time. "Boy of 12 faces death sentence" announced a headline in *The Times* in the summer of 1993. Now, following the shooting, there was international interest. While Cecil kept me abreast of developments (helped by another Pakistani contact called David Elisha), I continued to run media and parliamentary campaigns and to urge our supporters to keep praying for Salamat, Rehmat and John.

It was clear that the lives of all three were at risk. Rehmat and Salamat were out of hospital and on bail, pending their trial for the original offence. We needed to ensure their safety – a task that fell to Cecil, working with members of the police he knew he could trust. The badly injured John was in even greater danger. As a witness to the attack outside the High Court, he was a marked man and had to go into hiding. But he couldn't entirely disappear. Backed by Cecil and Asma Jehangir, the Catholic Bishops' Justice and Peace Commission was determined to pursue justice for the killing of Manzoor and issued a writ against his attackers. John's testimony would be crucial to the case.

Covertly, with the help of our Pakistani contacts, we began to make arrangements for all three to be spirited out of the country as soon as it became necessary.

When the case came back to the trial court, the judge – under pressure from the militants – found Salamat and Rehmat guilty and sentenced them to death. This was a shock and a setback, but not the end of the road. The men's next recourse was an appeal to the High Court. The process was set in motion and the case came before Judge Arif Iqbal Bhatti in February 1995.

This time the defendants were represented by Abid Minto, a Muslim barrister working *pro bono* because he believed in religious freedom and was a personal friend of Cecil's. As before, John Joseph stood alongside Salamat and Rehmat as their witness and bodyguard. Outside the High Court building, 200 Muslim extremists staged a noisy protest, kept at bay by a large contingent of armed police.

Judge Bhatti turned to the prosecuting barrister and asked him to produce his evidence. There was none. The story of the defacing of the mosque in Gjnanawala was exposed as a total fabrication. After two years of hounding, vilification and threats to their lives, Salamat and Rehmat were declared innocent and allowed to go free.

The decision came as no surprise to Rehmat. He told me later that while he and Salamat were in detention the night before the trial, Jesus himself had appeared to him in his cell. As Rehmat described it, he was dressed in brilliant white and told him not to be afraid because tomorrow they'd be freed.

Although their acquittal was excellent news, those involved in helping them were all too aware of what had happened the last time Rehmat and Salamat had been released by the court. Cecil had already made arrangements to have the men moved the instant they were free. Within hours, the two were smuggled from Lahore to the Pakistani capital, Islamabad, and put on a flight to Germany.

The weekend after their release, I flew to Dusseldorf to record their story. With me was the journalist, Andrew Boyd, who was then writing and producing our bi-monthly magazine, *Response*. Rehmat and Salamat were elated at being free but aware that they would never again be able to return to Pakistan. The events of the last two years had exacted a heavy toll not only on them but on their families. Twenty of Rehmat's closest relatives had been forced to flee their village for fear of reprisals. Salamat's family had also had to move.

Rehmat explained how the nightmare had begun. Back in Gjnanawala he'd been a successful farmer with a big house, a tractor and fourteen cows. Over time he became fed up with the music and calls to prayer coming from the mosque. He decided to retaliate. With the mayor's permission, he hired the village hall, installed a loudspeaker system and played Christian music to counter the noise. "Other people loved it," he told me. "People came to listen. So the mullahs got jealous that my music was attracting a crowd. They took their revenge by accusing me of insulting the Prophet."

For Salamat, now a teenager, the ordeal had begun in similarly innocuous circumstances. As a boy, he'd been friendly with the son of one of the mullahs in Gjnanawala. Like many of his age in Pakistan, he was fanatical about keeping pigeons. One day, one of his pigeons had strayed into his friend's loft. "I went round to fetch it," explained Salamat. "But my friend wouldn't give it back. Then my father went and spoke to his father, the mullah. Still they refused to give it back. Things got heated and, before I knew it, my friend's father accused me of writing insults to the Prophet Mohammed on the wall of the mosque."

When I asked Salamat what the whole experience had taught him, he answered simply: "Never to keep pigeons again!"

Although Rehmat and Salamat were now safe, John Joseph was not. While he waited to give evidence against the mullahs for the murder of Manzoor Masih, he had to endure a desperate life in hiding. He still had a bullet in him from the High Court shooting. He had a child and a pregnant wife to protect. The only way he could leave home was in disguise. At one point, the extremists discovered where he was living and surrounded the house, some carrying guns and cans of petrol. The siege lasted a couple of nights with John and his family hiding in the inside rooms and hoping the doors would hold if the mob tried to break in. He phoned me while it was happening to say he expected an attack at any minute and to urge me to tell his story to the outside world. It was only when Cecil put pressure on the local police chief that the police showed up and the mob dispersed.

As John tried to keep one step ahead of his pursuers, Cecil became more and more concerned for his safety. He knew that John had a brother and sister in London and asked if I could start investigating whether John and his family would be allowed to settle in Britain. I agreed to try.

So began a series of meetings with the UK Immigration and Asylum Department at Lunar House in Croydon, Surrey. With Cecil, David Elisha and our parliamentary officer, Tina Lambert, I also went to see Home Secretary Michael Howard and his junior minister, Ann Widdecombe. At the time, the Conservative government was clamping down on the thousands of applications from Punjabi Muslims wanting to settle in the UK. "There's no basis for those requests because they're not being persecuted," explained Michael Howard. "But if you bring me genuine cases of Christians in danger, I'll fast-track them."

With support from the top, we went back to the staff at Lunar House who forwarded John Joseph's case to the British High Commission in Islamabad. The High Commission initially wanted John to travel to Islamabad for interview, but Cecil and I insisted that getting him there from Lahore would be too dangerous. Instead, the senior visa officer, Bill Mulholland, flew from Islamabad to Lahore to interview John in hiding. He was shocked, both at John's physical state and at the grim life he was forced to lead in order to evade his would-be killers. He instantly recommended that John be given refuge in the UK.

Michael Howard personally signed the order allowing John and his wife and child into Britain. This was totally outside Home Office rules and a small miracle in itself. Visas were issued and we arranged for the family to be housed in the London Borough of Hounslow. The plan was in place. All that remained was for John to have his day in court.

The trial of the mullahs of Gjnanawala for the murder of Manzoor Masih finally took place in November 1995. John came to court in disguise, having grown a long beard to look like a mullah. He gave his evidence and was smuggled out of Pakistan the following day. Christian Solidarity paid for the air tickets and David Elisha accompanied the family as they flew out. We'd agreed that bringing them into Heathrow would be too risky (we knew the mullahs had supporters in London), so we chose a flight from Lahore to Manchester. Ethel and I were there to meet them as the family came through customs with just two suitcases between them. We drove them to a safe house in Devon for a couple of weeks to keep them out of the way, then transferred them to their new home in West London.

Back in Lahore, the court action against the mullahs fell foul of legal technicalities. In Islamic law, the testimony of a Christian – like that of a woman – is worth only half that of a Muslim man. Because John was a single witness, his evidence was not enough on its own to secure a conviction. Furthermore, the hearing was postponed after he'd given evidence. By the time it reconvened, John was out of the country and no witness to the shooting was available. The mullahs were released and remain free to this day.

As for John, he knows he's a marked man should he ever try to return to Pakistan. If he went back and was traced, it's more than likely that Islamic extremists would exact swift revenge.

Just when we thought the case was closed (albeit with no final justice for Manzoor Masih), it flared into life again. With John Joseph out of reach, the vengeance of the extremists turned on his brother, James, along with James' wife, Bimla, and their three little girls.

James, a Christian like his brother, owned a hardware store in Lahore. The extremists first cut the electricity to the business and the family home. A little later they burned down the store and attempted to set fire to James' house. Over time, the mullahs' supporters bought up the neighbouring houses so as to continue their campaign of intimidation. When I first met James on a visit to Pakistan in 1997, he had his arm in a sling after being attacked in the street.

It was clear that yet another family would have to be moved out of Pakistan. Once again, I began discussions with the Home Office and Lunar House to see if we could bring them to Britain.

We had just secured provisional agreement when James died of a heart attack at the tragically young age of forty-six. As if his loss wasn't dreadful enough for Bimla and the girls, they now found themselves homeless and still a target of the extremists. We pressed on with efforts to get them admitted to Britain, only to hit a roadblock when the Conservatives lost the 1997 election and Tony Blair's Labour government took over.

Whether through incompetence or the result of some new policy, Lunar House immediately lost 50,000 files in the course of moving offices and installing a new computer system. All communication between the government and human rights organizations slowed to a trickle. There was now just one phone line for anyone wishing to speak to UK Immigration and Asylum and it proved impossible to make contact. Before the election, Christian Solidarity had been on the point of training the government's case officers on the situation in Pakistan. The project was abruptly cancelled.

We sought help from Alan Keen, MP for Feltham in London where John Joseph was now living. Alan wrote to the Home Office who admitted losing the files relating to James and Bimla. We sent them fresh copies of all the relevant documents. These too went missing and we had to send them a second time.

All this time, Bimla and her daughters were still on the run in Pakistan. Cecil kept them in hiding, constantly moving the family from one home to another. With almost no means of support, they found it hard to get medical treatment and the girls' education was suffering. When they did make it to school for short periods, they were threatened by the children of Islamic extremists because they were Christians. A friend of mine called Don Rowley, an evangelist working in Peshawar, met the family twice to give them money and medicines and reported back on their condition. He found the girls undernourished and the family in a desperate state. He insisted we keep up the pressure to bring them to Britain.

Incredible to say, it wasn't until 2007 – ten years after James' death – that they finally left Pakistan for the safety of the UK. Accompanied by Cecil, they arrived at Heathrow on visitors' visas and claimed asylum. After their first application was rejected, it fell to me to write a report for the Home Office and argue their case in person at the appeal hearing. This time we succeeded and the family was able to begin a new life in London.

Every year on the anniversary of James' death, the Joseph family organizes a memorial service at which it's my privilege to speak and commemorate not only James but all those suffering for their faith in Pakistan. To this day, James' brother John carries the burden of how his Christian-inspired commitment to human rights brought such hardship to the rest of his family. It's a conflict that many in the persecuted church face day in, day out.

The circles of violence spreading out from the Gjnanawala

blasphemy case claimed one further victim. In October 1998, a Muslim extremist walked into Judge Bhatti's office in Lahore and shot him dead for having freed Salamat and Rehmat three and a half years earlier.

15

The Burning of Shanti Nagar

I had just finished speaking at a meeting of the Full Gospel Businessmen's Fellowship in Guildford, Surrey. I returned to my seat and the organizer asked us to take a moment to pray with the person sitting nearest to us.

I looked across the table at a middle-aged, slightly balding man in glasses who told me his name was Roger Salter. "And what can I pray for you?" I asked.

He gave a rueful smile and briefly told me his story. He was a Lloyd's "name" – one of the elite group of individuals rich enough to sink large amounts of money into the Lloyd's insurance market in the hope that profits in good years will outweigh the losses in bad years. Unfortunately for the names, a string of natural and man-made disasters in the late 1980s and early 1990s had left many of them ruined – Roger included. "I might have lost my money," he added, "but fortunately not my faith."

As we prayed, I felt God prompting me to say something. "Roger," I began, "I believe God has a message for you. He's saying, keep your eyes on him and he will restore all that you've lost – and more. He knows your situation. He's asking you to trust and to wait for him to act."

Roger didn't quite know how to react. "Thanks," he said, before praying in turn for me and the work of Christian Solidarity.

That was in the autumn of 1996. In February the following year I was in Washington for the National Prayer Breakfast hosted by members of the US Congress and Senate. Not so much a breakfast, more a series of events over several days, this annual gathering at the Washington Hilton brings together political, social and business leaders from around the world to pray and build relationships. The US President usually gives an address and speakers over the years have ranged from Mother Teresa to the rock star, Bono. This year I'd gone with our chairman, Mervyn Thomas, to try to raise the profile of Christian Solidarity.

A call came through to my hotel room and I picked up the phone to our Pakistani contact, David Elisha. This was a surprise: how he tracked me down to the Washington Hilton Towers I have no idea to this day. "Stuart," he said in some agitation, "a terrible thing has happened. Islamic militants have burnt down a Christian village in the Punjab and thousands of people are homeless. Please can you come and report it and see what Christian Solidarity can do to expose what these extremists are doing."

The situation was clearly urgent, so Mervyn and I flew back to London that night. On the way, we agreed that I should travel on to Pakistan with Tina Lambert, now our Director of Advocacy. The problem was how to pay for the trip. We simply didn't have the budget for two unplanned return air fares to Lahore, let alone for any aid we might want to give to the village. In addition, I'd always wanted to take my wife, Ethel, to Pakistan to introduce her to my good friend, Cecil Chaudhry. Here was an opportunity, but I didn't have the personal means to cover her costs as well.

It was a Sunday morning when Mervyn and I arrived at Heathrow Airport. The next morning I was back at my desk, wrestling with budgets and trying to figure out how we might afford a trip to Pakistan. The phone rang and I answered it.

"Stuart? It's Roger Salter from Guildford. Do you remember me?"

"Roger! Of course I do. How are you?"

"Great," he continued. "Never better. You'll never believe it, but God has done exactly what you said he would. To cut a long story short, I've got back all the money I lost at Lloyd's. With more on top!"

"That's wonderful," I replied. "Isn't God good!"

"Well, that's just it. Because you were obedient to God in what you said to me, I'd like to bless you in some way. What can I do for you?"

My heart warmed at God's faithfulness and perfect timing. "Well, funny you should say that, Roger…"

The upshot was that Roger Salter paid for three tickets to Pakistan and added a further amount to help rebuild the village. We left for Lahore the following week.

Once in Pakistan, our first meeting was with Cecil Chaudhry who briefed us on what he knew of the situation. The village was Shanti Nagar – "Land of Peace" in Urdu – originally built as a Christian settlement by the great grandfather of David Elisha. It lies in a hot, arid, cotton-growing region near the city of Multan and a smaller town called Khanewal. On the night of Saturday, 8 February, Cecil had had a distraught phone call from one of his many friends in the army – the local military commander, a Muslim, who had seen a mob burning the village. He could have intervened, he told Cecil, but as this was a civil matter he wasn't authorized to do so and had to leave it to the police, who were nowhere to be seen. (As we later discovered, the police were deeply implicated: they had actually escorted the mob to the village and forced the residents out at gunpoint.)

Cecil had travelled to Shanti Nagar the following day to inspect the damage for himself. He was told that 786 homes had been destroyed while others had been looted, crops had been wrecked and cattle, tractors and farming equipment had been stolen or burned. Around 20,000 Christians had lost their homes or had their livelihoods disrupted.

After a couple of days in Lahore, we flew on to Multan and drove via Khanewal to Shanti Nagar, accompanied by David Elisha who had family ties to the village and was anxious to see the damage. We parked on the outskirts and began picking our way through the ruined streets. Rubble and broken glass scrunched beneath our feet. People saw us coming and ran to meet us, desperate to tell us their stories and show us their devastated homes.

A short way in, we came across a burnt-out bus with the name, Full Gospel Assemblies, just legible on the blackened paintwork. Thousands of charred Bibles lay strewn in the wreckage. Villagers told us it belonged to the Full Gospel Pentecostal fellowship in Multan and had been in Shanti Nagar delivering Bibles when the mob attacked.

We walked towards the centre of the village, the smell of burnt remains still heavy in the air, and were shocked into silence as we saw the extent of the destruction. Several of the houses carried messages in English, daubed in paint by the villagers to catch the attention of any foreign visitors: "Is the crime to be Christian in Pakistan? Yes! Have we protection in Pakistan? No!" Alongside was the statement: "We should be strong."

We walked on past a ruined church and came to an imposing, brick-built building that had been the Salvation Army citadel. The local captain met us on the steps and showed us round the interior, now open to the sky. Standing by the charred stumps of the communion table, he remarked quietly: "With God's grace, we just have to forgive the people who did this and build our lives again."

As we spoke to witnesses and gathered more information, the causes of the event and what had actually happened on 8 February became clearer.

The spark was a seemingly trivial incident. Muslims in Pakistan are not allowed to hold liquor licences, so anyone wanting to buy alcohol has to rely on Christian licensees. With Ramadan coming to an end, a police inspector in Multan had wanted some liquor to celebrate the Feast of Eid. Accompanied by his sergeant, he'd come to his usual vendor in Shanti Nagar and demanded supplies. When the licensee explained he didn't have any, the inspector didn't believe him. The man invited him to search the house, which he did. In the process, the inspector angrily scattered some of his belongings and knocked a Bible to the floor, ripping one of the pages.

Annoyed by the way he'd been treated, the licensee lodged a complaint with the police. The inspector and his sergeant were subsequently suspended.

The quarrel escalated. The inspector joined forces with the local leader of a Muslim extremist party who had failed to win a recent by-election and was also nursing a grievance. In fact grievances were rife. Shanti Nagar was not only Christian, it was also the most prosperous village in the area and a cause of jealousy and resentment among local Muslims. When the police inspector and his politician ally decided to exact revenge on Shanti Nagar, it was not difficult to raise a mob.

Throughout the night of Friday, 7 February, several of the mosques in Khanewal and the surrounding villages announced over their loudspeakers that Christians had been seen desecrating the Koran by tearing out pages and scattering them on the outskirts of Shanti Nagar. The news brought thousands of Muslims out of their homes and a mob quickly formed. Worked to a frenzy by the extremists, they began marching on the village and attacking any Christian-owned premises they happened to pass along the route.

In the course of our investigations, we visited a convent in Khanewal which was one of the first places to come under attack. The priest accompanying us described how the rioters had advanced down the street and how the sisters and the priest-in-charge had feared for their lives. But then their Muslim neighbours had come to their aid, blocking the way and declaring they were willing to die rather than see the convent they loved destroyed by the mob. A nearby Catholic school was less fortunate and was set ablaze – as were thirteen churches in Multan, Khanewal and Shanti Nagar.

As the disturbance spread towards Shanti Nagar, the mob grew to an estimated 20,000. It now had a police escort, some of whom went ahead and informed the villagers that a demonstration – a *peaceful* demonstration – was coming their way and that everyone should leave their homes and head for the fields until it passed. Some refused, including the captain at the Salvation Army citadel. The police then fired guns into the air to force people out. Although they were clearly complicit and did nothing to stop the destruction, the police probably saved lives. Thanks to their warning and the grace of God, none of the villagers was killed.

After about ten days in Pakistan, we flew back to the UK. Tina and I wrote up our report and sent it out to the media, to Members of Parliament and peers, to the European Union, to the US State Department and to representatives of the US Congress and Senate. Although it took several years, Shanti Nagar village has now risen from the ashes. So far, thankfully, we've seen no repeat of the destruction of Christian property on such a scale.

Pakistan has probably kept us busier than any other part of the world. Over the years we've quietly moved thirty-one Christians out of the country to help them escape charges of blasphemy or apostasy. And these are just the high-profile cases in which the people concerned have faced particular danger. We've helped many others to move within Pakistan in order to start life again in a new community.

Our 1997 visit to the Punjab in the aftermath of the Shanti Nagar fire was a chance to meet more persecuted Christians. One was Sam Chand Baba, a convert from Islam and a member of one of the most prominent Muslim families in Sindh province. His father was a *pir*, a Muslim cleric with his own personal devotees – in his case around 80,000 including some well-known politicians. From childhood, Sam Chand Baba was groomed to follow his father and also become a *pir*. By his teens he'd learned the Koran by heart and he remains an expert on Islam. But his life changed as a young man when he travelled on a train from Sahiwal to Karachi and someone gave him a New Testament. He began reading it, was gripped by the message of Jesus and declared himself a Christian shortly afterwards.

It was a dangerous move. After his father died, his mother and uncle issued a *fatwa* requiring all true Muslims to seek him out and send him home to face the death sentence. Undeterred, he joined a theological seminary in Gujranwala and became a travelling evangelist – a very effective one, judging by the large numbers of converts he left behind on his journeys.

Tina, Ethel and I met Sam Chand Baba – a large, dark-haired man then in his forties – at Cecil Chaudhry's home in Lahore. With him were his wife, dressed as a Muslim for safety, and their five children. By this time he was permanently on the run with as much protection as Cecil could give him. But being the son of a *pir*, he was well known and was in and out of police custody, constantly being beaten up but somehow managing to escape every time. Cecil was convinced that the time had come to move the family out of Pakistan and asked if Christian Solidarity could help.

We followed the now familiar routine of applying to the Home Office. This involved sending in detailed reports with full particulars of all those we wished to move and then praying we'd get a positive response. Throughout the process I worked closely with Cecil who arranged for Sam to be interviewed for a visa at the British High Commission in Islamabad. The family eventually moved to the UK in 1998, their exit masterminded by Cecil who accompanied them on the plane to London. One of our supporters, Dr John Herbert, Earl of Powis, provided accommodation in a house belonging to his estate in the small Welsh town of Welshpool.

Even then, Sam was not safe. Out in the town one day, he was stopped in the street by a Muslim visiting from Birmingham. "I know you," said the stranger. "Aren't you Sam Chand Baba?" With his cover blown, we thought we should move him again and he's now in the north of England in a house donated by a local Assemblies of God church.

The *fatwa* against Sam exists to this day and the uncle who issued it has since served as Chief Minister of Sindh province. Sam has been back to Pakistan temporarily, but his latest visit in 2008 had to be cut short when he was recognized and threatened. He lives in the knowledge that he'll never again be able to live permanently in the land of his birth.

Another to fall foul of Pakistan's religious laws was a young farmer called Ayub Masih. Ayub lived in the Punjab in a village near Faisalabad and his case – like many – began with a local dispute. An argument over the ownership of some land led to an accusation of blaspheming the Prophet Mohammed and Ayub was arrested. A full five years later in April 1998, his case came to court in the town of Sahiwal. Ayub denied the blasphemy charge but was found guilty and sentenced to death.

The case was of great concern to the Catholic Bishop of Faisalabad and Chairman of Pakistan's Justice and Peace

Commission, Dr John Joseph (not to be confused with the John Joseph in the Gjnanawala case). Bishop John had long campaigned against Pakistan's blasphemy laws and had told Cecil Chaudhry that he wouldn't tolerate another Christian being sentenced to death. At the time of Ayub's trial, he'd been trying to arrange an appeal. When sentence was passed, he wrote to Pakistan's *Dawn* newspaper saying that Christians and Muslims should act together to get the blasphemy laws repealed and Ayub's sentence lifted.

On 5 May, ten days after Ayub was sentenced, I made one of my regular calls to Cecil to catch up on events and see how he was. He picked up the phone, but kept having to break off to talk to someone on another line.

"Who've you got there?" I asked him.

"It's Bishop John Joseph," said Cecil. "He's telling me to take care of things here. He's just going to visit Ayub Masih in prison and say a mass for his safety."

That was the last time they spoke. Shortly after phoning Cecil, Bishop John summoned his driver and asked to be taken to the courthouse in Sahiwal. There he got out, told the driver to wait, walked a few metres to the front of the building and shot himself dead with a pistol.

The bishop's suicide was deeply shocking, both inside Pakistan and in the worldwide church. It seems that when all other avenues failed, this saintly man saw the taking of his own life as the only way to protest at Pakistan's blasphemy laws. The act was clearly premeditated. For some time the bishop had been saying in public that he was ready to sacrifice his blood for the sake of the Lord's people. He had also written a report for the Vatican describing the problems Christians faced in Pakistan and setting out the reasons for his action – a document we later distributed to the media. In the light of his death, his letter to the *Dawn* newspaper took on new significance. "Dedicated persons," he wrote, "do not count the cost of the sacrifices they have to offer."

In the event, Ayub was spared the death sentence but kept in prison in appalling conditions. Cecil and the Pakistani Catholic church took care of his family while Christian Solidarity and other human rights organizations continued to campaign on his behalf. He was finally freed by the Supreme Court in 2005, thanks partly to the brave Muslim barrister, Abid Minto, who regularly defended Christians accused of blasphemy and had earlier secured the release of Rehmat and Salamat Masih.

Fulfilling a promise made to Bishop John Joseph, Cecil personally escorted Ayub to America where he now lives in safety.

In 1993, the same year that Ayub Masih and the Gjnanawala trio were first arrested, Anwar Masih, a Christian living in Faisalabad, got into a dispute with his Muslim grocer over a bill. One problem with the Pakistani penal code is that people can all too easily use it to settle scores with their neighbours. Anwar's grocer did just that, lodging a complaint under clause 295C that Anwar had blasphemed the Prophet Mohammed. As a result, Anwar ended up in prison facing a possible death sentence. Christian Solidarity took up his cause and began campaigning for his release.

It took three years for the case to come to court and Anwar was in solitary confinement for most of that time. In Pakistan, a blasphemy case involving a Christian almost never remains a local issue. The anger and outrage reverberate around the mosques and across the country and the defendant, guilty or not, is invariably branded as deserving death. As the day of Anwar's hearing approached, members of an Islamic extremist party built a gallows outside the prison in Faisalabad – a message to the court that Anwar should hang for insulting the Prophet and, if he happened to be acquitted, that someone else would do the job instead.

In the end, the hearing was called off and Anwar was left languishing in prison until 1998. Finally brought to trial, he was acquitted of blaspheming the Prophet but found guilty of insulting the Islamic religion. Given that the normal penalty was five years in prison and Anwar had already served his time while waiting to be tried, the judge set him free.

The verdict enraged the extremists. After they vowed again to kill Anwar and his wife and children, Bishop John Joseph personally took him into hiding. But the day before his suicide, he called Cecil and told him it was becoming more and more difficult to keep Anwar safe. He was therefore transferring him to Lahore to place him under Cecil's protection.

Anwar was still in serious danger. The extremists were after his blood and made at least one attempt to abduct his children. Cecil came to the conclusion that Anwar and his family could no longer stay in Pakistan and urged Christian Solidarity to bring them to the UK. After the usual arrangements with the Home Office and the High Commission in Islamabad, we succeeded in bringing them to Britain. Once again, Cecil organized the exit from Pakistan and accompanied the family to London. I met them at Gatwick Airport and drove them to Newport in Wales where they started life under a new name in the care of the local evangelical church.

Although the family are now thoroughly acclimatized and the children speak English like any Welsh kid, Anwar has never recovered psychologically from his years in solitary confinement, solely on the word of his grocer. He carries the mental scars to this day.

Through contacts such as Cecil Chaudhry and John Joseph (he of the Gjnanawala case), Christian Solidarity has learned of further instances in which Christians have suffered for their faith.

Tariq Iqbal was a Muslim chaplain in the Pakistani Air Force before converting to Christianity. In 1990 he was arrested under clause 295C of the penal code for blaspheming the Prophet Mohammed and thrown in prison pending trial. John Joseph's Christian Organization for Human Rights took up his case and visited him in jail. Disabled as a result of polio, Tariq Iqbal needed help getting in and out of court whenever he was called for hearings. His guards wouldn't touch him physically on account of his being a Christian, so John and his colleagues would help him from the police car and support him as he limped from the street into the building.

According to John, Tariq Iqbal had a tiny cell with a hole in the floor as a toilet. Because he was an apostate, the authorities removed his light and fan and blocked the outflow from the toilet so the contents backed up into his cell. For two months he ate and slept in his own faeces. But, says John, he was willing to endure it for the sake of Jesus, his Saviour. He expected to be killed and eventually died in prison in July 1992 through a combination of beating and poisoning. When Tina, Ethel and I later visited Lahore, we laid flowers on his grave and on that of Manzoor Masih as a gesture of solidarity from the church in Britain.

Another to suffer was Gul Masih, a young Pentecostal Christian who was seen by his neighbour placing newspaper in his fireplace and falsely accused of desecrating the Koran. For this he spent two years in prison, his ankles shackled to his wrists. Cecil told me that when he came out of prison, he walked as though still in chains. As with so many other victims of persecution, Cecil took care of him until he could be moved out of Pakistan.

On my trip to Pakistan in 1997, I met a devout Christian called Aftab Mughal in Peshawar. Aftab was a journalist and human rights activist working for Cecil and was vocal in his protests against the blasphemy laws. I met him subsequently in Geneva when he gave evidence on human rights abuses to the UN High Commissioner for Refugees in his capacity as Secretary to the Pakistan Justice and Peace Commission. Inevitably, his international profile made him a target for militants and extremists. Violently attacked on at least two occasions, he was forced to flee to Britain and seek asylum. He and his wife are now looked after by Christian Solidarity in Blackburn, Lancashire.

As well as introducing the Sharia-based penal code that has caused such trouble for Pakistani Christians, President Zia ul-Haq's reform of the constitution in 1979 changed the electoral system. Under the new rules, Muslims, Christians, Hindus, Buddhists and other faith groups could only vote for parliamentary candidates of the same religion. This immediately denied any of the minority faiths a voice in parliament because each seat was invariably won by the Muslim candidate. It also meant that Muslim Members of Parliament had nothing to gain from helping non-Muslim citizens because they'd never get their votes. This unjust system probably explains why Muslim MPs constantly failed to protest at the persecution of minorities.

For a human rights activist like Cecil Chaudhry, the main priority was always to get rid of the blasphemy laws. He recognized, however, that the only way to repeal them was first to change the electoral system and give non-Muslims an effective political voice.

He expressed this view when he spoke to the Christian Solidarity board at an away-weekend in Surrey in 1994. "You don't have to tell me about the blasphemy laws," he told us. "I live with them every day. The notorious 295 clauses are wreaking havoc among Pakistani Christians." He then explained why groups such as Christian Solidarity should put their weight behind electoral change. Only when minorities had representation in Parliament, he said, could attention switch to the blasphemy laws themselves.

It was an ambitious and long-term strategy, but Cecil is a determined man and we agreed to support it. In the years that followed, we helped him present his case around the world – to British MPs and the Foreign Office, to officials in the European Union and to the US Congress and Senate – all with the aim of putting international pressure on Pakistan to change its electoral system. Success finally came in 2003 when President Pervez Musharraf was forced to restore the joint electorate system after Pakistan's minorities boycotted local elections – a move spearheaded by Cecil who addressed over a hundred public rallies to win support. There's no doubt that Cecil's tireless campaigning both inside and outside Pakistan was largely responsible for securing a more representative system.

At this point I need to introduce another key figure in the fight for religious liberty in Pakistan. Shahbaz Bhatti is a Catholic whom Cecil got to know in the early 1990s when he headed a youth organization called the Christian Liberation Front. Recognizing his talents, Cecil set about mentoring Shahbaz to take over some of his own work in the human rights field. Shahbaz subsequently became Christian Solidarity's main link in Pakistan, filing reports whenever Christians became the victims of discrimination. As Cecil's right-hand man, he also shared the work of speaking out for Pakistani minorities in the centres of influence in Britain, Europe and the USA.

In 2002, Cecil and Shahbaz founded APMA – the All-Pakistan Minorities Alliance – to campaign for equal rights for religious minorities and the repeal of Pakistan's blasphemy laws. When the electoral system changed in 2003, the Alliance was able to field parliamentary candidates with a reasonable chance of success and now has a number of MPs. In another welcome development, Shahbaz himself was appointed Federal Minister for Minorities Affairs (the first Christian to hold the post) and became a member of the cabinet under President Asif Ali Zardari in November 2008.

In his new role, Shahbaz has made great strides in protecting the rights of religious minorities. He was the driving force behind a bill to outlaw discrimination against non-Muslims and is currently preparing a bill that will realize Cecil Chaudhry's dream of repealing the blasphemy laws. Speaking to the US Commission on International Religious Freedom in Washington in September 2009, he declared: "The stand of the Pakistani government is to review, revisit and amend the blasphemy law so it will not remain a tool in the hands of extremists." That's a far cry from the situation just a few years previously.

Shahbaz has also been effective in prosecuting Pakistani officials who disregard minority rights. In one instance in 2009, a young Christian man was arrested in the town of Sialkot and garrotted in prison. Through Shahbaz's intervention, the prison governor and police superintendent who should have ensured his safety were suspended.

At about the same time in the village of Gojra in the Punjab, a Christian wedding party was accused by extremists of tearing up the Koran when all they'd been doing was throwing paper money at the bride and groom in the traditional way. After the wedding a number of Christian houses were set alight and the police stood by as five people burned to death in their homes. Shahbaz visited the scene and began proceedings against the individual policemen who had failed to stop the murders. In addition, the Christians of Gojra who lost their homes have been compensated – something that has never happened before. In Shahbaz, Pakistan's minorities know they have a voice at the highest level.

Shahbaz is a brave man who understands the risks of taking such a public stand. Acknowledging the frequent threats to his life, he states simply: "I personally stand for religious freedom. Even if I pay the price of my life, I live for this principle and I want to die for this principle." When he addressed Christian Solidarity's annual conference in London in October 2009, he spoke movingly of the need for prayer to uphold persecuted

Christians and repeated his willingness to give his life for the gospel and for the church in Pakistan.

Although much remains to be done, Pakistan has moved a long way since the rule of President Zia when anti-Christian discrimination was enshrined in law. The roles played by Cecil and Shahbaz as God's men in the right place at the right time bring to mind the words of Mordecai to Queen Esther in the Old Testament: "And who knows whether you have not come to the kingdom for such a time as this?" (Esther 4:14, RSV). Without their courage and commitment, Pakistan might still be the dark and difficult place I first came to know in the 1990s.

16

The Russian in Dhaka Jail

It must have been in 1994 that I boarded a flight to London at the end of a Christian Solidarity meeting in Zurich. I squeezed my way down the aircraft, tucked my briefcase into the overhead locker and dropped into my aisle seat. As the other passengers gradually got settled, I glanced across to the young man in the window seat on the same row. He was flicking through the pages of the in-flight magazine and I thought he looked weary. At times like this I usually make a point of saying hello: you never know what opportunities for conversation the Holy Spirit might open up. He returned the greeting and flopped back into his seat.

"I really don't know why I'm on this flight," he sighed.

"Why do you say that?"

"I've just come from the Congo. There's been some fighting, some kind of rebellion, and my company decided to ship me straight back to the UK. Via Switzerland. But my wife's in Bangladesh. So that's where I'm headed."

I pointed out that this particular flight was not going to Bangladesh. At least, I hoped not.

"I know," he replied. "I'm stopping off to see family in the UK on the way. It's all happened so suddenly, I hardly know if I'm coming or going. I'm a consultant engineer, by the way.

Sorry, your name was...?"

"Stuart Windsor," I replied. "I'm a Christian."

"Are you really? So am I. What do you do?"

I told him I was UK National Director of Christian Solidarity, speaking up for persecuted Christians around the world.

"That's interesting," continued my new acquaintance. I would tell you his name, but it seems to have disappeared from my records and I can't now remember what it was. I think it might have been Steve, so let's go with that. He went on: "Does the name Vladimir Lankin mean anything to you?"

I confessed it didn't and Steve went on to explain. "Vladimir Lankin was attached to the Russian Embassy in Dhaka, the Bangladeshi capital. Due to some mix-up over a container, he found himself implicated in an illegal shipment of gold. He's innocent, but he's now in prison. While he's been there he's become a Christian. I'm part of the international fellowship in Dhaka that's trying to help him. We're trying to get support from Christians in the UK."

He paused and fastened his seat-belt, then turned back to face me. "I don't suppose your organization would be interested in helping a Russian in jail in Bangladesh?"

I had to tell him that helping convicted gold-smugglers, even innocent ones, was not really our brief at Christian Solidarity. Nor was Bangladesh one of our target countries. But I made a note of Vladimir's name and took Steve's phone number in Dhaka with the promise that I'd see what we could do.

I discussed the case with our Chairman, Mervyn Thomas, when I got back to the office. Technically, Vladimir Lankin was not in prison because he was a Christian. However, if Steve's story was true, he was nonetheless a Christian in prison. We agreed we'd do some more research and pray for guidance as to whether we should take up his cause.

About three weeks later the staff at Christian Solidarity were gathered in the office for morning prayers when I felt an overwhelming urge to call the Dhaka number. When God wants me to do something, I don't normally hear instructions like some people do. It's more often an inner conviction from the Holy Spirit and I know what I'm supposed to be doing. This was definitely one of those occasions.

As soon as we'd finished praying, I hurried back to my desk and dialled the number I'd taken on the plane. I didn't even know whether Steve had arrived home or was still in the UK, so was slightly surprised when he picked up the phone.

Steve was even more surprised – and elated to hear me. "Stuart!" he exclaimed. "How did you know I was here? I've just this second walked in through the door from the airport."

"I didn't know," I replied. "But I'm glad I've caught you."

Steve went on: "I was just telling my wife I'd met this guy on the plane who might be able to help Vladimir, but I didn't think you'd remember. And now here you are. What can I do for you?"

I explained that we were interested in helping Vladimir but would need some more details. Steve agreed to send me a brief. He also mentioned that Vladimir had a daughter, Tomila, studying at St Antony's College in Oxford and that she might have more information to help with any campaign.

I felt God had answered. We had to take the case.

As well as the details from Steve, we found out more from some of our supporters, including a couple called Peter and Stella Grant. Now the International Director of Tearfund, Peter then worked for the UK Department for International Development (DfID) and was attached to the British Embassy in Dhaka. He and Stella were members of Dhaka's international Christian fellowship which had found out about Vladimir Lankin and was trying to take care of him and his family.

Gradually we pieced together the story. A career diplomat, Vladimir had been brought up in Siberia. In 1942 his father had been sent to a labour camp in Russia's Far East for telling jokes about Josef Stalin (the charge being "anti-Soviet agitation and propaganda"). Released after his seven-year sentence, he stayed on in Siberia and raised his family there. While other branches of the Lankins were Baptists and as such had been persecuted by the Bolsheviks, Vladimir's immediate family was not in the least religious. Indeed, young Vladimir's first contact with Christianity came when his grandmother arrived to live with the family and used to ask him to read the Bible for her.

His grandmother's faith had little effect and Vladimir became a Communist – not from conviction (he claimed to hate the Soviet system) but because it was the only way to get on in the diplomatic service. He studied Indian languages at Tashkent University and became fluent in Hindi and Urdu as well as English. In 1989 he was appointed head of the Press Information Department at the Russian Embassy in Dhaka with the rank of First Secretary.

His downfall came in January 1993 at the hands of a Bangladeshi called Kalim who supplied duty-free goods to the diplomatic corps in Dhaka. Kalim persuaded Vladimir that it was possible to short-cut the usual bureaucratic delays in getting consignments through customs if a well-dressed foreigner went to Zia International Airport and signed for them. To do his friend a favour, Vladimir signed a form ("a small formality", he was told) authorizing Kalim's company to receive a consignment of biscuits and chocolates from Singapore on behalf of the Russian Embassy. In so doing, he accepted responsibility for the two boxes in question.

When the boxes were opened by Bangladeshi Customs, they were found to contain 80 kg of illegally imported gold. Given that Bangladesh imposed a 100 per cent duty on gold, smuggling could be very lucrative and the penalties were harsh. Vladimir's plight was made worse by the fact that he'd just left his post at the Embassy and had therefore lost his diplomatic immunity.

Nor could he look to Kalim for help: by the time the scam was discovered, Kalim and his family were on a flight to Bangkok.

Abandoned to his fate by the Russian Embassy, Vladimir was arrested, tortured with electrodes and detained on the grounds that he was "a dangerous criminal – a leader of an organized crime network aimed at destroying the economic and social structure of Bangladesh". He found himself in squalid conditions with torture rife and prisoners made to sleep on floors swimming in excrement and vomit. At one point he signed what he thought was a statement in Bengali. This was then filed as a "confession" which only got him deeper into trouble. He eventually ended up in Dhaka Central Jail, built by the British a century earlier to house 1,500 inmates and now holding 6,000.

One night, as his prison diary relates, he saw a dimly glowing vision of a cross on his cell wall when the lights went out. With his atheist, Communist background he knew nothing of the Christian significance of the vision, but he scratched the outline on the wall with a teaspoon and spent much of his time during the day looking at it. The vision recurred on other nights. He was convinced it had some kind of spiritual meaning but he couldn't figure out what it was.

The mystery began to lift when someone randomly gave him a book from the prison library. Written in the days of the British Raj, it turned out to be the history of the Salvation Army under the guise of a not-very-good love story. But this book, says Vladimir, was a gift from God in helping him to unravel the meaning of the vision. He later got hold of a Bible and a book called *Loving God* by Charles Colson, President Nixon's former Special Counsel and founder of Prison Fellowship International. Through his reading and through words and verses that came to him in dreams, he pieced together the basics of the faith and committed himself to Christ.

He then began to find other Christians among his fellow prisoners – two Catholic Filipinos, a Nigerian Anglican and an

American ex-Buddhist called Thomas whose father was a retired NASA officer and who'd been imprisoned for tearing pages out of scientific journals in Dhaka National Library. A church began to form – the First Congregational Church of Dhaka Central Jail.

On Christmas Day 1993, nearly a year after his arrest, Vladimir was baptized by Thomas in the water butt in the corner of his cell.[9]

By the time Christian Solidarity became involved, Vladimir was receiving visits from members of the international fellowship in Dhaka and his case was becoming more widely known. He even had letters from Charles Colson and the British preacher and writer, John Stott, after both were informed that Vladimir was studying their books.

Having ascertained the facts – helped by Vladimir's daughter, Tomila, who visited our offices from Oxford and brought us a photograph – we began a campaign for his release. This followed the usual Christian Solidarity strategy of asking our supporters to pray, circulating the story to the press and putting pressure on the authorities to re-examine the case.

Someone who played a vital role was Dr John Herbert, Earl of Powis, who has been a longstanding supporter of our organization and served on our board for a number of years. A descendant of Clive of India (and also, as it happens, the poet, George Herbert), John has a particular interest in the subcontinent. When he asked what he could do to help, I suggested he talk to the Bangladeshi High Commissioner and explain the miscarriage of justice that this poor Russian was suffering in Dhaka Central Jail.

"I'll do better than that," he said. "I'll take him to dinner." Which he did – and I'm sure he pulled no punches in informing the High Commissioner of Vladimir's plight.

Over a period of months, our campaigning, along with pressure from Christian expatriates in Dhaka, began to have an effect on the Bangladeshi government. In the meantime, Vladimir's defence lawyers had been urging him to ask for clemency. Given that he was technically guilty of authorizing an illegal gold shipment, it was difficult to ask for the case to be reviewed. The best option, they said, was to write a grovelling letter to the president, acknowledging his mistake in signing the form and asking for a pardon.

He did so and it worked. In September 1997, after four and a half years in jail, Vladimir was told he was free to go and was taken from prison to the Russian Embassy. (Aware of the international pressure, the embassy itself had suddenly discovered a new concern for its former employee.) There he was reunited with his wife and children and a little while later the family flew back to Moscow.

A few months afterwards, I travelled to Moscow with Mervyn Thomas and fellow board member, Franklin Evans, to visit our *Nasha Semya* foster care project and was able to meet Vladimir in person. What I most remember about him was his radiant smile and self-effacing manner – not what I expected in a man who had just been through such a brutal experience. But then, the grace of God is a wonderful thing. We took him to speak at two Moscow churches where large congregations turned out to hear his testimony. His imprisonment, he said, had been God's trap – "his merciful trap, a trap of grace, where he caught me and laid his hand upon me and claimed me as his own".

The following summer I was speaking at a seminar at the New Wine conference and retold Vladimir's story. As soon as his name came up, a lady in the audience called out: "It's true! I was there! I went and saw him in prison!" This was Stella Grant, whom I hadn't met but who, with her husband, had played such a large part in supporting Vladimir in jail and publicizing his plight. It was a great pleasure to meet one of our fellow campaigners.

At about the same time, we contacted Vladimir again to ask if he'd speak at Christian Solidarity's next annual conference. He willingly agreed. Before he could come, however, we had to get him a visa from the British Embassy in Moscow. As well as writing to the Embassy, we contacted the Foreign Office in London for permission for Vladimir to enter Britain. The answer was a firm "no": it was not government policy to allow former prisoners into the country. This was disappointing, but we accepted the decision and made other plans for the conference.

A little later, Christian Solidarity hosted a delegation from the Russian Federation Ministry of Education and the Moscow Education Department in connection with our work among Russian orphans. We happened to mention our attempts to get Vladimir Lankin into the country and the British government's policy of barring ex-prisoners.

"That wouldn't exactly be the case," explained our guests.

"Oh? Why's that?"

"This Mr Lankin of yours. He would have been ex-KGB. That's why the British government wouldn't let him in."

If that's true, it's good to know that even the dreaded KGB was not beyond the reach of God's love.

17
Civil War in Sudan

The tiny six-seater seemed to hang motionless under the vast African sky. Scrolling beneath us, almost imperceptibly, was the dark green smear of Sudan's Sudd swamp, glistening with silver lakes and marshlands and the White Nile snaking its way north towards Khartoum. I listened to the thrum of the single engine, alert for any change in its note and wondering how far a heavily-laden Cessna Caravan would glide if the engine cut out. Far enough, I hoped, to get us over the crocodile-infested swamp that stretched away towards the heat-haze shimmering on the horizon.

I looked across at Caroline Cox on the opposite side of the plane. Head pressed against the window, she seemed equally absorbed in the unfolding terrain. I recalled her account of her visit to Khartoum some years earlier when she'd gained an audience with General Omar al-Bashir, President of Sudan and friend of Osama Bin Laden, who is thought to have spent at least four years in Sudan. With the President was his Islamic adviser, El Turabi. Caroline had challenged both men on the government's plan to subdue and Islamize the south of the country. When Bashir seemed not to care about the rights of southerners, she retorted that she'd be back, with or without official permission, and continue monitoring human rights abuses.

"In that case," the President replied, "we will have to shoot down your plane."

Undeterred, Caroline had since made several visits to Sudan on behalf of Christian Solidarity. Now I was travelling with her into Africa's largest country and the theatre of its longest-running war. The trip was illegal, with no official flight plan and no permission to enter Sudanese airspace. As on all our trips into Southern Sudan, our safety depended on keeping the lid on our visit until we were out of the country.

The Sudd still stretched as far as the eye could see. I tried not to dwell on Caroline's assessment of what the Sudanese authorities might do if they locked onto our flight. It was possible they'd try to shoot us down with a surface-to-air missile. Possible but unlikely: the Sudanese wouldn't waste a valuable missile on a tiny plane like ours – unless, that is, they happened to know that Baroness Cox was on board. They might, though, buzz us with a fighter plane or track us onto the ground and bomb us as we landed.

I glanced at my watch. Another hour and a half to our destination, the tiny airstrip at Turalei in the Bahr El-Ghazal district in the northern part of Southern Sudan. I closed my eyes and prayed for a safe landing.

Civil war had raged in Sudan almost continuously since the country's independence from Britain in 1956. The northern half of this huge, sparsely populated land is Arab and Muslim while the south is home to black African animists and Christians – tribes such as the Dinka, the Nuer and the people of the Nuba Mountains south of the central town of El-Obeid. Over the years, these groups have suffered appallingly from the Khartoum government's desire to impose Islam on Southern Sudan and exploit the oil reserves in the north of the territory.

After years of sporadic unrest, the civil war re-erupted in 1983 when President Numeiri attempted to enforce Islamic

Sharia law across the country and redrew the boundaries to bring the oilfields into Northern Sudan. When 500 southern troops refused to be shipped north, Numeiri sent one of his officers, southern-born Colonel John Garang, to put down the mutiny. It was a bad move. Garang switched sides, taking charge of the rebel forces and establishing the Sudan People's Liberation Army (SPLA) and its allied political movement, the SPLM, as the focus for southern aspirations.

The war intensified after the 1989 military coup that brought President Bashir to power. Determined to Islamize the country once and for all, Bashir's government began handing arms to Arab tribes in the southern areas of Northern Sudan and urging them to wage holy war (or *jihad*) against the black African *kaffirs* ("unbelievers") to the south. Anything they could seize in the process – chattels, animals or even people – was theirs to keep. At the same time, southern Sudanese fleeing north to escape famine and drought were captured, interned in so-called "peace camps" and forced to become Muslims – partly by having food aid withheld until they complied.

Bashir's strategy was first exposed by the Sudanese church, its main spokesman being the Catholic Bishop of El-Obeid and friend of Christian Solidarity, Macram Gassis. In 1992 the bishops of Southern Sudan made an international appeal for help, warning that swathes of the southern population faced being massacred or deported to the north in the name of *jihad*. Caroline Cox spoke passionately on behalf of the Southern Sudanese in the House of Lords in December 1992. She then extracted an invitation to the country from the Sudanese ambassador to London, demanding unrestricted access and the presence of her own TV cameraman wherever she chose to go. It says much for Caroline's powers of persuasion that the hapless ambassador, having merely invited her to the Sudanese embassy to put the government's case, ended up agreeing to her demands.

So followed a series of visits, both legal and illegal, in which Caroline and John Eibner of Christian Solidarity in Switzerland investigated the conduct of the war and the suffering of its victims.

A horrifying picture emerged. In its offensive against the people of the Nuba Mountains, the government had starved the region of aid and cut off its water supplies. Food and medicines were made available only to those who agreed to move to peace camps in the north. Then came military force with reports of burnings, poisoned wells, deportations, torture and execution.

Here and elsewhere, Caroline and the Christian Solidarity team recorded instances of villages strafed by helicopter gunships and terrorized with crude bombs rolled from the back of Antonov cargo planes. The targets were often busy markets or churches packed with Sunday worshippers. It also emerged that many of the pilots flying Bashir's helicopters and aircraft were Armenian mercenaries made redundant when the war in the Caucasus came to an end in the 1990s.

A particularly savage aspect of the war was the slave raids, mainly against the Dinkas of the Bahr El-Ghazal region which lies at the southern end of the El-Obeid to Wau railway. The worst to suffer was Abyei County which borders the north and has the misfortune to sit above a huge oilfield. Throughout the dry season, the government would run trains packed with militia down into the south. These were accompanied by nomadic, horse-mounted, Baggara Arabs who would launch attacks on nearby villages, striking before dawn when the inhabitants were asleep. The mud-built, straw-thatched *tukuls* or huts would be torched, the men shot or burned to death and the women and children rounded up, roped into lines and marched away to the north. Captives could be made to walk for ten days or more. If they survived, they'd end up as slaves or concubines, either to their captors or to others who bought them from the raiders. Families were often split so that siblings and mothers and children would lose contact. Women were systematically raped while children were given Arabic names and forced to become Muslims.

Caroline and John were determined to bring this twentieth-century slave trade to the world's attention. One way they did so was by buying back small numbers of individuals from sympathetic Arabs who were willing to act as go-betweens, purchasing southern slaves from their northern owners and marching them back to their villages. Once they'd redeemed them, Caroline and John would record their testimonies to include in their reports.

The world started to take notice and journalists from around the world began asking to join the team on future trips. When Caroline and John visited Bahr El-Ghazal in October 1995, they were able to take a reporter and photographer from *Der Spiegel*, a cameraman from Channel 4 News and a reporter for the BBC and the *Sunday Telegraph*.

Caroline's findings were endorsed by other bodies. In a report to the UN General Assembly, the rapporteur of the Commission on Human Rights listed a series of abuses on the part of the Sudanese government – aerial bombardment of civilian targets by government forces; food and relief used to force people to convert to Islam; the killing by soldiers in uniform of displaced people in the south who refused to convert to Islam; and arbitrary rounding up of children to be sent to special camps to be ideologically indoctrinated and forced to become Muslims.

A further report by two Southern Sudanese politicians supported the claim that children from Bahr El-Ghazal were being taken as slaves. One of its authors, a former government minister called Santino Deng, revealed that the slave trade also had an international dimension. "Some of our children," he said, "are sent to Koranic schools in Djibouti, Mauritania, Gabon and Cameroon, the Kingdom of Saudi Arabia and Libya."[10]

While Caroline was occupied with Sudan, I was finding my feet as Christian Solidarity's UK National Director and attempting to expand the organization – as well as handling our other crises in Nagorno Karabakh, Pakistan and elsewhere. But Caroline is a hard woman to ignore. As a trustee of Christian Solidarity, she was determined that Christians in the UK, and our organization in particular, should be speaking out more vigorously for persecuted Christians in Sudan.

All of which led to the trip that Caroline and I were now undertaking.

Our objectives in travelling to Bahr El-Ghazal in May 1998 were the same as for every other Christian Solidarity mission – to show solidarity with persecuted Christians and others; to ascertain the facts of what was happening and record examples of persecution; to deliver aid; and to visit and encourage church leaders. The fact that Bahr El-Ghazal was now suffering famine as well as raids made it all the more important to give practical help and to show the people of the region they were not forgotten. Having collected our data as professionally and accurately as we could, our aim was to circulate it to the press when we got home and to raise awareness of the situation.

Accompanied by the author and film journalist, Damian Lewis, and his cousin and assistant, Hanna Lewis, Caroline and I flew British Airways to Nairobi. Emerging from Jomo Kenyatta International Airport into Kenya's dazzling sunlight, we crossed to the small domestic airfield at nearby Wilson Airport. Here we'd arranged to catch a Beech King Air twin-propeller aircraft operated by a company called Trackmark. Run by expatriate air force pilots, mainly British, Canadian and Australian, Trackmark provided the local air transport for most of our Sudanese trips.

Before taking off, we took on board a consignment of aid and medicines including anti-malarial tablets and dehydration kits for babies. These, we knew, could make the difference between life and death among the famine-stricken people we planned to visit. Then we lifted out of Nairobi and set course for Lokichokio in Kenya's extreme north-west. As the mountains of Ethiopia shimmered into view on our right, the landscape below grew harsher and drier – a prelude to the vast, empty scrubland of Southern Sudan.

Lokichokio, an airstrip and cluster of settlements in the baking red dust of Kenya's northern plains, was our base for the next twenty-four hours – a chance to become acclimatized to the African heat and to finalize plans for the next few days in Sudan. Here we met a number of BBC, ITV and Fleet Street journalists who'd been covering the Bahr El-Ghazal famine and were now heading back to Nairobi. The worst was over, they told us. As far as news was concerned, Bahr El-Ghazal was off the radar.

A different story emerged from two humanitarian aid officers from the SPLM who had now joined our party as advisers. The journalists, it seemed, had just missed a ferocious raid in which Baggara horsemen had massacred thousands of victims in the marketplace at Wun Rok, a short distance from our intended destination at Turalei.

A day after landing in Lokichokio, we reloaded our aid and baggage onto a Trackmark Cessna Caravan and took off in a north-westerly direction. As we flew over the border and began crossing the Sudd swamp, we huddled together between the seats and prayed that our entry into Sudan would not attract the attention of government forces.

The flight from Lokichokio to Turalei takes two and a half hours and ends on a bare-earth airstrip in the bush. Landing at any time outside the dry season is hazardous. When the rains begin, incoming pilots have to touch their wheels on the surface to gauge the state of the mud. If the ground seems solid, they'll circle again and land on the second approach, hoping they've made the right call. On several of our trips in and out of

Sudan, we passed the rusting carcasses of Sudanese government Antonovs that had crashed on take-off or landing.

This being the dry season, our landing was straightforward. But even as we circled, we could see the aftermath of recent Baggara raids in the still-smoking *tukuls* below us. Stepping out from the Cessna once we'd landed, we were greeted by two Dinkas carrying a cross – the traditional Christian welcome for incoming travellers. But the singing crowds that Caroline had come to expect after her previous trips to Sudan were simply not there. Turalei was deserted.

"The people have fled," explained our welcomers. "To see what's happening, you must get back in your plane and fly to Wun Rok. That's where the people have gone."

We climbed back on board and made the ten-minute flight to Wun Rok. As we taxied to a stop on the dusty strip, the crowd appeared. Hundreds of men, women and children emerged from the bush and swarmed around the Cessna, dancing and singing to welcome us in. Willing hands took our bags and carried them into the village where we set up our tents. (On all our trips, we made a point of taking our own food, water and shelter so as not to be a burden on the people we were there to help.) Once this was done, there was no putting off the task we dreaded – inspecting the market.

The massacre had taken place less than twenty-four hours before. Our SPLM companions guided us to the scene and explained what had happened.

Wun Rok's enormous Abin Dau market was famous throughout the region, attracting traders from as far away as Uganda, Kenya and Northern Sudan. The previous day when the place was packed, the Baggara had attacked on three sides, corralling the crowd and funnelling them towards the waiting guns. Many were abducted and thousands more were shot and hacked to death. Bodies of people and animals still lay strewn on the ground and among the surrounding thickets. At every turn there were more horrors – corpses buzzing with flies; body parts; dead horses; weeping relatives. The stench turned my stomach.

Damian had his camera out and was filming the scene. Where we could, we stopped people and asked them, through our translators, to tell us their stories. One witness we met was an SPLA officer who had fought with the government forces before defecting to the south. He'd been a short distance away when the raid took place and had hurried back with his men to defend the market. Though he'd arrived too late to prevent the killing, he told us many of the raiders had been in army uniforms and that he'd recognized the leader as a northern commander.

The process of gathering evidence continued through the following week. Each day, after praying and asking God to lead us to the right people, we set off across the dry scrubland in a Land Rover provided by the SPLA to track down witnesses to the massacre. At each village, we'd sit with the elders under the village tree and hear their stories. Others would come and join us and contribute what they knew or had seen. Amid the tales of horror were moving accounts of slaves who had escaped; of enslaved Christian mothers who kept their faith and culture alive for the sake of their children; of parents and husbands who had travelled north to find their loved ones and made enormous financial sacrifices to buy them back.

Most of the villagers were Catholics and several of our meetings ended in a mass conducted by the local priest. These were a chance to pray with our Sudanese brothers and sisters and let them know that the church in other parts of the world had not forgotten them. Simply being there meant as much as the small amount of practical aid we were able to bring.

Even as we toured the area, other raids were taking place not far away. Though we were never attacked personally, the villagers we met lived in constant fear that they might be next.

After a week, we had enough notes, pictures and testimonies to make a powerful case to the press. Using our satellite phone, we called Trackmark and waited at Wun Rok airstrip for the Cessna to pick us up. Once back in Lokichokio, we found one journalist still in town writing up the Bahr El-Ghazal famine for the British press. This was Paul Harris, also known for his contributions to Jane's military publications. Our arrival gave him something of a coup. He knew nothing of the Wun Rok massacre and seized on our stories and pictures to file a story back to London.

We arrived home via Nairobi a couple of days later to find, on the front page of the *Daily Telegraph*, a picture I'd taken of Caroline Cox cradling a former slave girl on her lap. Alongside was Paul's account of the massacre as we'd related it to him. I bought a copy as we left Heathrow, amazed at how God had intervened to get our exposé into the press even before we arrived home.

A further trip to Sudan in June 1999 was organized with the help of Stephen Wondu, a tall, well-educated Dinka whom I'd met in Washington where he represented John Garang's SPLA. (He's now Southern Sudan's ambassador to Japan.) Stephen agreed to set up a meeting with the elusive Garang himself.

Flying in from Nyam Lell, another recently raided village near the El-Obeid to Wau railway, Caroline and I, along with Stephen and an SPLM adviser, landed on a remote strip near Sudan's border with Uganda – the co-ordinates known only to Stephen and the pilot. As we'd been ordered, we immediately camouflaged the Trackmark Cessna with branches to avoid detection from the air. Then we settled down to wait, swatting away the flies and wondering what would happen next.

After a couple of hours, a dozen or so SPLA commanders emerged from the scrub. They shook hands warmly, then sat in a circle on the ground, their Kalashnikovs balanced across their knees. Next we heard a vehicle revving through the bush and John Garang himself bounced into view in a Jeep bristling with armed bodyguards. He dismounted, greeted Caroline with a pumping handshake (they'd met on one of her previous visits in 1994) and squatted down among his commanders.

I was intrigued to be face-to-face at last with Sudan's legendary rebel leader. Garang was a Dinka, a big, bearded man with a bulky physique and obvious charisma. Proud, persuasive and articulate, he'd studied at Grinnell College in Iowa, gained a PhD in Agricultural Economics and later returned to the USA for military training. He carried his Bible wherever he went and consulted it often. By the time we met him, he'd spent sixteen years waging bush war against the government in Khartoum and would carry on for another six before peace was eventually signed.

Caroline began by reminding Garang of our interest in Sudan and how we wanted to gain an accurate picture of the war and the effect it was having on the population. In reply, Garang thanked us for making the journey. Not many Westerners were brave enough to visit his war-torn country, he said. He then described some of the SPLA's recent gains and losses and painted his vision of a united Sudan in which all citizens would enjoy equal rights. As he spoke, I could understand how this powerful personality had managed to unite so many quarrelling factions across the south and hold his alliance together for so long. I also warmed to his sense of humour. Christian Solidarity in the UK had recently split from its parent organization in Zurich and he laughed that he now had two Christian Solidarities to represent him. I agreed we were twins, but pointed out that we were not identical. It was a mild quip, but it tickled Garang and he flashed me a massive smile. "Reverend Windsor," he said, "you can be my pastor any time you like!"

Impressive as he was, Garang was nevertheless a complex and shadowy figure – Marxist as well as Christian and said to be brutal with anyone on his own side who disagreed with him. His SPLA was certainly guilty of atrocities, especially in the early stages of the war. All the same, I believe he'd have made an excellent leader of his country.

The fruits of his long campaign came with the peace agreement of 2005 which gave a measure of self-government to the south and installed Garang as Bashir's vice president. By then the civil war had claimed more than 1.5 million Southern Sudanese lives, either by violence or from starvation and disease. Over the same period, between 3.5 and 5 million were displaced from their homes and became either refugees or slaves.

Garang was vice president for just three weeks before being mysteriously killed in a helicopter crash.

Our 1999 trip also took us to the Nuba Mountains and the Blue Nile and Upper Nile regions on the Ethiopian border. The aim, as on our earlier visit, was to uncover evidence of human rights violations, show solidarity with the victims and deliver aid to areas not being reached by other organizations.

Landing in the Nuba Mountains was risky, both because the rains were about to begin and because government troops were known to be in the area. We disembarked as quickly as we could to allow the Cessna to take off again and were taken by local church leaders on a two-hour walk to the nearest village. Dinkas walk quickly with an easy, rolling gait that puts us shambling Westerners to shame. I remember my boots on this occasion being slightly too tight and my feet were raw and bleeding by the time we arrived.

But my own discomfort quickly vanished as we began to record the stories of people attacked and captured by northern forces. A small, frightened boy described how militia had raided his village and captured his family. His parents had been taken to Khartoum and he hadn't seen them since. He himself had ended up in one of the notorious peace camps where he was repeatedly beaten and tortured with cigarette burns before managing to escape. His body still bore the scars.

A young man called Kamis was ambushed by government soldiers while driving his cows and goats to market. He, too, was taken to a peace camp and tortured to make him confess to being an SPLA soldier. He spoke of seeing other prisoners having their toenails and fingernails pulled out and some even dying under torture. After two months in prison, he was sent to work as a forced labourer on a soldier's farm. One night he was able to escape and spent four days walking back to his village.

"Many civilians were forcibly converted to Islam," he told us. "If someone was a Christian, he was tortured, beaten and told, 'You should not be a Christian; you should become a Muslim.'"

"We're fighting to restore our dignity, to preserve our culture as Christians," added a veterinary surgeon called Abdul. "We are people of the Nuba Mountains and we want to keep our historic culture. If the Arabs destroy us, Sudan will become an Islamic country."

Further testimony came from Farouk, abducted by government soldiers while looking after his goats in the forest. After being beaten and burned, he was forcibly recruited into the government army to fight the SPLA. He reported seeing large numbers of Nubans and Dinkas in the same situation. Black African soldiers, he said, were always placed on the front line. Their officers referred to them as slaves and many died from harsh treatment and bad food.

It was moving to hear his gratitude at being able to tell his story. "Thank you very, very much for coming from so far away and for walking so far to find us here in the forest. All we ask is peace, education and the opportunity to develop ourselves."

It was here that we started to uncover evidence of the use of chemical weapons in the Nuba Mountains. According to local SPLA commanders, shells containing chemicals were being manufactured in El-Obeid. Witnesses had seen them being fired by modified artillery or dropped from Antonov bombers. They produced smoke that caused unusual respiratory diseases and killed off vegetation. Our post-trip report included a plea for the international community to put pressure on the government of Sudan to allow a full investigation of the chemical weapons claims. The possibility that Sudan had obtained its chemical weapons from Saddam Hussein's Iraq added further urgency to our request.

From the Nuba Mountains, our journey took us east to the village of Yabus in the Blue Nile region. There we met Malik, the local SPLA commander, who happened to be a Muslim but was clearly much loved by the Christians in the area. Malik had driven over 100 kilometres on a tractor to come and meet us, and he was able to update us on the military situation. Government forces, he said, had launched several massive assaults since the start of the dry season the previous November and for four months had besieged the SPLA garrison at Ulu near the border with Upper Nile. In a tough battle, the SPLA had broken the siege and put eleven government battalions out of action. Southern forces had since been consolidating their position in the Blue Nile region.

Yabus was a mixed Muslim–Christian community recently liberated by the SPLA and now strewn with tanks and trucks abandoned by the northern forces. As Malik showed us around, we came across several *tukuls* stacked high with guns, mortar rockets, grenades and shells left behind by retreating government troops. We took pictures that we later showed to the Ministry of Defence in London who were interested to see what kind of weapons the Sudanese government was using. They confirmed that these were NATO-standard armaments manufactured in China and were even able to identify which factory they'd come from.

At Malik's invitation, we agreed to make a ninety-kilometre journey north to the Ethiopian border and the village of Kurmuk where the SPLA was holding 140 prisoners of war. Even in the dry season (and this, being June, was the cusp of the wet season), it's a four- to five-hour drive through trackless bush and across thirty or so river-beds. We made a slow, bumpy journey (six hours in this case) in a truck provided by the SPLA and found the prisoners under guard behind bars in a mud-walled compound. We interviewed four of them. Two were southern Sudanese who'd been kidnapped on visits to the north and forcibly recruited. One of these – a young Nuba press-ganged while on holiday in Khartoum – had more evidence of chemical weapons. Every government battalion, he explained, included at least one officer responsible for such weapons. We asked him how he could be sure. "Because," he said, "they keep these munitions in a special place and put on masks and gloves to handle them."

Through the Red Cross, the SPLA had offered its prisoners of war back to the Sudanese government but the government didn't want them. For their part, the prisoners seemed more than happy to stay where they were.

While in Kurmuk, we visited a church-run medical compound responsible for the health of some 180,000 people in the southern Blue Nile region. Christian Solidarity had sent medical supplies to the centre the previous year. In a joint effort with Safe Harbor International, the mission arm of Calvary Chapels in the USA, we were now able to bring a further consignment. Among the patients we met soldiers injured by artillery shells and a nine-year-old goatherd who'd picked up a landmine and had his left arm and three fingers of his right hand blown off. With TB and malaria adding to the toll of war injuries, the handful of staff were doing magnificent work under intense pressure.

A highlight of the visit was a service at Kurmuk's ecumenical church. The pastor, Timothy Nyra, invited me to speak and handed me a Bible. I turned to a passage which has particular resonance for Christian Solidarity – the story of the prophet Jeremiah thrown into a pit and rescued by Ebed-Melech the

Cushite (Jeremiah chapters 38 and 39). I preach from it often on the basis that Ebed-Melech trusted in God, was informed about the fate of one of God's servants and took action to save him – not a bad summary of what Christian Solidarity seeks to do. I knew, too, that the biblical land of Cush from which Ebed-Melech came covered Ethiopia, parts of Egypt and Sudan. What I didn't know was that the version of the Bible from which I was speaking actually describes him as "Sudanese". It wasn't until I hit the word in the passage and a roar of delight went up from the congregation that I realized what a beautifully appropriate translation this was and silently thanked God for prompting me towards this passage.

I later asked various Sudanese Christians which parts of the Bible they felt held particular promise for their own country. In the same way that Iranian Christians refer to biblical Elam as meaning part of modern-day Iran and hold to the promise that God will restore its fortunes (Jeremiah 49:38–39), I wanted to know if and where they thought Sudan featured in the Bible. The answer, they told me, was Isaiah chapter 18 – a passage directed at Cush which ends with a prophecy of gifts being brought to the Lord "from a people tall and smooth-skinned… whose land is divided by the two rivers". Interpreting these as the White and Blue Nile and believing that all of Sudan will one day worship God, the country's hard-pressed Christians have drawn great strength and comfort from the Bible's promises.

The final leg of our June 1999 trip was to Ruweng County in the western Upper Nile region. In the month before our visit, 1,200 government forces had swept through a 100-kilometre swathe of the county, killing scores of civilians with Antonov bombers, helicopter gunships, artillery and tanks. A hospital, 17 churches and over 6,000 homes had been burned and hundreds of people had been abducted. The government had deliberately destroyed food stores and livestock, so survivors were now living in the bush without shelter, food or medical care. Thousands were facing a slow death from starvation.

Ruweng County borders the southern Sudan oilfields and the Khartoum government was about to begin pumping oil down a 1,600-kilometre pipeline to Port Sudan on the Red Sea coast. The revenue from the oil exports would be used to buy more military hardware to prosecute the war against the south. But the strategy depended on clearing the SPLA and the black Southern Sudanese from the areas surrounding the oilfields. As our own report later stated, "The presence of large oil reserves is a major factor in the government offensives designed to drive the indigenous African peoples from their lands and to claim these areas as Arab territory."

There was also a Chinese connection in that Chinese companies were involved in extracting the oil and China supplied the arms bought with the proceeds. To guard their installations, the oil companies had flown in thousands of Chinese nationals. A Dinka rebel commander told us that he and his forces had killed a number of these men in skirmishes around the Bentu oilfields and found that they were ex-prisoners released from Chinese jails.

Our report concluded:

> *The systematic destruction of life and community by the government of Sudan in the Nuba Mountains, Southern Blue Nile and Western Upper Nile which we witnessed on this visit as well as in other parts of Sudan demands strong action by the international community. Christian Solidarity therefore calls on the international community, and in particular the member states of the United Nations Security Council, to prevail upon the government of Sudan to cease hostilities against its own people.*

By the time we returned to Yabus for our final day and night before flying out, the wet season was almost upon us. On a sweltering, humid afternoon with the coming rains heavy in the air, our SPLA hosts took us walking in the bush to see a UN-chartered aircraft, a twin-engined Antonov AN28, that had crashed a few years before while taking off from the village airstrip. The UN fact-finding team had survived, so we were told, but the wreckage lay where it had landed – a forlorn symbol of the world's failure to stop the war.

Ten minutes into our return trip, our guide glanced up at the sky. "This is it, Stuart! Here comes the rain. Run!"

We pelted back to the village, arriving just as the rain dropped from the sky, drumming on the parched earth and turning everything to a sticky red morass. We made a cup of tea and sat on the veranda of our house while the slower members of the party limped in out of the rain. A sopping Caroline squelched onto the veranda and flopped into a chair. The Deputy Speaker of the House of Lords looked so bedraggled, we had to laugh.

Caroline had her revenge. Before we'd gone out, we'd been warned to fasten the flaps of our tents, front and back. I'd done the front of mine but not the back. When the rain eased off and we sploshed back to our tents, I found that mine had filled like a paddling pool – which Caroline thought was hilarious. "Serves you right for laughing at me!" she snorted.

But the tables turned again. As my blow-up mattress was unusable, our hosts somehow procured another tent and equipped it with a proper bed – and not just a bed but a mattress! This was a luxury I'd never known in Sudan and for one night I slept in almost total comfort.

Until, that is, I was woken in the small hours by a roar and a whoosh like a train blasting through the village. I spent the rest of the night wondering what this sudden sound could have been. It certainly wasn't a train. Nor was it traffic – there isn't any in Southern Sudan – and I knew it wasn't an aircraft. If I'd had to guess, I'd have said it was a waterfall, switched on for a few moments and just as suddenly switched off. It left me mystified.

When the village chief came by in the morning, he had a message. "Well, Pastor and Lady Cox, I've got good news. The aircraft is on its way to pick you up."

After a gruelling, sweaty week with nothing but wet-wipes to keep ourselves clean, this was good news indeed.

"I've also got bad news," he went on. "The river flooded during the night. And the airstrip is on the other side."

When we got down to the river-bank with our possessions, the sandy, bleached-dry bed of the day before had turned into a torrent some forty metres across. But the SPLA hadn't fought a sixteen-year bush war to be beaten by a river. Our host, the local commander, hoisted Caroline onto his shoulders and stepped out into the chest-high water. One of his men did the same for me (I was somewhat lighter in those days) and carried me over as I held my gear above my head.

Dignified it wasn't. But they got us over the river in time to meet the plane.

18

Haggling for Slaves

The buying back of slaves is a contentious issue. The argument is often made that it feeds the slave trade and puts money into the hands of raiders and slave-owners – money that could be used to buy arms and fund future attacks. Those involved have been fiercely criticized, not just by Sudanese government sympathizers who claim slavery doesn't exist in Sudan, but also by organizations such as Save the Children and Anti-Slavery International who believe slave redemption makes the situation worse.

We don't pretend there are straightforward answers. Redeeming slaves is a repugnant business and at Christian Solidarity we're well aware of the moral dilemmas it brings. The board, not surprisingly, has tended to be divided on the issue and eventually decided not to be involved. That said, Caroline Cox and I took the view in the 1990s that redemption is sometimes justified.

One reason is straightforward Christian compassion. A slave is a human being, made in the image of God. Turning anyone into an object to be owned and traded is surely the worst violation of the human spirit and one we cannot ignore. I believe we have a biblical responsibility to free the captive, trusting that God will take care of the bigger picture if we do what we can at the individual level. I never heard a rescued slave or a parent reunited with a freed child say that redemption was wrong – or that the longer-term risks outweighed the joy of a family reunited.

Our other reason for buying back slaves has been more pragmatic. The number we've redeemed as an organization is a few hundred compared to the thousands who've been carried into slavery during Sudan's civil war. The reason we've done it, apart from helping the victims where we can, has been to expose the practice of slavery and put pressure on Sudan's government to stop supporting it. That's why we always recorded and published the testimonies of the slaves we redeemed. The deterrent effect, we hoped, would be greater than any encouragement to make further raids.

Although Caroline had previously been involved in slave redemption with Christian Solidarity International in Zurich, our first such venture at Christian Solidarity in the UK was in February 1999. From my filming days I knew the team running a Christian TV programme called *100 Huntley Street*, broadcast from Toronto. The programme assistant was a Pentecostal pastor by the name of Cal Bombay. Born in Africa, Cal had a deep interest in Sudan and used his programme to raise funds to take tractors and other agricultural equipment into the Southern Sudanese district of Equatoria. Some of the money he raised was earmarked for redeeming slaves – which brought him into contact with our organization.

We decided on a joint trip to a remote part of Southern Kordofan, twenty miles from the front line and the government garrison at Abyei town. Although I planned the logistics, I wasn't able to go on this occasion. Instead, Caroline and two of our advocacy team, Elizabeth Batha and Tina Lambert, travelled with Cal and a party of Canadian, British and Australian journalists.

The area had been devastated by raids from the north –

roughly one a year for the previous sixteen years. As a result, 90 per cent of the population had fled their homes. Knowing that rebuilding would lay their villages open to more attacks, the people lived in the open and scratched a living as best they could. Despite the immense needs, Southern Kordofan appeared to be beyond the reach of international aid: nothing had got through since a single airdrop in 1996. So as well as redeeming slaves, we wanted to deliver much-needed medicines.

The local community had records of 634 individuals who'd been taken as slaves since 1994. Caroline and Cal were able to redeem 325 and left money to buy back any more who might be traced in the future. According to the Commissioner for Abyei County, a Christian called James Ajing Path, the financial help the team was able to bring was invaluable. For people who'd lost everything in the raids and had no cattle or money left to buy back their loved ones, a few dollars from the West represented the only hope they had of ever being reunited.

The delegation took testimonies from people who'd escaped or been redeemed. These built up a consistent picture of physical abuse, forced labour, harsh conditions and pressure on slaves to become Muslims. Freed slaves also described government troops as having been involved in their original capture and the destruction of their villages.

While in Southern Kordofan, Caroline and her team made contact with some of the Arab middlemen who made a living by tracing slaves in the north, securing their release and returning them, at a price, to their relatives. While they clearly had a financial motive, many also expressed sympathy for the victims and said they were in it to try to counter the evil effects of the slave trade. For their trouble, they risked the anger of the Sudanese government for exposing the lie that abduction and slavery didn't exist. We heard of several middlemen who'd been seized by government agents and never seen again. Within the complex morality of slave redemption, these were the people with whom we had to do business.

While the team was at work, the much-feared El-Obeid to Wau train passed through the district and the accompanying militia swept through the countryside, causing further misery and destruction.

Aware of unfinished work, we returned in August 2000. Arab militia had continued to spread terror in the intervening eighteen months while the Sudanese government added to the mayhem by attacking civilian targets with Antonov bombers. Our supporters had given generously for more slave redemptions and the media were increasingly interested in the story. At this point a Christian film producer called Paul Egglestone approached the BBC *Everyman* programme to see if they'd be interested in filming one of our missions. (Paul supported our work and was keen to see it covered by the mainstream media.) When *Everyman* responded positively, we decided to ignore official advice not to travel to Sudan and began planning another trip with a BBC film crew. This time I was able to go as well.

The trigger for action was news from Stephen Wondu, the SPLA's man in Washington, that Arab middlemen in Northern Sudan had rounded up a party of about 300 slaves and were preparing to walk them to Abyei County in the south from where they'd originally been taken. Stephen wanted to know if Christian Solidarity would be willing to redeem the captives when they reached their destination.

We said we would. The *Everyman* team filmed the preparations as Caroline and I got ready and I went with a colleague to collect the ransom money from a branch of NatWest Bank. They then recorded the staff at Christian Solidarity gathering round and asking God to bless our trip – the Chairman praying "not only for Stuart, but those going with him, that they'll be able to cope with him" (thanks, Mervyn!). The cameras continued to follow us as we checked in at Gatwick Airport for the flight to Nairobi.

My own luggage included the most valuable item of all – a battered black briefcase containing US$24,000 in 50-dollar and 20-dollar bills.

While flying into danger was nothing new for Christian Solidarity, the *Everyman* crew were obliged to go through the BBC's war zone training and what they saw and heard was enough to put them off the whole idea. To add to their concerns, the Khartoum regime had recently bombed a UN aircraft on the ground and the UN had responded by banning all flights into the south of the country. Faced with this health-and-safety nightmare, they filmed us as far as Gatwick and then stood down. To cover the rest of the trip, the producers had to borrow a team from the BBC's South Africa correspondent, Fergal Keane. Cameraman Roger Chapman and sound engineer Mark Hatch had worked in a variety of African trouble spots and were unfazed by dangerous missions. They flew up from Johannesburg and met us in Lokichokio near the Sudanese border.

The other members of the party included the *Everyman* producer and director, Nick Gray, and Paul Egglestone who'd first suggested the project and who came along as consultant producer. Also on the team was Andy Jacobson, the officer responsible for Christian Solidarity's aid projects. Andy had come to us from the Ministry of Defence and was invaluable in helping to plan the logistics. He'd recently returned from Sudan with more evidence of government atrocities including photos and video showing a Russian-built Antonov dropping bombs on a school. One had fallen on a class sitting under a tree, killing fourteen children and a teacher.

The trip followed the usual route via Nairobi to Lokichokio. There I made the mistake of spending too long in the toilet at the airfield (knowing you're not going to find another flush toilet for several days certainly concentrates the mind on seizing the last opportunity!). In my defence, I also wanted to make sure that everyone else had been before I took my turn. When I emerged and hurried across the tarmac to the waiting Cessna Caravan, the Trackmark pilot was clearly irritated at having to wait. The UN flight ban was making the next leg of the journey difficult enough and my dawdling hadn't helped. If Caroline hadn't made him wait, I think he'd have taken off without me.

In the event, he took off his headphones and refused to fly at all. I suspect he didn't want to go anyway and my being a nuisance provided the excuse. After a tense exchange, he ordered us off the plane and told us to make our own way to wherever the hell we wanted to go. Irritating as this was, we knew that the UN flight ban gave him the right to refuse to fly. We had no choice but to pick up our luggage and disembark.

It was not a happy moment. Stranded in remote Lokichokio with a film crew and no aircraft, Caroline, Andy and I gathered in a huddle and prayed for God to do something – anything – to get us on our way. Then, not knowing what else to do, we walked over to the Trackmark office and asked if we could use the phone to try to find another carrier.

The chances were slim. But that, I find, is when God acts. Despite an up-country phone line that crackled like a warthog rootling in a pile of twigs, we made contact almost immediately with someone who could help. A commercial Canadian crew just happened to be flying into Lokichokio in a twin-engined De Havilland Buffalo. They could be with us in a few minutes and were willing to fly us into Southern Sudan and back for £20,000, half of it payable up front.

God was stretching our faith. Against all the odds he'd provided a replacement flight, but we now had to pay for it. The Trackmark flights were covered by pre-arranged bank transfers from NatWest Bank in the UK. There was no such arrangement for unplanned flights like this and I certainly wasn't going to break into the $24,000 in my briefcase. I decided all I could do was phone my bank manager, the excellent John Mackenzie of

Barclays Bank, Walton-on-Thames. John was a busy man (he personally handled the accounts of some of the highest-paid stars at Chelsea Football Club) and I knew I was most unlikely to catch him at his desk.

Rather than use the crackly Trackmark phone, I thought I'd try with the marine satellite phone we'd brought with us. That meant unpacking it and swivelling the lid that contained the aerial to try to align it to where I thought the satellite should be – always a hit-and-miss affair. Eventually I found a connection.

As the phone rang in far-away Surrey, I shut my eyes and prayed. "Please let him be in."

He was.

"John," I said, still struggling with the signal, "I'm calling you from Lokichokio in northern Kenya."

"Uh, huh." John was a fellow church member and knew me well. I think he guessed there was an unusual request to come.

"I've got a problem," I continued. "I and my companions – we're marooned in the middle of Africa. I need to write a cheque from my personal account. Quite a large one."

"Oh yes? And how much would that be for?"

"Ten thousand pounds."

I sensed an intake of breath. "You haven't been kidnapped, have you?"

"No, it's not that. I have to pay for a flight into Southern Sudan."

"Southern Sudan? Where the civil war is? And the UN flight ban?"

"That's the one. Can you authorize it?"

"When do you need it?"

"Right now, if you could."

I shall always be grateful that John, sitting in his office in leafy Walton-on-Thames, instantly approved a £10,000 personal cheque from me to the pilot of the Buffalo on the understanding that Christian Solidarity would repay it into my account. As soon as the pilot showed up, I wrote him out a cheque and handed it over. Once satisfied it was sound, he was ready to fly.

Little more than an hour after being thrown off the Trackmark Cessna, the three of us plus the film crew, Stephen Wondu and a couple of other SPLA representatives who'd met us in Lokichokio were installed in the far more spacious cabin of the De Havilland Buffalo. It was still pretty basic – a few seats bolted to the floor behind the cockpit – but at least we had room to put our heads together and thank God for opening a way through yet another impossible situation.

Caroline had been a thorn in the side of the Sudanese government over many years and we knew they wanted her, dead or alive. (In 1994 they'd tried her in her absence and sentenced her to death.) There was no way they could know she was on this particular flight, but we couldn't take chances. Across 800 kilometres of no-fly zone, the pilot kept radio silence and flew low to avoid radar, all the time watching out for Sudanese missiles and fighters. As we circled to land at the prearranged Point Alpha in Abyei County in Bahr El-Ghazal, we could tell from the greenness of the vegetation that the wet season was well under way. The pilot would need all his skill to get down and away safely.

He made it with a few bumps and skids and taxied to a stop. "You've got three minutes," he yelled. "Anyone who's still aboard then is coming back to Loki!"

The surrounding woodland was already disgorging people who sprinted towards the plane with smiles and waves. As boxes were unloaded, they hoisted them onto their shoulders and carried them the short distance to Bahr El-Ghazal village. There, under a deal brokered by the SPLA, the Arab traders with their consignment of rescued slaves were waiting to do business.

The slaves had walked for three weeks from the north and had already been waiting five days for our own party to arrive.

Guarding them were eight well-armed, white-robed Arab middlemen, their faces swathed in their turbans to preserve their anonymity in case of reprisals when they returned north. The slaves sat listlessly under the trees, herded like goats to be haggled over in the last stage of their journey to freedom. A few metres away in the shade of one of the houses sat the relatives, agonizingly close to loved ones that in many cases they hadn't seen for years. Their patience was monumental.

The tension of the wait was captured in the BBC film. "I have seen my wife and son," said a man called Manut, speaking through our interpreter. It was four years since he'd lost them, his son only a baby at the time. The eyes in his gaunt, bearded face betrayed an immense sadness. "I've been told I must wait here until they're officially delivered to me. I'm not allowed to collect them."

A lady called Awel had lost her children in a raid two years ago. She told us what had happened. "While I was away fetching water, the Arab raiders attacked the village and everyone ran and hid. When I came back to the house, there were dead bodies all around. When I couldn't find my children among them, I knew they'd been taken by the raiders. I wanted to kill myself.

"But I can see them from here," she went on. "When I can go and get them, I'll run at them with joy as any mother would who's been separated from her children for such a long time."

Achchong had lost all eight of her children to the raiders and was frantic with worry. "Losing a child by abduction is a terrible thing," she told us. "Such a gift from God to be stolen from you by a stranger. It's the worst thing that can happen to you in your life. We pray a way can be found to stop those people who rob mothers of their sleep and happiness for the rest of their lives."

We moved from relative to relative, recording their stories. They were harrowing to hear and soon I was barely able to speak for emotion. I wanted to sprint across the few metres of sandy earth that separated relatives and slaves, to scoop up armfuls of lost children and bundle them back to their waiting parents. But I couldn't, any more than the relatives themselves. The dreadful business of recording and bargaining still had to take place. I found myself profoundly moved by the stoicism and dignity of those waiting on both sides of the sandy divide – and enraged at the callousness of those who had caused their misery.

As the sun set on our first day, it was clear that negotiations would have to wait until the morning. Before we put up our tents for the night, Caroline addressed the squatting slaves. "We know that you have suffered a terrible thing. You know and we know that slavery is a very bad thing. But we look forward to making friends with you tomorrow and hearing your stories."

Before the haggling began, we wanted to be sure that the people offered for sale by the middlemen had genuinely been abducted and enslaved. It didn't take us long to be absolutely certain that slavery was the right description for what these people had endured.

Nyan, aged twenty, was one of a party of women abducted in 1994 and beaten continually during a seven-day walk to the north. When they arrived they were distributed to different masters and raped repeatedly by their owners and the owners' relatives. The result was a child, now aged two. She'd called him Ayii ("Something Noisy") in memory of the anguish of his birth.

Ajok, nineteen, was force-marched from Abyei, barefoot and naked, and given to a man called Mohammed Issa in the town of Muglad. She told us: "I had to sleep on the floor in the kitchen and eat the leftovers. I had to work hard washing clothes and cleaning. I was forced to sleep with one of his sons and became pregnant. They wanted me to become a Muslim and tried to force me to go to the mosque, but I refused." She eventually escaped and spent nine days in the bush looking for traders to bring her home.

Madelina, also nineteen, had been a slave for four years. She'd been a schoolgirl in Abyei town and was travelling with other pupils to Muglad to sit exams when their lorry was stopped by Arab militia. The twenty-eight Dinkas on board were ordered off and taken. She was raped and became pregnant, but managed to escape and find a trader who took her to Khartoum where she gave birth. "Please tell the world about the hardships we're suffering," she pleaded.

Amona was eighteen when she was taken from the village of Ganga. "All the men and older boys were killed because the raiders believed that the boys would become soldiers." Amona was roped in a line behind a horse with sixteen other women, girls and young boys. The walk north took thirteen days, during which seven of the group who tried to escape were shot or hacked to death with machetes.

Kabissa, twenty-eight, described being caught in a surprise attack between Wun Rok and Turalei. "One of my sons, aged one and a half, was pounded to death in a wooden tub in front of my eyes. I was enslaved for about four years, kept in a cattle compound and never given enough food. An Arab raped me and I became pregnant. I gave birth in the cattle compound." She called the baby Mam, meaning "suffering".

Ajing, fifty, had been forced to work the land of his master, Mohammed Abdur Ahim. One day Mohammed beat him so severely he lost the sight in both eyes and was then good for nothing except cleaning the house. He and his young son were forced to live outside under a tree, eating only the scraps from Mohammed's table. "My owner said that their plan was to enslave the entire Dinka population and to occupy their land," said Ajing.

As we and the film crew recorded this inventory of suffering (and these are just a handful of the many stories we heard), I was particularly moved by a slight, timid-looking boy called Joseph who said he was nine years old – or so he thought. He sat on the ground in ragged khaki shorts, his face old before its time, and told how his owner had whipped and starved him and given him the Arabic name Taban, meaning "weak". His parents had been away from home tending their goats when he was captured and he hadn't seen them for two years. I think he touched a memory of mine, that of losing a mother at about the same age, and I found his story heartbreaking. As it happened, Nick Gray, the *Everyman* producer, had a nine-year-old son called Joseph and he, too, could barely contain his emotions at hearing the boy's story. Joseph said he hoped his parents would be there to meet him, but he hadn't seen them. If they weren't among the waiting relatives, he'd walk back to his home in Ganga village and keep looking for them.

Before the haggling began, Caroline and I squatted on two piles of bricks under a tree and prayed that the money in my briefcase would be enough to free all the slaves. The thought that some, even now, might be hauled back north because we'd run out of dollars was too painful to contemplate. The arithmetic was stark: with 300 slaves to be redeemed, we had to secure a price of $80 or less. With the translator and the two traders hunkering down beside us and the *Everyman* camera rolling, Caroline opened the bidding.

"We're happy to offer $50 because of the time and distance of your journey. So $15,000 for 300 women and children."

Back came the opening shot from the traders: "Tell the lady that every person we have delivered, we have bought for 1 million in Sudanese currency – that's $200."

This was a blow. We'd expected the traders to start high, but not this high.

Caroline stayed cool and shook her head. "We've never heard the figure of $200. The most we paid last time was between $50 and $60, and those were special circumstances. We cannot give more than a fair price. We know from some of the people we've spoken to that you did not buy every slave. Some escaped and came and found you, so they cost you nothing."

"Yes, but these people would not have arrived here without our help. And we had to feed them on the journey."

At this point the translator tallied up the numbers. Pointing at the traders in turn, he told us: "This man here has brought 180 slaves and this man 173." Not 300 slaves as we'd been led to believe, but 353. It became even more imperative to keep down the unit cost. Our maximum was no longer $80, but something under $70.

Caroline repeated her $50 offer, conceding that she'd pay the same amount for the extra 53. "That would bring the total to $17,650," she added. "Which is a lot of money."

The traders countered with a new claim. "Don't forget we had additional costs. We lost three camels on the journey. Does the lady have any idea what the price of a camel is?"

"Stuff the camels," I thought. "What about the kids?" While we pondered the absurdity of valuing a camel more than a child, the traders softened their stance. "We propose a compromise price of $75. But you must compensate us for the camels that died on the way. Let me remind the lady, the cost of a camel is $200."

In a slip of the tongue – either that or she hadn't heard properly – Caroline replied: "We hear what you say about losing your donkeys and are prepared, out of goodwill and for this time only, to give $55 for each person."

I could see the traders bristling. "Donkeys!" they hissed when the words were translated. "Let us be clear they were camels, not donkeys! And a camel is not cheap."

One of the village officials now leaned over and murmured to the traders that they ought to accept $60 per slave. The traders conferred and announced their decision. "This $60 is less than we wanted, but to make a deal we will accept, even though it doesn't cover our costs."

"We, too, accept," said Caroline. "But only because of the extra distance and time. That's the only reason we're prepared to give this very large sum of $21,180 for 353 slaves."

We stood up and shook hands. Then squatting down again, I clicked open my briefcase and counted out the money in $1,000 bundles into the hands of the traders. The slaves were at last free to go and they and their relatives streamed across the divide to seek each other out. I watched, close to tears, as Manut and Awel and Achchong and hundreds of others greeted their loved ones and led them away.

Manut's wife, Adol, had had her leg broken in captivity. His son, Deng, had a broken right arm that flopped uselessly at his side. Adol spoke to our film crew before the family went home: "No one treated our injuries. When I asked the Arabs to help us, they said they wouldn't waste medicine on an African. 'You're only a Dinka, so if you die it's not a problem.' We both suffered greatly. My redemption today is like being brought back from death and restored to life."

Awel hugged her children close. "I feel very happy now. I believe that God's love for me and my children has brought us back together. It has always been my prayer that they would one day return."

As for Achchong, she discovered six of her eight children among the slaves. The two oldest, it seemed, were still captive in the north. "Despite not having these two," she told us, "I'm so happy. Now we'll go home and share our joy together."

Amid the bustle I noticed Joseph, his young face clouded in anxiety as he realized his parents were not among the crowd. I knew that his village, Ganga, had been burnt down the previous year. My heart went out to him and I prayed he'd one day find his parents alive.

Once the deal was struck and the slaves freed, we had to leave as quickly as we could. We called the Canadian crew on our satellite phone and settled down under a tree for the two to three hours it would take for the De Havilland Buffalo to arrive from Lokichokio. At one point a drone overhead had us squinting into the sky. It turned out to be a government Antonov bomber, fortunately flying too high to notice anything unusual on the ground. It was a relief to hear the friendly engines of the Buffalo swinging in to collect us.

Back in Lokichokio, we transferred to a Trackmark Cessna flown by a young Kenyan and took off again for Nairobi. Although we'd escaped rain during our week on the ground, the clouds thickened as we flew south. Soon the rain was hammering on the canopy and the little Cessna was bucketing about in the turbulence. When the sky turned black and bolts of lightning sizzled past the wingtips, we realized we were flying through a thunderstorm. It was too late to go over or round: we simply had to grip our seats and hope our fragile aircraft would survive without being flipped over like a pancake.

The sky grew even darker. Through the howl of the storm I could hear the engine altering pitch, slowing, speeding, faltering again. I remembered gazing down on the Sudd swamp on my first-ever flight into Southern Sudan and hoping we'd glide if the engine failed. If it failed now, we'd be gliding nowhere. We'd be tossed through the air like a shuttlecock.

Nick Gray leaned across and yelled to make himself heard. "Stuart! I think it's time for one of your prayers!"

Then the pilot shouted back that he couldn't find Nairobi's Wilson Airfield. After battling the controls for a few more minutes, he managed to lock onto the international airport and knew that if he turned left just before arriving he'd find Wilson. It was a wonderful moment when we shot out into the sunlight to see Nairobi on the horizon. Though I've flown a great many flights in horrendous conditions, I think Lokichokio to Wilson Airfield at the end of our slave-redemption trip was the most frightening. The pilot admitted afterwards it was touch and go whether we'd get through.

Entitled "The Dangerous Adventures of Baroness Cox" and narrated by the journalist and former hostage, John McCarthy, the *Everyman* programme was shown on BBC television on 29 January 2001 and watched by an estimated 5 million people.

The following day I was flying out from Heathrow for the National Prayer Breakfast in Washington. Having checked in, I stopped at Wetherspoons for some breakfast and placed my briefcase on the floor. A young lady approached. "If you don't mind me asking," she said, "was that the briefcase you had in the programme – the one with the money for the slaves?"

I assured her it was.

"That was fantastic," she continued, and lightly touched the briefcase as if to share the adventure it had been through. Before I'd finished eating, several other people came up and said they'd watched the programme. One or two handed me money for the work to continue.

Over the following weeks, letters and donations poured in from people who had seen the programme. It was heartening to see its impact in bringing the plight of Sudan's slaves to the outside world.

My last trip to Sudan was in February 2006 with Caroline and our Malawian officer for sub-Saharan Africa, Dr Khataza Gondwe. This was a few months after the signing of the peace agreement between the Sudanese government and the SPLA. Under John Garang's successor, Salva Kiir, Southern Sudan now enjoyed a degree of autonomy and the promise of a referendum in 2011 on whether to become fully independent. It's a measure of the changes that instead of flying in covertly from Lokichokio, we were able to catch a scheduled flight into Southern Sudan from Kampala.

Our main contact this time was Bishop Maban, a Sudanese

Presbyterian minister in Yei near the Uganda–Zaire border who'd been a chaplain to the SPLA during the war and was now doing wonderful work building clinics and schools in this deprived region. We asked him what he thought had most contributed to the SPLA's success. His answer was clear.

"At the start of the war, the SPLA troops were undisciplined and unethical in their conduct. They were carrying out atrocities, just as the north was, and the war was going badly. So we chaplains spoke to John Garang and all the senior commanders and told them that unless they repented before God and asked for forgiveness, they'd never win the war. We had a big meeting to pray and ask for forgiveness. From that time on the war swung in favour of the south."

Despite the relative peace, tensions remain – mainly to do with the sharing of oil revenues and President Bashir's creeping Islamization of Southern Sudan by changing the names of rivers and villages and encouraging Arabs to settle further south, especially in oil-rich Abyei, in order to swing the result of the 2011 referendum. Since the agreement, the International Criminal Court has issued an arrest warrant for Bashir on charges of war crimes in Sudan's Darfur region. In the warrant he's accused of "intentionally directing attacks against an important part of the civilian population of Darfur… murdering, exterminating, raping, torturing and forcibly transferring large numbers of civilians and pillaging their property".

Some things, it seems, have not changed. Substitute Bahr El-Ghazal for Darfur, and that's more or less a description of Bashir's tactics against the south during the civil war. Yet still he walks free while thousands of slaves are thought to remain in captivity.

Christian Solidarity continues to monitor the situation.

19

Nigeria: the Advance of Islam

"If you survive, tell my brothers I died well and am living with Christ. And if we all die, we know that we die for the Lord!"

These words were spoken by Pastor George Orji in a dusty compound in the northern Nigerian town of Maiduguri. The date was 27 July 2009. A violent Islamic faction called Boko Haram – the name means "Western education is a sin" – had launched an offensive against police and Christian targets in the north-eastern states of Borno and Yobe. Intent on imposing Islamic Sharia law, Boko Haram had already burned down twelve churches and killed at least 150 people in two days of bloodshed. By the time the rampage ended a couple of days later, the teaching hospital in Maiduguri was reporting a thousand bodies piled up in its morgue.

In Maiduguri, the militants rounded up a group of some 250 Christians. If they didn't recant their Christianity, they told them, the women would be used as human shields against the military as Boko Haram prepared to fight to the death. As for the pastors in the group, they would be beheaded.

According to eyewitnesses, George Orji had no need to be in

the compound but had come to look for his wife. Seized by the militants, he encouraged the group to remain faithful. "Never give up," he urged. "Stand for Christ." At that point his fellow pastor, Sabo Yakubu, a father of seven, was hacked to death and his heart torn from his chest. George Orji continued singing and praying and speaking to his executioners about the love of Jesus.

His final plea was addressed to his fellow Christians: "Tell my brothers I died well."

Moments later, the Islamists cut his head off.

Nigeria is home to a large and vibrant Christian community that has grown spectacularly in the last half century. In the southernmost states, Christians make up an estimated 80 per cent of the population. In the north, however, the situation is reversed, with Muslims accounting for over 90 per cent. In the country overall, Christians and Muslims exist in almost equal numbers.

At present, the country's constitution is secular and guarantees freedom of religion for all Nigerians. Nonetheless, the country's thirty-six states have considerable autonomy to frame their own legislation. In recent years, twelve Nigerian states have introduced Sharia law to consolidate their Muslim identity and to increase the pressure for the whole of Nigeria to become Islamic. If nineteen states succeed in introducing Islamic law, they'll form a majority. It will then be possible to change the constitution to make Nigeria officially Muslim. This is more than just a possibility: it's the declared Muslim agenda.

In seeking to create an Islamic state, Nigeria's Muslims enjoy the moral and financial support of countries such as Saudi Arabia, Libya, Egypt, Sudan and Iraq. Saudi Arabia bankrolls development agencies that target their aid at Muslims and those converting to Islam. When Sharia was introduced in Gombe – one of the first states to take this step – the ceremony was attended by the Saudi ambassador whose staff handed out free burkas to local women. At Christian Solidarity we've heard reports from former Muslims that money given by Saudi Arabia has been used to buy and destroy huge quantities of Bibles. There's clearly a co-ordinated and well-funded international strategy to bring Nigeria into the Islamic fold.

Although Christians, in theory, are not bound by laws designed for Muslims, their freedoms have been severely curtailed in Nigeria's Sharia states. As in Pakistan, it's hard for Christians not to fall foul of the Islamic code. If converts from Islam face the death penalty and Christians are constantly vulnerable to charges of blasphemy from malicious neighbours or zealous officials, there's no way they can practise their faith freely. In many northern states, there appears to be a process of attrition designed to make life as difficult as possible for the Christian community.

A case in point is the closure and demolition of city-centre churches. As a result, by 2003, there were no churches left in the central areas of Kaduna, Kano and Bauchi. Churches further out from the centre are then frequently targeted by violent mobs, widening the church-free cordon and pushing Christian congregations out to the suburbs and the surrounding countryside. Disturbingly, the militants involved are often better armed than the police and are known to include foreign mercenaries. In attempting to rebuild their ruined churches, or extend existing ones, Christians are often thwarted by the fact that all religious buildings have to be registered. In many cases, permission is simply refused.

With Islamists determined to introduce Sharia law and the church equally determined to resist, Nigeria's Christians have agonized over how to respond. Pastor Victor Musa, a former leader of the Evangelical Church in West Africa, put it to me this way when I met him in Jos: "How many times must we turn the other cheek? We turn this cheek and they slap it. We turn the other and they slap it. We turn the first one and they slap it again. Do you think we're being stupid?"

Goaded by attacks on their property and communities, many Nigerian Christians have seen no option but to take up violence themselves. Before we condemn them for doing so, we need to understand how isolated and vulnerable they often feel. As Pastor Musa continued: "They destroy our churches, they burn our homes, they kill our pastors. What in God's name does the church in the West expect us to do if they don't come and help us?"

It was against this background that Caroline Cox and I travelled to Nigeria in March 2000. Five months previously, Zamfara in north-western Nigeria had become the first state to adopt Sharia law and a handful of other states had followed suit. But in February 2000, the process was halted and Sharia law suspended after religious riots in Kaduna killed more than 200 people.

Christians in the north might have gained a breathing space, but tensions were still high and the Islamization of Nigeria was a live and urgent issue.

Our purpose in travelling was to show solidarity with Nigerian Christians, discuss the situation with Christian and Muslim leaders, investigate the Kaduna riots and hold a meeting, we hoped, with the newly elected Nigerian president, Olusegun Obasanjo. With us was Christian Solidarity board member, Sam Solomon, a scholarly, full-bearded, Arabic-speaking Egyptian who qualified in Sharia at Cairo University before converting to Christianity. A world expert in Islamic law, Sam was to prove invaluable in our discussions with Muslim leaders and in helping Christians to understand the Muslim agenda.

The violence in Kaduna had broken out four weeks before our visit when Christians marching to Government House to demonstrate against the imposition of Sharia law had been attacked by Muslim fundamentalists. Homes, shops, businesses and churches were torched. The Christians retaliated, destroying a number of mosques. Killings continued on both sides until the army and state police restored order.

It soon became clear that the initial attacks were pre-planned. A week before the riots, the police commissioner, a Muslim, had transferred all his senior Christian officers out of Kaduna and replaced them with lower-ranking Muslim policemen, some of whom were later seen taking part in the riots. In many cases, Christians arriving at their places of work on the day the riots began found their Muslim colleagues absent – obviously forewarned of what was about to happen.

Foreign hands were also in evidence. During our interviews in Kaduna, we heard reports that President Gaddafi of Libya had sent 300 armed troops to Nigeria the previous month. Exactly why was not clear, but links to the riots could not be ruled out. It also emerged that rockets and rocket launchers had been found in the house of one of the Muslim ringleaders. Where they had come from was never explained.

One of our Kaduna contacts, Saidu Dogo of the interdenominational Christian Association of Nigeria (CAN), spoke of seeing the police directing rioters towards his home and shots being fired at his house. When he was arrested five days later, he saw Muslims whom he knew had been involved being sent home from the police station without charge.

Our hosts in Kaduna took us to inspect the damage. Picking our way through the Christian quarter, we saw burnt-out homes and churches and the wreckage of the Baptist Theological Seminary. Many of Kaduna's Christian leaders were distraught at what had happened. Still determined to resist the march of Islam, they grieved at the breakdown in relations and were ashamed that Christians had taken part in the violence.

"The Muslims will try again to take control of Nigeria," said Kaduna's Anglican bishop, Josiah Fearon. "They won't stop until they've achieved Sharia." He added that 300 Anglicans had lost their homes and everything they owned. Seven Anglican buildings had been destroyed and eighteen church members murdered. Despite the suffering within his community, his mind was on reconciliation. "My goal is to create an atmosphere of peace so that I can continue to share the gospel. I'm willing to be challenged in my witness by the Muslim if he so desires, but I must be free to do it."

Given that part of Christian Solidarity's mission is always to understand the opposing point of view, Caroline, Sam and I held a meeting with the imam of Kaduna's central mosque. A sharp, articulate man in his thirties, Imam Muhammed Murayn Ashref spoke excellent English and surprised us all by quoting a large chunk of Isaiah 43 from memory. He was also robust in defending the efforts of Nigeria's Muslims to implement Sharia law and their determination to see it extended not just in Nigeria but elsewhere in Africa. Sitting with him on the floor in the traditional manner, we raised the issue of the UN Convention on Human Rights, notably Articles 18 and 19 that deal with freedom of worship. How, we asked, did the UN Convention apply to Christians in Muslim states?

"It may suit the West," replied the imam. "Here in Africa, we Muslims have our own definition of human rights – one that includes the right to live under Sharia law."

"That's fine for Muslims," we countered. "But what about Christians who don't want to live under Sharia law?"

"They have nothing to fear," said the imam with a smile. "Christians must accept the word of Muslims that those living in Sharia states will not be adversely affected."

Having seen how Christians were suffering in similar circumstances in Pakistan, we found his promises far from reassuring.

The same trip took us to the capital, Abuja, for our planned meeting with President Obasanjo. Trained at Aldershot in the

UK, Obasanjo was a career soldier who became Nigeria's military head of state in 1976. Three years later he handed over to a democratically elected civilian – the first Nigerian leader ever to leave office voluntarily. In the 1990s he spoke out against the dictatorship of President Sani Abacha and was thrown into jail for his trouble. Released after Abacha's sudden death in 1998, he announced he'd become a born-again Christian, stood in the 1999 election and became president a second time.

Obasanjo was criticized by many Nigerian Christians for not doing enough to stop the spread of Sharia. In the aftermath of the Kaduna riots of February 2000, the Nigerian Catholic bishops condemned him roundly. "It is the duty of government to ensure law and order," they wrote. "The tragedy could have been avoided if government had heeded our warning. Even now it is not too late for government to take vigorous action to halt this mad rush to national suicide."

Obasanjo was not immune to the criticism. "What happened in Kaduna is a shame to all of us and we have all sinned," he said at the scene after the riots. "We must all pray and seek forgiveness." He and his council of thirty-six state governors then voted to suspend the adoption of Sharia, granting Christians in the north at least a temporary respite.

We arrived in Abuja on a Saturday evening. On the Sunday we met one of Obasanjo's chaplains, Bishop William Okuyi, who escorted us to the morning service at the president's residence. His chapel was still being built, so the worship took place in the presidential gym. The congregation came from different fellowships and denominations in Abuja and included several cabinet ministers and their wives, along with diplomats and senior civil servants. Obasanjo himself, a large, bespectacled man in flowing Nigerian robes, sat at the front and led the intercessions for the nation.

We then joined the president and some of his other guests for lunch. He welcomed us warmly and offered to meet us privately once lunch was over. This was our chance to voice concerns about the spread of Islamic extremism and to urge support for Christian freedoms in the north. Under vigorous interrogation from Caroline, Obasanjo replied that he preferred to delegate the northern issue to his Muslim vice-president rather than interfere himself.

Tragically, in 2002, Kaduna erupted again.

The background was the 2002 Miss World competition, scheduled to take place in Abuja. The contestants were under pressure to pull out even before they arrived. In the northern state of Katsina, an Islamic court had sentenced a young woman to death by stoning for bearing a child out of wedlock after she was raped. Campaigners around the world had taken up Amina Lawal's cause and were urging a boycott of the competition. With Miss World already making headlines, many Nigerian Muslims opposed the event for very different reasons. Not only was it an affront to conservative ideas of female modesty, it would also be taking place in the holy month of Ramadan.

The touch-paper was lit when a young, female journalist wrote in an article in Nigeria's *This Day* newspaper that the Prophet Mohammed would probably have enjoyed the contest and might have married one of the contestants.

Four days later, Muslims in Kaduna attacked and burnt the local office of the newspaper in protest at the article. The violence spiralled as rival gangs of Muslims and Christians took to the streets. Troops and police responded in force. By the time the bloodshed subsided three days later, 120 churches had been burnt down and the number of dead stood at over 200, all but a handful Christian. Those murdered included four clergymen – a Catholic priest, a Pentecostal pastor, a Methodist minister and a Baptist pastor.

The Methodist, we were later told, had left Kaduna on 20 November, the day before the riot, to visit members of his church. The following day he returned to town with two friends in a taxi driven by a sympathetic, moderate Muslim. As they approached the outskirts, they were stopped at a barricade by a crowd wielding knives and sticks. One of the ringleaders gestured to the driver to wind down his window and asked if there were any Christians in the car.

The driver's first thought was to protect his passengers. "Oh no," he replied. "We're all good Muslims in here."

He was about to drive on when the minister corrected him. "Excuse me, Sir," he said to the ringleader. "I am a Christian."

The mob hauled him out of the car and murdered him on the pavement.

Six weeks later in January 2003, Caroline, Sam and I were once again on our way to Nigeria to visit centres recently targeted by Islamic militants – not just Kaduna but also Jos, Kano and Bauchi. Our aim, as on the previous visit, was to show solidarity with persecuted Christians, investigate the violence with the help of first-hand testimonies and interview religious leaders, both Christian and Muslim. This time we had a further objective. With life becoming increasingly perilous for northern Nigerian Christians, we wanted to set up an affiliated organization in Nigeria to monitor the state of persecution at close hand.

In Kaduna we were guests of CAN, the Christian Association of Nigeria whose local chairman was Saidu Dogo. He and his team briefed us on the events of 21 November 2002, claiming that the attacks on Christians had been deliberate and systematic. That day, they told us, there were very few Muslim teachers or students in the schools. The police and army, who could have quelled the violence at an early stage, were unusually slow to respond. Muslims arrested after the riot had been sent to the Sharia court for trial and were later released because no Christians would venture into the court to testify against them. In contrast, the twenty-eight Christians arrested had been brought before the civil magistrate's court and were still in jail facing serious charges.

We then toured Kaduna to see the damage. This was heart-breaking: we'd done exactly the same less than three years earlier. At each point on the route, we recorded testimonies from the victims.

Pastor Sam Kujiyat, Saidu Dogo's vice chairman at CAN, showed us his gutted church. His expensive audio and video equipment had been looted and the church photocopier, too heavy to move, had been torched. He had hurried down to the church when the riots began and found it already destroyed. As he stood in the smoking ruins, a rioter with a knife had sprung at him from the shadows and pinned him down. The assailant raised his weapon to plunge it into Sam's chest. Sam prayed a lightning prayer and the man found himself transfixed. By a miracle, said Sam, he wasn't able to strike the blow. Three times he tried before giving up and running away. Tears in his eyes, Sam thanked us for coming to share the church's suffering.

A man called Danjuma reported seeing vehicles on the move on the morning of 21 November and asking a Muslim colleague what was happening. "You'll soon know," was the reply. He then saw groups of Muslims carrying knives and chanting, *"Alla-u Akbar"* ("God is great"). He hurried home to alert his family. He was helping his 70-year-old mother out of the house when the mob broke in and set it ablaze. His brother was murdered and his body thrown down a well. Another occupant of the house had his hand and head cut off. The mob, said Danjuma, included his own neighbours. When he reported what had happened to the police, one of the attackers was arrested but later released. All the police had done otherwise was advise him to forget the whole incident.

We spoke to a Christian schoolteacher called Marwi. On the day of the riots, he'd arrived at his school and found most of his Muslim colleagues absent. Within minutes, he heard the chant of *"Alla-u Akbar"* and a crowd came into view with machetes and iron rods. He left swiftly to collect his children and tried to find a taxi to escape the area. With none available, the family tried to flee on foot. On the way they saw a mob of about 300 attacking a man in his twenties. They poured a can of petrol over him, set him alight and burnt him alive. The crowd then recognized Marwi as a Christian and turned on him. Slashed on the wrist with a knife (he showed us the scar), Marwi sprinted away with his children. "Christ gave me speed," he commented. He managed to escape, but his home was destroyed.

Similar testimonies emerged elsewhere in Kaduna and in other towns affected by the violence. In Jos, Bishop Benjamin Kwashi and his team described an attack just six days earlier that had claimed the life of the vice-president of the Church of Christ in Nigeria (COCIN, a sister organization to CAN). Altogether, the attackers in this case had killed fifteen Christians. The police had been unable to stop them because their weapons were no match for those of the militants.

In the mixed Muslim–Christian village of Kassa, not far from Jos, we heard how a well-armed gang, including mercenaries who could have been from Chad or Niger, had targeted Christian homes in a surprise attack the previous October. Hearing the commotion and the cries of *"Alla-u Akbar"*, the Christians ran into the bush. Five died as shots were fired and houses set on fire. Some villagers drove to the nearest police station, thinking they'd be safe there. The police, however, were outnumbered and outgunned and fled as the attackers approached. All the cars in the police compound were set alight and gutted.

As on our previous visit, we wanted to hear the Muslim side of the story. In a room adjoining the main mosque in Kaduna, Caroline, Sam and I sat cross-legged on the floor to interview the senior imam and some of his elders. Imam Bakar began the proceedings in Arabic, apologizing for his complete lack of

English and looking to Sam to translate.

Sam, who looks like a mullah, clearly made an impact with his knowledge of Islamic law. In previous interviews with Muslim leaders, we'd heard him referred to as *galalltak*, a name reserved for esteemed scholars. We could see the elders nodding and agreeing whenever he spoke.

The imam explained he had no knowledge of what lay behind the recent riots but thought they might have been caused by unemployed young people. Certainly no one from his community had been involved – and any that were would be guided onto the right path through the mosques. As far as the judicial process was concerned, the imam confirmed that a few Muslims were still in prison after the riots. Any that were guilty would receive fair treatment in the Sharia courts. When we asked why so many Christians were still being held, he replied that they could have been charged or freed more quickly if they'd gone through the Sharia courts instead of the civil system. In practice, though, no Christian would ever choose to be tried under Sharia law.

After about an hour, the imam looked at his watch. "I'm very sorry, but I have to go," he said in perfect English.

His alleged lack of English was a minor deception, but it cast doubt on the trustworthiness of his testimony. And the issue of deception came up again when we spoke to the chief registrar of the Sharia court in Kano. He repeated several times that a good Muslim must never cheat a Christian. Sam, quoting the Koran, pointed out that Muslims did have permission to deceive in pursuit of their cause. The registrar was forced to backtrack. Under Sam's probing, he agreed it was acceptable Islamic practice to cheat Christians in any way that would advance the Muslim faith. By the same token, any promises or reassurances given to Christians could be broken with moral impunity.

So much, we thought, for all those assurances that Christians had nothing to fear from Sharia law.

Our interviews with Muslim leaders in Kaduna, Kano and elsewhere produced a number of consistent themes. It was clear that there was indeed a Muslim agenda to Islamize Nigeria's constitution; that Muslims were duty-bound to establish Sharia wherever possible; and that Nigerian Christians in the future, while not technically subject to Sharia, would have to accept the status of *dhimmi*, becoming second-class citizens with fewer legal rights than their Muslim neighbours.

Our Muslim interviewees also defended the strategy of expelling Christian congregations from city centres and refusing permission to rebuild wrecked churches. They told us it was inappropriate and undesirable for churches to be built near mosques, not least because the sound of their worship was offensive to Muslims. Furthermore, as Sharia became the dominant legal system, it was unreasonable for Christians to expect redress for churches that had been destroyed or to seek permission to rebuild on the same sites.

Our 2003 trip sowed fresh fears for the future of Nigeria's Christians. At the same time, we saw much to inspire us in the faith and heroism of individual Christians and sign after sign that God was at work on behalf of his church.

If we ever doubted that God was in control, our experience on an empty road between Kaduna and Abuja was a powerful corrective.

Caroline, Sam and I were travelling in a car driven by our trip co-ordinator, Edwin Ringwat, who was also the head of corporate relations for the Governor of Plateau State. We were hurrying to Abuja to catch a plane to Lagos to connect with a British Airways flight home. Caroline was due to speak in the House of Lords as soon as we returned, so we couldn't afford to be late. The car was a Honda Accord with about 130,000 miles on the clock. The previous day I'd asked Edwin if it had ever been serviced and he'd laughed.

About 100 kilometres south of Kaduna the inevitable happened. We began hearing an ugly and unwelcome noise in the region of the back wheels. We tried to ignore it, but it grew steadily worse. Soon we realized this was one sick car and we weren't going to make it to Abuja any time soon. Edwin pulled over. Caroline and Sam were asleep in the back, so Edwin and I got out to see what was wrong. On both back wheels we found oil leaking from the hubs.

"It's the wheel bearings," I said helpfully. "They've gone. We won't be going anywhere."

There's not much between Kaduna and Abuja and the spot where we'd broken down was possibly the emptiest stretch of all – nothing but flat, deserted scrubland as far as we could see. No traffic. No signs of habitation other than a cluster of mud huts a little distance from the tarmac. The only sounds were the buzzing of the flies and a slow, rhythmic creak. Some fifty metres away, three teenage boys in ragged clothes swayed listlessly on a makeshift swing slung beneath a tree.

By now Caroline and Sam had emerged and we explained the problem.

"What on earth are we going to do?" asked Caroline.

The answer was obvious. We gathered in a huddle and prayed. "Lord, you can see the fix we're in. You know we have a flight to catch. It's an awful long way to Abuja. You know we depend on miracles and now we could really, really do with one. Please help us."

"Please open the boot, Sir."

Surprised at this interruption, we stopped praying and looked up. The three boys from the swing stood respectfully in front of us.

"Pardon?"

"We've come to help. Please open the boot."

Edwin flipped up the lid. Without a word, the boys pulled out the tools and began jacking up the rear of the Honda like professional mechanics. All we could do was stand and watch and wonder what would happen next. Off came the wheels, and the youngest boy was dispatched to one of the nearby huts. He disappeared inside and emerged a moment later with a cardboard pack.

I couldn't believe what I was seeing. In the middle of the Nigerian bush, this young lad had managed to lay his hands on a brand-new pair of wheel bearings for a Honda Accord.

The boys hadn't finished. They replaced the bearings, refitted the wheels, lowered the jack and stowed the tools tidily in the boot.

"Lord, I know we asked for a miracle," I breathed in amazement. "I didn't expect it this quick!"

For a few moments we remained speechless, our jaws hanging foolishly as we struggled to comprehend what we'd just seen. I was about to ask how this had happened – how the exact wheel bearings we needed had ended up in a mud hut at precisely the point where we broke down – when the youngest boy announced he had something to say.

"My name is Godwin," he said, rubbing his calf with the sole of his foot like a shy child.

"It would be!" I thought, my mind turning to the three angels who visited Abraham in the book of Genesis. Had I just met the second angel in my life?

It turned out Godwin was a real boy with a real problem. "That hut there is my home," he continued. "My mother and father are dead and I live there with my aunt. But she's very poor and she can't afford to send me to school. Master..." – this was directed at me on account of my white hair – "please will you educate me?"

I couldn't refuse. We'd seen enough to know that God was in this situation, so the four of us made a pact that we'd somehow make it possible for Godwin to go to school. We didn't know how, but we knew we had to do it.

Back in the UK (yes, we did make our flight home), I was preaching the following Sunday at West Thurrock Brethren Chapel in Essex and told the story of Godwin and the miraculous provision of a set of Honda wheel bearings. I also described the pact we'd made to get him educated. As I was leaving, one of the elders handed me a cheque for Christian Solidarity. With it was a brown envelope containing £300 and a note to say that this was for Godwin's schooling.

Three days later I had a call from Edwin Ringwat in Nigeria. After dropping us at Abuja Airport, he'd gone back and traced Godwin at his home. He'd already made arrangements for Godwin to start school, but he now needed to find the first year's fees.

"How much are we talking?" I asked.

"In sterling," said Edwin, "that would be about £300."

So Godwin had his wish. The church's money covered his first year at school and Sam Solomon made separate arrangements after that.

Incidentally, I never did discover how a brand-new set of Honda wheel bearings came to be stored in Godwin's aunt's hut on the Kaduna–Abuja highway. It remains a mystery to this day.

One other result of our visits was the setting up of Christian Solidarity Worldwide Nigeria in Abuja. Launched in 2007, it's headed by Dr Solomon Lars, an eminent Christian politician and General Secretary of the Christian Association of Nigeria (CAN). The board includes a number of national figures including Archbishop Benjamin Kwashi. The office continues to monitor incidents of violence and the state of persecution throughout the country. Its mission has been well summed up by Archbishop Kwashi: "When a Muslim is touched, all Muslims respond. Whenever a Christian is attacked, there must be one voice. This is what Christian Solidarity is trying to do."

The 2009 martyrdom of Pastor George Orji and the bloodshed in Jos in 2010 are evidence that Nigeria's Christians continue to face persecution. As Sam Solomon constantly reminded the suffering Nigerian church, Islam is all-embracing for its followers. It affects every part of life from religion and politics to law and economics. It teaches that the whole earth is a mosque and that all the prophets, including Jesus, were Muslims. From the time of Mohammed, the Muslim agenda has been to establish a world religion with a single caliphate or system of governance under which Muslims will dominate non-Muslims. In the face of such an absolutist creed, events unfolding in Nigeria are part of a continuing and predictable pattern.

With the country a prime target for world Islam, Archbishop Kwashi has called on Nigerian Christians to act in a spirit of forgiveness and not to seek revenge. Meanwhile Sunday Ola Makinde, the Methodist Archbishop of Abuja, has appealed for help from the West. As he told Christian Solidarity, "We need your support to keep Christianity. Please educate the world about the plight of Christians in Nigeria."

Like their Sudanese brothers and sisters who also face persecution from the north, Nigeria's Christians form a strategic line of defence against the march of Islam within Africa and are paying a heavy cost for their stand. If Nigeria and Sudan were both to become Islamic states, other countries could follow and the future of Christian Africa could be in peril. Now, more than ever, it's essential for Christians in the West to pray, speak out and stand in solidarity with the persecuted African church.

20

Adventure of Faith

At the time of writing, I've been UK National Director of Christian Solidarity for seventeen eventful years. As retirement looms, my thoughts turn frequently to that scary moment in May 1993 when I first sat down at my overflowing desk in Witney and prayed to know which of the many calls on my time I should answer first.

It was then, you'll remember, that Susanna, my assistant, handed me a fax announcing the release of three house-church leaders in Vietnam. The timing, it seemed to me, was God's confirmation that I was indeed in the right place at the right time and that under his guidance we'd see more captives freed in the years to come.

This was a huge encouragement, but it didn't answer the question of where to start in an organization consisting of myself and Susanna. So I threw myself at everything. While the unflagging Susanna continued to write our bi-monthly prayer digest, I took over the editing of *Response* magazine which went to the 7,000 supporters on the Christian Solidarity database. Together we researched cases of persecution, put out press releases, maintained the database, organized exhibitions and speaking tours and tried to broaden our links with UK churches.

With Ethel still in Widnes, I lived during the week in a bed &
breakfast close to the office and worked every available moment.
Fourteen-hour days were the norm rather than the exception.
When possible I drove home to Widnes on a Friday evening, but
sometimes, for weeks at a time, the weekends would be taken up
with speaking engagements around the UK or missions abroad
to Moscow or Nagorno Karabakh. Not for the first time in my
life, I was hugely grateful for the patience and understanding of
Ethel and the family.

By my second year I'd had more than enough of bed
& breakfast living and moved in with Ethel's sister, Sue, and
her husband, Fred, who offered me a home at Hucclecote in
Gloucestershire, some forty minutes' drive from Witney. Life
there was a lot pleasanter, but it meant more time travelling
to and from the office. Also eating into the time was the fact
that more of our work was now in London with frequent visits
to Parliament to speak to MPs and peers. A trip to the capital
meant parking at Oxford Station and taking the train, all of
which took up most of the day in travelling.

The answer, in November 1995, was to move our office
from Witney to New Malden in south-west London. The family
home was still in Widnes, so I took up lodgings in Surrey with
a couple called Spencer and Grace Nash whom I'd got to know
through Zilla Harrod and her friend Esther – these being the
two ladies who'd caused consternation at Charles de Gaulle
Airport by asking the passengers if they were the ones God had
told them to find.

As Caroline and I carried out more missions to Nagorno
Karabakh and the *Nasha Semya* foster-care project began
to get off the ground in Moscow, the organization became
better known and was able to take on more staff. In 1996 we
appointed Dr Simon Qadri, an Indian convert from Islam who
had been on the faculty of Islamic and Arabic Studies at Nagpur
University before his new-found Christian faith forced him to

leave the country. Born into a wealthy Islamic family, Simon spoke Hindi, Urdu, Arabic and English and was also the cousin of Mansoor Ali Khan, Ninth Nawab of Pataudi and captain of the Indian cricket team. Simon's knowledge and language skills were a huge asset to our work in the Middle East and the Indian subcontinent. When he left us, he moved on to the Foreign Office where he monitored the Indian and Pakistani press for the then Foreign Secretary, Jack Straw.

We then took on our first parliamentary officer, Emma Joynson-Hicks, and gave her the task of raising our profile and publicizing the plight of the persecuted church among MPs and peers. When Emma returned to her family's coffee business, the role was taken by Tina Lambert. Both were excellent at the job and instrumental in expanding our work.

Others who joined in the early years were Elizabeth Batha, an expert in international human rights who also oversaw the foster-care programme in Russia, and a young Finnish woman named Joanna Chellapernal who became one of our country officers for the Caucasus. Another valuable member of the team was Shireen Aguire who came from Goa and transferred to Christian Solidarity from Sam Yeghnazar's Elam Ministries.

Along with the indefatigable Caroline Cox, the main inspiration behind the now expanding Christian Solidarity was our Chairman, Mervyn Thomas. In a previous career, Mervyn had been a part-time researcher for Conservative MP David Atkinson who, in 1978, screened a film about the persecuted church to some of his Westminster colleagues. From that meeting was born the UK arm of Christian Solidarity International with David as President and Mervyn stepping in as Chairman. As we've seen, Mervyn was instrumental in bringing me into Christian Solidarity and there has hardly been a day since when we haven't spoken and prayed together.

Mervyn's qualities are many and unique. His compassion for the persecuted church is deeply felt. His sense of humour has defused countless tense situations while his tenacity and determination have made him excellent at managing the board of trustees. He's the best chair of meetings I've ever known. As our Chairman, Mervyn flung himself into our advocacy work with energy and passion. But he always wanted to do more and in 1999, once the organization was big enough to warrant it, he left his day job (Sales and Marketing Director of Dietary Foods, the makers of "Sweet 'n' Low") and became Christian Solidarity's full-time Chief Executive.

With a few later additions, this was the team that turned the tiny organization of 1993 into a substantial and well-respected human rights agency in the space of just a few years. And what a team it has been. I'm hugely grateful for the talents and dedication and sense of common purpose among the wonderful group of people with whom I've had the privilege of working.

Of course there have been bumps along the road. 1997 turned out to be a difficult year when differences with our parent organization in Zurich came to a head. Our colleagues at Christian Solidarity International wanted to expand the aid side of the work. We in the UK felt there were plenty of Christian aid organizations already doing a good job and that our particular niche should be advocacy on behalf of the persecuted church. We also had concerns about CSI's management and the way particular projects were being run. The upshot was a painful but necessary split when we in the UK broke away, changed our name to Christian Solidarity Worldwide and began operating independently. Shortly afterwards the American, Australian and German arms of CSI followed suit and set up their own independent organizations.

One of my first priorities on joining Christian Solidarity was to make the organization better known among the churches in Britain. That meant, among other things, gaining a platform at big Christian conferences such as New Wine.

I was familiar with New Wine from my filming days and was surprised to find that Christian Solidarity had no official links. So I felt we should try to make our mark. In 1993 I took a stand at the conference exhibition to see if I could find a way of getting our name and mission in front of the 18,000 visitors who come to one or other of the two New Wine weeks every summer. At the very least, I thought, the organizers might agree to put Caroline Cox on the programme for the following year.

That week I happened to spend a lot of time with Chris Cocksworth, Chaplain of Royal Holloway College and son-in-law of New Wine's visionary founder, David Pytches. When I raised the suggestion that Caroline would make a good speaker, David was non-committal. Chris, on the other hand, was eager to have her speak to the students at Royal Holloway. She and I paid a visit a few weeks later and Chris was bowled over by Caroline's moving account of persecution in Nagorno Karabakh. He went straight back to his father-in-law and told him he absolutely must invite Caroline Cox to speak at New Wine.

When the conference came round the following year, I sat in the main auditorium and listened to Caroline describing her work among Armenian Christians fighting for their very survival. After she'd finished, the audience of six or seven thousand sat in shocked silence for several long seconds – one of those proverbial pin-drop moments. The organizers then announced they were taking an offering for our work. We didn't know this was going to happen and weren't able to wait for the money to be counted. Caroline and I were due to take a cargo of aid to Nagorno Karabakh the next day and had to leave to finalize our preparations.

As we were driving to Manston Airport the following morning, I had a phone call from David Pytches' assistant, Joyce Wills.

"Stuart," she said, "we've counted the offering. Will eighty be enough for you?"

"Of course, Joyce," I replied. "We didn't expect an offering anyway, so we're happy with whatever you've got. Eighty pounds, you said?"

"No. Eighty thousand. And there's more to come."

In the end, Caroline's New Wine debut raised about £100,000 for Christian Solidarity. This not only made a huge difference to individual projects, it also marked a step change in the scale of our work. Given that New Wine at the time was the main annual conference for about a thousand UK churches, Caroline's appearance helped enormously in raising our profile and publicizing the plight of persecuted Christians around the world. The result was many more churches and individuals signing up to pray and campaign for the suffering church.

With more support, the work expanded, which in turn attracted more donations – many with remarkable stories attached to them. On one occasion the postman delivered a brown paper package to the office. I opened it up and found a note from a young man in Brighton who explained he'd recently walked into a church and picked up a leaflet about Christian Solidarity. He had just sold his small antiques business and was leaving to join the Christian outreach organization, Operation Mobilisation. In his note he said that God had clearly told him to give the proceeds to Christian Solidarity. I continued unwrapping the package and out dropped £6,000 in £50 notes.

Another donation arrived on a day when all the usual staff were out of the office and we'd called in our parliamentary officer, Tina Lambert, to answer the phone and do the banking. It wasn't her real job, of course, but she was happy to help. At the end of the day I called to check that everything was all right.

"Oh yes," said Tina. "You'll be pleased to know we had a cheque for £1,000 which I've put in the bank."

A few days later I was looking through our bank statements and noticed credits amounting to £103,000. "Surely some mistake," I thought. I had no recollection of that much money going in and I didn't want to spend it if it wasn't ours. I phoned the bank to see if they could explain.

"I don't see what the problem is, Mr Windsor," said the person at the other end. "You've had a few smaller cheques and one for £100,000 that was paid in last Thursday."

Last Thursday, I thought. That was the day Tina was in charge. Maybe she could clarify the mystery.

I took it up with Tina and we concluded she must have misread the number of noughts on the cheque and put it down as a hundred times smaller than it actually was. (Tina has many wonderful talents, so can be excused for miscounting noughts at the end of a busy day.) The gift was from a young couple who'd had a legacy from a dead relative and decided they didn't need it. Like the ex-antiques dealer in Brighton, they'd felt God telling them that the money should go to Christian Solidarity.

Looking back, I'm deeply thankful to our army of supporters for enabling Christian Solidarity to grow as it has. The 7,000 names on the original database have increased to 25,000 across a spectrum of UK churches and denominations. Hundreds have become personal friends – and though I've only been able to mention a handful in this book, all are important to me. Our staff, meanwhile, has grown from two to thirty-two and we now help persecuted Christians in over twenty countries. This we do principally by gathering information and compiling reports on the difficulties they face. Our findings go to the churches for prayer, to the media for publicity and to those in the centres of power to bring pressure to bear on repressive regimes. Known for their accuracy and impartiality, our reports are trusted and respected in Parliament, in the European Union, at the UN Human Rights Commission and in the US Congress and Senate where we also have a growing body of supporters.

I mention this not because the organization itself is important. In the greater scheme of things it isn't. What does matter is the growing awareness that Christians around the world are suffering for their faith. Under the guidance of the Holy Spirit and in partnership with many other organizations, Christian Solidarity has been able to play a part in keeping the world informed and rallying God's people in support of the persecuted church.

The fax that Susanna placed in my hand as I sat wondering where to begin was indeed prophetic. Over the years we've seen captives freed and the church of Christ continuing to advance in many parts of the world. Yet still our freedoms are under threat – perhaps more so now than ever before.

I would like to think that Christian Solidarity could one day disband because its work was done and Christians were no longer being persecuted. Unfortunately, that's not the way persecution works. "If they persecuted me, they will persecute you," said the church's founder and Christianity, by its nature, will always attract opposition. This will rise and wane and take different forms at different times and places, but persecution remains a constant in the history of the faith.

At present, I believe, the trend is towards greater persecution. The twentieth century saw more Christian martyrs than the previous 1,900 years put together, mainly through the rise of atheist, totalitarian regimes which elevated man above God and the state above the individual. When that happens, there's little tolerance of those who claim allegiance to a higher power. As in Rome when Christians refused to worship Caesar, so in the Soviet Union when sections of the church refused to bow to Communism and paid a heavy price for doing so.

When I first took over the job at Christian Solidarity in 1993, our focus was on those parts of the world emerging from Communism. Although religious freedom subsequently returned to most of the Eastern Bloc countries, we continue to be concerned about Communist China. Here the church has grown explosively and there are more Christians than there are members of the Communist Party. The authorities know that if Christians were to organize themselves politically, they'd be an unstoppable force. That's unlikely to happen and would probably be a retrograde step if it did. All the same, the sheer growth of Christianity is seen as a threat and the government remains determined to keep the church in check.

Among the world's other Communist regimes, North Korea remains high on our list of priorities. The same goes for Vietnam, Laos and Cuba, all of which have questionable records on religious freedom. In the historically Christian country of Eritrea, today's neo-Communist government is thought to have locked up around 20,000 political opponents, including 3,000 whose only crime was their Christian faith. Somalia, too, is a dangerous place to be a Christian.

Even in the countries that threw off the Communist yoke, the freedoms won in the 1990s are now, in many cases, being rolled back. Russia and Romania, for example, are tightening up on religious organizations outside the Orthodox Church. In a throw-back to the Communist era, there are calls for the registration of Protestant places of worship and for those with smaller congregations to be closed down.

Although the Communist world is still a concern, our attention in the last seventeen years has gradually swung towards the threat posed by Islam. Like Communism, Islam is an absolutist creed. Conversion to another religion is equated with blasphemy and in some countries is punishable by death. Even where the death sentence is not officially sanctioned, Islam inflicts enormous shame on an apostate's family. In Pakistan, for example, it's not uncommon for a family disgraced in this way to ask the local mullah for a *fatwa* – in effect, a licence to kill the offending member. Quite apart from the threat of death or imprisonment, converts are often ostracized by their communities, thrown out of work and forced to flee abroad or to another part of the country.

At the same time, there's a spiritual thirst throughout the Muslim world that Islam is failing to satisfy. The advent of satellite TV now makes it possible for Christian broadcasters to reach people and places that were previously closed to non-Muslim influences. Often made by Middle Eastern nationals who understand how to present the gospel attractively to Muslims, Christian TV programmes are reaching millions and finding an eager response in countries such as Iran with its young and disaffected population. It remains to be seen whether Islam, like Communism, will be hollowed out from the inside, prove inadequate to the needs and longings of ordinary citizens and start to lose its grip. I have to admit it's hard to see it happening, but I cannot doubt that God has his plans for the Muslim world.

In sub-Saharan Africa, we see Islam and Christianity in tense equilibrium in countries such as Sudan and Nigeria. Christians in both countries are on the front line and dealing every day with the expansionist ambitions of their Muslim neighbours, particularly over the issue of Sharia law. More than ever, they need the prayers and support of Christians in the West.

And so to Western Europe, where I feel we're at a watershed. The receding of the Christian tide in the twentieth century has removed faith to the margins of society and allowed a secular agenda to take hold. In a society with no bedrock of belief, it's not surprising that tolerance and equality have supplanted truth and justice as society's highest values. The result is political correctness which refuses to elevate any lifestyle or belief above any other. While tolerance is an admirable quality, a society divorced from God moves inexorably towards intolerance of those who express belief – especially Christian belief. Nothing stands still and the creed of tolerance is even now mutating into a militant secularism that sees Christianity as an active threat to reason, rights and equal opportunity.

All the while Islam continues to gain ground, both through

growing weight of numbers and as its fierce certainties provide an often attractive answer to Europe's spiritual vacuum. If the headlines tend to focus on militant Islam, that's because the moderate voice of Islam is strangely muted. I long to hear more of Europe's Muslims disowning the extremists and condemning the treatment of Christians in their own countries. For whatever reason, it doesn't seem to be happening.

Again and again in Christian Solidarity, we've seen the road to persecution follow the same route. First comes disinformation about Christians and Christianity. This is followed by discrimination and harassment, leading in time to persecution, imprisonment and finally martyrdom. For present-day martyrs we need to look to countries like Iran, Pakistan and Nigeria. We're a long way from that point in Europe, though I'd say we've reached the discrimination stage. The question is whether the pendulum will need to swing all the way to martyrdom before it returns, or whether we, the church, can reverse the trend and restore Christianity to the heart of European culture before that happens.

The Amnesty International report for 2009/10 lists sixty-six countries in which Christians and others suffer unjust imprisonment and torture. Christian Solidarity operates in about a third of those countries, of which just a small number make it into this book. There are many more places in the world where persecution is on the rise.

Though the skies appear to be darkening in many parts of the world, I cling to the words of Jesus that he will build his church and the gates of hell will not prevail against it. The building continues, often through the witness and sacrifice of brave individual Christians. Looking back through this book, I'm reminded of Aslan Krikorian in Stepanakert; Pastor Ivan Fedotov surviving twenty years in the Siberian gulag; Paul Tran Ai imprisoned in Vietnam; Mehdi Dibaj and his fellow martyrs in Iran; Manzoor Masih murdered in Lahore; Bishop John

Joseph, taking his own life for the sake of the church in Pakistan; Bishop Macram Gassis and his stand against slavery in Sudan; John and Altaa Gibbens carrying the torch in Mongolia; George Orji martyred in Nigeria, and many more who have poured themselves out for the sake of Christ's church in recent years. I pay tribute to the heroes of the faith whom it's been my privilege to meet and help through Christian Solidarity.

Most of all I thank God that in all the dangers and mishaps and hardships and impossible situations of the last seventeen years, he has never failed me. My simple testimony is that faith works. When you believe God's promises – when you step out in faith and take risks on his behalf, however crazy they may seem – God is there and God acts. If telling my story can persuade more Christians to discern his voice, obey in trust and discover the difference it makes to their own and other people's lives, I shall be more than satisfied.

Appendix 1

The testimony of Revd Mehdi Dibaj, martyred in Iran in July 1994

(Reproduced in Bernard Levin's column in *The Times* on 13 January 1994.)

In the holy name of God who is our life and existence. With all humility I express my gratitude to the Judge of all heaven and earth for this precious opportunity, and with brokenness I wait upon the Lord to deliver me from this court trial according to his promises. I also beg the honoured members of the court present to listen with patience to my defence and with respect for the name of the Lord.

I am a Christian, a sinner who believes Jesus has died for my sins on the cross and who, by his resurrection and victory over death, has made me righteous in the presence of the holy God. The true God speaks about this fact in his holy Word, the gospel. Jesus means Saviour "because he will save his people from their sins". Jesus paid the penalty of our sins by his own blood and gave us a new life so that we can live for the glory of God by the help of the Holy Spirit and be like a dam against corruption, be a channel of blessing and healing, and be protected by the love of God.

In response to this kindness, he has asked me to deny myself and be his fully surrendered follower, and not fear people even if they kill my body, but rather rely on the creator of life who has crowned me with the crown of mercy and compassion, and who is the great protector of his beloved ones and their great reward.

I have been charged with "apostasy"! The invisible God who knows our hearts has given assurance to us Christians that we are not among the apostates who will perish but among the believers so that we may save our lives. In Islamic law an apostate is one who does not believe in God, the prophets or the resurrection of the dead. We Christians believe in all three!

They say, "You were a Muslim and you have become a Christian." No, for many years I had no religion. After searching and studying I accepted God's call and I believed in the Lord Jesus Christ in order to receive eternal life. People choose their religion but a Christian is chosen by Christ. He says, "You have not chosen me but I have chosen you." From when? Before the foundation of the world.

People say, "You were a Muslim from your birth." God says, "You were a Christian from the beginning." He states that he chose us thousands of years ago, even before the creation of the universe, so that through the sacrifice of Jesus Christ we may be his! A Christian means one who belongs to Jesus Christ.

The eternal God who sees the end from the beginning, and who has chosen me to belong to him, knew from everlasting whose heart would be drawn to him and also those who would be willing to sell their faith and eternity for a pot of porridge. I would rather have the whole world against me but know that the almighty God is with me, be called an apostate but know that I have the approval of the God of glory, because man looks at the outward appearance but God looks at the heart, and for him who is God for all eternity nothing is impossible. All power in heaven and on earth is in his hands. The almighty God will raise up anyone he chooses and bring down others, accept some and reject others, send some to heaven and others to hell.

Now because God does whatever he desires, who can separate us from the love of God? Or who can destroy the relationship between the Creator and the creature or defeat a heart that is faithful to his Lord? He will be safe and secure under the shadow of the Almighty! Our refuge is the mercy seat of God who is exalted from the beginning. I know in whom I have believed, and he is able to guard what I have entrusted to him to the end until I reach the Kingdom of God, the place where the righteous shine like the sun, but where the evildoers will receive their punishment in hell-fire.

They tell me, "Return!" But from the arms of my God whom can I return to? Is it right to accept what people are saying instead of obeying the Word of God? It is now 45 years that I am walking with the God of miracles, and his kindness upon me is like a shadow and I owe him much for his fatherly love and concern.

The love of Jesus has filled all my being and I feel the warmth of his love in every part of my body. God, who is my glory and honour and protector, has put his seal of approval upon me through his unsparing blessings and miracles. This test of faith is a clear example. The good and kind God reproves and punishes all those whom he loves. He tests them in preparation for heaven. The God of Daniel, who protected his friends in the fiery furnace, has protected me for nine years in prison and all the bad happenings have turned out for our good and gain, so that I am filled to overflowing with joy and thankfulness.

The God of Job has tested my faith and commitment in order to strengthen my patience and faithfulness. During these nine years he has freed me from all my responsibilities so that under the protection of his blessed Name, I would spend my time in prayer and study of his Word, with heart-searching and brokenness, and grow in the knowledge of my Lord. I praise the Lord for this unique opportunity. "You gave me space in my confinement, my difficult hardships brought healing and your kindness revived me." Oh what great blessings God has in store for those who fear him!

They object to my evangelizing. But "If you find a blind person near a well and keep silent, then you have sinned" [Persian poem]. It is our religious duty, as long as the door of God's mercy is open, to convince evildoers to turn from their sinful ways and find refuge in him in order to be saved from the wrath of a righteous God and from the coming dreadful punishment.

Jesus Christ says, "I am the door. Whoever enters through me will be saved." "I am the way, the truth and the life. No one comes to the Father except through me." "Salvation is found in no one else, for there is no other name under heaven given to men by which we must be saved." Among the prophets of God, only Jesus Christ rose from the dead, and he is our living intercessor forever.

He is our Saviour and he is the Son of God. To know him means to know eternal life. I, a useless sinner, have believed in his beloved person and all his words and miracles recorded in the gospel, and I have committed my life into his hands. Life for me is an opportunity to serve him, and death is a better opportunity to be with Christ. Therefore, I am not only satisfied to be in prison for the honour of his holy name, but am ready to give my life for the sake of Jesus my Lord and enter his kingdom sooner, the place where the elect of God enter everlasting life, but the wicked to eternal damnation. May the shadow of God's kindness and his hand of blessing and healing be upon you and remain forever. Amen.

With respect. Your Christian prisoner, Mehdi Dibaj.

Appendix 2

Christian Solidarity Worldwide
A voice for the voiceless

Christian Solidarity Worldwide (CSW) is an international human rights organisation which specialises in religious freedom, works on behalf of those persecuted for their Christian beliefs and promotes religious liberty for all.

Its primary work is advocacy. By standing in solidarity with those persecuted for their faith, and speaking up on their behalf, CSW seeks to influence the legislation, policies, attitudes and behaviour that reinforce religious discrimination and persecution and which hinder and prevent religious freedom. In so doing, CSW aims to bring about lasting cultural, social and political change.

Central to CSW's mission is to speak up for those who have no voice and ensure they are heard in the international community. This means drawing attention to people's suffering and lobbying those with power to improve their situation. CSW urges governments and other international bodies such as the United Nations to take specific action to address violations of religious freedom and other human rights.

CSW also engages the wider church in praying, protesting

and providing for the needs of victims of persecution around the world.

To achieve its objectives, CSW follows four main strategies:

1. Documenting and raising awareness of religious persecution
2. Influencing key decision-makers whose policies or actions affect the oppressed
3. Empowering victims of religious freedom violations
4. Offering support and solidarity to the persecuted.

To find out more, visit www.csw.org.uk.

Acknowledgments

The bulk of this story is drawn from Christian Solidarity's reports and my own records and memory. Where my memory is faulty (and at the age of sixty-seven I'm willing to admit that it might be), I offer my apologies and am more than willing to be corrected.

Elsewhere I've relied on information provided by others, especially for those parts of the book where friends and colleagues have been out on the front line and I've been back at base co-ordinating their mission.

In this respect I'm indebted to Andrew Boyd whose book, *Baroness Cox: A Voice for the Voiceless* (Lion, 1998), has been a valuable source of material for the chapters dealing with Nagorno Karabakh, Russia, Burma and Sudan. His is a masterly analysis of events in these particular countries and I thoroughly recommend his book.

The chapter on Vladimir Lankin, the Russian in Dhaka Jail, draws on his story as told in *The Trap*, jointly written by Vladimir and his friend John Thorpe. The book is unpublished, I believe, but deserves a wider audience.

In writing about our work with Russian orphans, I'm indebted to two reports – *Trajectories of Despair: Misdiagnosis and Maltreatment of Soviet Orphans*, edited by Caroline Cox and published by Christian Solidarity International, and *A Trajectory of Hope: an evaluation report on the Moscow Our Family Project* by Professors Christina Lyon and Chris Jones of the University of Liverpool.

Others who have helped to refresh my memory of past events include my RAF buddy, Malcolm Trist; Maria Ternovskaya of the *Nasha Semya* project in Moscow; Robin Brodie and Dr Alan Johnston who undertook our mission to Mongolia; our contact in Burma, Dr Martin Panter; Group Captain Cecil Chaudhry; John Joseph, shot and nearly killed in Lahore; and members of my own family. I'm grateful to them all for their assistance.

Finally, my thanks go to writer Graham Jones, my collaborator in producing this book.

Stuart Windsor
New Malden, February 2011

Notes

1. Could this really have been the legendary Boris Volynov? Though I've often wondered, all my subsequent research points to the fact that it was.

2. The basis for this view is 1 Corinthians chapter 13 where Paul speaks of the imperfect (prophecies, tongues and knowledge) disappearing "when perfection comes" (verse 10). If you interpret "perfection" as the complete canon of Scripture, you can see the point. But we're told this will happen when we "see face to face" and "know fully" (verse 12), which hasn't yet happened.

3. In 1997, the UK arm of CSI split from the Zurich-based parent organization and took the name Christian Solidarity Worldwide (CSW). In this book, the term "Christian Solidarity" refers to CSI before 1997 and CSW afterwards.

4. For the full text, see Appendix 1.

5. To protect identities, the names of the children in this chapter have been changed.

6. For more on this story and the *Nasha Semya* project, see Andrew Boyd's book, *Baroness Cox: A Voice for the Voiceless* (Lion, 1998).

7. The story is told in more detail in Andrew Boyd's book, *Baroness Cox: A Voice for the Voiceless.*

8. Ben has written a number of books on Burma including the recently published *Than Shwe: Unmasking Burma's Tyrant,* Silkworm Books, 2010.

9. For much of this information I'm indebted to John Thorpe, a member of the Dhaka international fellowship, who wrote up Vladimir's story in a book called *The Trap* (unpublished).

10. Quoted by Andrew Boyd in *Caroline Cox: A Voice for the Voiceless.*